CAMBRIDGE LIBRARY COLLECTION

Books of enduring scholarly value

History

The books reissued in this series include accounts of historical events and movements by eye-witnesses and contemporaries, as well as landmark studies that assembled significant source materials or developed new historiographical methods. The series includes work in social, political and military history on a wide range of periods and regions, giving modern scholars ready access to influential publications of the past.

Memoirs of the Life and Labours of the Late Venerable Hugh Bourne

Hugh Bourne (1772–1852) was a Methodist preacher who is best known as the co-founder of the Primitive Methodist movement. After converting to Methodism in 1799, Bourne became influenced by the American evangelical American Lorenzo Dow (1777–1834) and together with William Clowes held an open-air evangelical meeting in 1807. Such gatherings were prohibited by the Methodist Conference, and the two were expelled by the Methodist Society in 1808. They formed the Primitive Methodist Connexion in 1810, with Bourne assuming a leading role in the movement. This volume, first published in 1854 and written by Bourne's nephew John Walford, contains a detailed biography of Bourne. Using private papers inherited on Bourne's death, his childhood, conversion and the founding of the movement are described, with his leadership of the Connexion also discussed. This biography provides valuable information concerning Bourne's life and motivations during and after the founding of the movement.

T0370950

Memoirs of the Life and Labours of the Late Venerable Hugh Bourne

By a Member of the Bourne Family

JOHN WALFORD

CAMBRIDGE
UNIVERSITY PRESS

CAMBRIDGE UNIVERSITY PRESS

Cambridge, New York, Melbourne, Madrid, Cape Town, Singapore,
São Paolo, Delhi, Dubai, Tokyo, Mexico City

Published in the United States of America by Cambridge University Press, New York

www.cambridge.org
Information on this title: www.cambridge.org/9781108024983

© in this compilation Cambridge University Press 2010

This edition first published 1854
This digitally printed version 2010

ISBN 978-1-108-02498-3 Paperback

Memoirs

OF

The Life and Labours of Hugh Bourne.

CHAPTER I.

ANCESTORS—GRANDFATHER OF HUGH BOURNE—ABBEY FARM—GREAT IN-
DUSTRY—ACCUMULATES WEALTH—MARRIAGE OF JOSEPH AND ELLEN THE
PARENTS OF H. BOURNE—STAFFORDSHIRE POTTERIES—SCOTLAND—FORD-
HAY FARM—CHILDREN BORN—STRONG DRINK—H. B'S. MOTHER—HER
PIETY AND CAPABILITIES—DECLINING YEARS—AFFLICTION AND DEATH—-
DEATH OF H. B'S. FATHER.

The ancestors of the Bourne family were Normans, and came
into England with William the Conqueror. They settled in
North Staffordshire, where their descendants, bearing the name
of Bourne, are very numerous; but the estates obtained by the
conquest have long passed from the family, and are now in other
hands.

The father of Mr. Joseph Bourne, and grandfather of Hugh,
the subject of this memoir, lived at the Abbey Farm, near Milton.
As well as being a farmer, he carried on the wheelwrighting and
timber trades. He was a man of great industry and frugality, and
was prudent in the management of his farm and other businesses;
and by these means he accumulated wealth, which enabled him to
place his children as they arrived at manhood on farms, or in
trades, that put them on a level with the respectable yeomen of
the neighbourhood.

Mr. Joseph Bourne, the father of Hugh, married Ellen, the daughter of Mr. Steele, farmer, of Hatchley, near Cheadle.   At the time of their marriage, science was beginning to develope new and important resources in the manufacturing of earthenware in the Staffordshire Potteries, and commercial enterprise soon greatly enlarged and extended the trade, to the great benefit of the district.

Many of the farmers' sons, and others in the surrounding neighbourhood, were induced to become travellers, or (to use what was then a more popular term) pot sellers, or hawkers of earthenware. Among the numerous adventurers in this business, Joseph, the son of John, of the Abbey, was numbered.   Scotland was the place to which he and   his wife directed their   attention ; and having purchased from the earthenware manufacturers to the extent of their united means. the brittle ware was despatched to the appointed mart.   Joseph and his wife embarked at Liverpool, and arrived in safety at Greenock.   Here they commenced their perambulations ; and in the Moorland style, from house to house, they hawked the pots they had brought from their native home to the land o'cakes !   This journey to Scotland was remunerative : they made money, and returned to the Abbey Farm. Ere long Joseph took the Ford-Hay farm, in the parish of Stoke-upon-Trent, in the county of Stafford ; and at the same time he commenced business as a wheelwright and a dealer in timber.

At Greenock—in merry Scotland, as he used to call it in his better mood of mind, when inclination led him to be jocular—his eldest two sons, John and Joseph, were born ; and at Ford-Hay, three daughters and three sons : in all, five sons and three daughters were born to Joseph and Ellen of the Ford-Hay farm.

It was generally believed that the pot-selling journey to Scotland fixed in Joseph Bourne a fondness for strong drink, which was a besetment to him through a protracted life.   In addition to this propensity for tippling, he was a man, who, for violence of temper and wrathful passions, had few equals : these unhappy failings in the father caused grief and sorrow to the mother, and fear and dread in the children.   The paroxysms of anger and passion in the father estranged the better feelings of the children, and caused them to avoid the father's presence, and caress with fondness the mother; and we think the veneration of Hugh Bourne for his mother, from the earliest dawn of reason, considerably surpassed that of his brothers and sisters. In consequence of the intimate connection between the mother and the son's early life, we shall present the reader with a very brief memoir of Mrs. Ellen Bourne.

Ellen was strictly brought up from childhood, and habituated to the Church of England mode of worship, consequently she became strongly attached and devoted to the religious practices and duties of the religion of her fathers, who for generations had been staunch churchmen. The return of each Sabbath brought Ellen to her accustomed seat in the parish church. The principles of industry and prudence in the management of household affairs, which qualified her for a farmer's wife, were communicated by the example and precept of her own excellent mother; and on her marriage with Mr. Joseph Bourne, she commenced the duties of her own domestic circle as a prudent, God-fearing woman should do. And first, with devotedness to her religious duties, as having prior claims to all secular and other domestic duties. Secondly, with steady frugality and industry in the management of her house and family—her diligence and assiduity in the care of her children and servants were of the first order. Her son says "My mother was a woman of such prudence, management, industry, and economy, that could not be surpassed, if equalled."

The interest she took in training her children to fear God in the morning of their youth, and in inculcating sobriety, industry, frugality, and the proper method of husbanding time, was characteristic of her virtue. Her son says "She often taught her children to read while spinning at the wheel." At the wheel! while "She spun her wool and flax to clothe her husband and children, that they might be known in the gates." At the wheel! the spinning wheel! "She dictated to her children lessons of greater worth than ' *classic lore*'—lessons of the child's first duty to its Maker—reverence for the Supreme Being—prayerful devotion—sanctity of the Sabbath, and strict morality; urging upon them the importance of shunning evil, and cleaving to that which was good."

At the knee of his kind and affectionate mother, the child Hugh was first taught the principles of godly sincerity, self-denial, and the temperate use of God's good creatures; and as a counteracting principle to their father's propensity for strong drink, this excellent woman taught her children to abhor the sin of *drunkenness*, that they might " Live soberly, righteously, and godly in this present world ; looking for the blessed hope, and the glorious appearing of the great God and our Saviour Jesus Christ." —*Titus* ii, 12, 13. These motherly counsels to the child Hugh, laid the foundation of that Christian temperance by him so long and rigidly adhered to in after life. This noble-minded woman, according to the light and means she possessed, instructed her family, both children and servants, in the duties connected with the ordinances of the established church, of which she was a consistent member.

Soon after her son Hugh's conversion in 1799, she was fully brought to God ; and learned a more excellent way ;—" Not by works of righteousness which we have done, but according to his mercy he saved us, by the washing of regeneration, and renewing of the Holy Ghost ; which he shed on us abundantly through Jesus Christ our Saviour."—Titus iii, 5. 6. No sooner did she taste of the grace of her heavenly calling, but she united herself along with her son Hugh, in church fellowship with the Wesleyan Methodist Society ; and they met in class at a village called Ridgway, half a mile from Bemersley. Soon after her connection with the Methodists, she had the heart-felt pleasure of seeing her youngest son, James, brought to God, and joined in the same class with herself and his brother Hugh. This, to so excellent a mother, was a consolation of no small magnitude ; and a still greater was afforded her when her two sons, Hugh and James, were called to exercise in the public ministry as preachers of the everlasting gospel.

And when by a chain of circumstances, brought on in the providence of God, her son Hugh was led to plant the standard of gospel light and truth in the open air upon Mow Cop, on Sunday, July 12th, 1801, and at the same time to lay a *foundation* for extensive open air worship, and the establishing of the English camp meetings on a firm and substantial basis in the face of the most formidable opposition from friends and foes, this good woman greatly rejoiced : and she subsequently rendered her sons, Hugh and James, great help by motherly and prudent counsel. She became, indeed, a mother in Israel to the infant and rising cause. In her the fathers, or first race of Primitive Methodist Preachers, found a

true and special friend ; a soother of their sorrows :—in the good
Samaritan style she supplied their wants in time of need, cheered
their spirits, and encouraged their efforts in the field of gospel
toil.

By her husband she was called, in sarcastic derision, a BISHOP ;
—for often when inebriated, and amongst his pot companions, he
would boast of his munificence to the cause of Methodism ;
saying "I keep a *bishop* and *two parsons*," alluding to his wife
and two sons, Hugh and James.   At some times she suffered much from the violence of her husband's temper, for he was
strongly opposed to Methodism, and to every community that
dissented from the church, considering himself—although
destitute of the realities of religion—a firm and staunch
churchman.   And there was not wanting in some the baseness
to influence his mind against his wife and sons, on account of
their Methodistic tendency ; and many a time she, her sons,
and the early fathers of Primitive Methodism that have tarried
at her house for the night, have had to retire and dedicate the
upper garret, or chamber, as a bethel in which to offer their
oblations of prayer and thanksgivings to the God of all their
mercies ; otherwise they could not have escaped a volley of
abuse, and storms of rage and insult from him.   From this source
Mrs. Bourne had much to pass through on her way to heaven,
which was extremely repugnant to the feelings of so good a
woman.   Still she could say through divine assistance "*Thy will
be done;*" and many a time has her sorrowful spirit been upraised,
when under severe trial from her husband, with this sweet and precious promise—"My grace is sufficient for thee,"—and with her
heart uplifted to the throne of grace, she prayed with the Psalmist
" Set a watch, O Lord, before my mouth : keep the door of my
lips."   Thus she breathed out her soul to God, "Taking
heed to her ways lest she should sin with her tongue."   She
guarded, with the skill of a master mind, the words and actions
of herself and children, teaching the latter to walk by rule.

The moral and religious principles which Mrs. Bourne had
been taught in early life by her own prudent mother, were as follows :—" To fear God, and honour the king upon the throne of
Great Britain ; water baptism, as the regeneration propounded by
the church of England ; and the religious duties and alms-giving

enjoined by the book of common prayer, and inculcated by the
parochial clergy." These were the fundamentals which she had
been taught from the dawn of reason, and to which she in early
life had been strictly trained ; and the strict morality laid down
at the onset of housekeeping, for the government of her own
household, had been firmly adhered to. But now having found
the " Pearl of great price," and the new and living way to the
throne of God's mercy, through the blood of the covenant and
the renewing influence of the Holy Ghost, she could exclaim with
implicit confidence, " Old things are passed away, and behold !
all things are become new ;" experimentally knowing that " If any
man be in Christ he is a new creature." The former rules and
injunctions enjoined upon herself and children were now more
strictly and cheerfully observed by herself and two sons, Hugh
and James ; avoiding at the same time as much as possible all
cause of offence that might arise in her husband's mind against
principles, so diametrically opposite to his own notions of religion
as practiced by churchmen generally. Everything consistent with
conjugal duty and affection, (except what God and conscience
forbade,) Mrs. Bourne did with cheerfulness :—" Her feet in
sweet obedience moved " to the commands of her husband, and
the calls of the domestic circle—taking up, and bearing with
holy meekness and resignation to the divine will, every cross that
lay in the way to the footstool of mercy ; permitting no difficulty
to stop the course of that divine consolation which she daily
received from the fountain of life.

When declining years and afflictions reduced her physical
powers and energies to feebleness, and signs that nature was fast
decaying were manifest, even then, while her frame was tottering
upon the verge of the silent tomb, her soul was as the garden of
the Lord, blooming with life and immortality. Her mental faculties and spiritual energies were fresh and vigorous ; and when
confined to the couch and chamber—

" Where the good man meets his fate"—

the rapturous bursts of triumphant praise and thanksgiving to
which she gave utterance, were delightful to hear. Her acclama-
tions of praise and glory to the LAMB that sits upon the throne,
rang through the house !—All who came within the range of her

voice were faithfully exhorted to love and fear God. To her sons, Hugh and James, she gave a solemn charge, the import of which was as follows:—" Stand firm and unshaken by the infant cause, fan the holy flame, follow the openings of divine providence, and when I am no more with you, the God of Abraham will be your guide. And *thou, my beloved Hugh*, son of my right hand, let not my affliction and death prevent thee from fulfilling thy appointments. Go, my son, preach the gospel; and if we never meet upon earth, when thou hast fulfilled thy mission in this lower world, and served thy day and generation, my son, I hope to greet thee with an eternal welcome to Zion's Holy Mount, where we shall realize an eternity of happiness together!"

Hugh soon after took a final farewell; went out from the presence of his affectionate and revered mother, followed by her benedictions and prayers, to preach God's Word! To him this final separation was a trial of no common kind: the guide of his youth, and the staff and stay of his maturer years, was about to be taken from him. "And when," he said, "I took a last farewell of my mother; and when I first heard of her death, my heart throbbed with *grief and gratitude!*—grief, at the thought of seeing my mother no more upon earth: gratitude at the thought, my mother's salvation is safe and secure." The last words she uttered were—" Come, Lord Jesus, and come quickly!" and she then peacefully fell asleep.—Thus lived, and thus died, the mother of Hugh Bourne.

Of her it might have been truly said, "She openeth her mouth with wisdom; and in her tongue is the law of kindness: she looketh well to the ways of her household, and eateth not the bread of idleness: her children rise up and call her blessed; her husband also, and he praiseth her."—Prov. xxxi. 26-29.* Mrs. Bourne died on Thursday, August 7th, 1817, in the 81st year of her age.

* Notwithstanding her husband's violence of temper, and opposition to Methodism, he, in his collected and sober moments, well knew the worth of such a wife; and even at the festive board of mirth and jollity, he would sometimes speak in praise of his wife's high virtues, and care and management of his household.—J. W.

On referring to Hugh Bourne's Journal, it appears he was at that time labouring in the neighbourhood of Belper, in Derby-shire, and we find the following entries :—

" *Thursday, August* 7.—At Windley, abroad, my mother died on this night.

" *Friday, August* 15.—Came home : my mother died on Thursday, August 7th, and was buried on Sunday, August 10th, 1817. My mother has been pious for a long time; she was quite worn down with old age.   She has had a rough road through life, a very rough road, but she has weathered the storm.   On Friday, August 1st, she broke through all, and praised God almost the whole day. She spoke aloud, " Glory to God ! Come Lord Jesus, and come quickly," &c. . . . . In the same way she proceeded till the Thursday night following, when about six o'clock she fell asleep in the Lord.   Well, from her, under the Lord, I received my first religious impressions, and to her care I owe a great deal....... Her industry and labours in the things of this life have been great and continued.   We were a large family, and my father a very drinking, violent, passionate man, but my mother's industry and great labours kept the family from want.   But her road through the world has been rough indeed ; now she rests from her labours. On the Friday, August 1st, when she broke through into the full victory, my brother James thought that death was near.   I was out labouring in the ministry when she died, and they did not think it necessary to send for me.*   When I first knew of her death I was filled with sorrow ; but this was mixed with joy, when my brother James gave me an account of her death.   O Lord, prepare me to follow her ! "

With little ceremony, and less pomp, the remains of this blessed woman were conveyed to the silent grave, while her beloved son Hugh continued his ministerial labours in the Home mission field, which labours were of much more importance than the *obsequies* of a beloved mother!   Such devotedness to the rising community of Primitive Methodists as was found in the

---

* He had taken leave of his mother on Friday, July 25th, when the scene was affecting ; but his native bashfulness and timidity always throw a veil over his own feelings and sufferings. Happily, we have the testimony of an eye witness of the parting benediction of the dying mother to her Benjamin, the son of her right hand, and the tears and grief which were seen when the son went out-from his mother's presence.

dying mother and her two sons, is worthy of a finer touch than the biographer is capable of giving to it; * but we must leave the mother of Hugh Bourne slumbering in the tomb, until the morning of the resurrection, when mortality shall put on immortality, and soul and body be re-united, and "Shine as the stars in the firmament for ever and ever."

The Husband and Father.—Mr. Joseph Bourne, the husband of Ellen, and father of the subject of this memoir, held the Ford-Hay farm twenty-two years. He then removed to a large farm at Bemersley, in the parish of Norton-in-the-Moors, in the county of Stafford, where he lived to within a few months of his one hundredth year, and then went the way of all flesh. His two sons, Hugh and James, agonized in prayer with strong cries to God, for the salvation of their father's soul: and the Lord so graciously condescended to pour out his Holy Spirit in answers of mercy, that they had hope in their father's death; so that we trust this man, in answer to the many prayers of his wife and sons, found his way to heaven, where no difference of opinion in religion can mar the comfort and happiness of man and wife.

* The Nazarite, under the law, was not only forbidden wine and strong drink, but it was strictly enjoined upon him that he should not make himself unclean, "For his father, or for his mother, or for his sister, when they die; because the consecration of his God is upon his head; all the days of his separation he is holy unto the Lord."—Num. vi, 7, 8; and our Lord is supposed to have had reference to the vow of the Nazarite, when he said,—" Let the dead bury their dead; but go thou and preach the Kingdom of God."—Luke ix, 60. This injunction was strictly carried out, first—by the mother in her last charge to her son; second—by her son James, in carrying out his mother's wishes in not sending for his brother; third—in Hugh's devoted labours and perseverance in the prosecution of his sacred duty.—J. W.

CHAPTER II.

HOMELY DIET AND EXERCISE—PHYSICAL AND MENTAL CHARACTERISTICS OF DIFFERENT CLASSES AND PERSONS—FORMATION OF CHARACTER—MO-THER'S INFLUENCE—THOUGHTS OF GOD—A LETTER—GOD IN THUNDER —SPIRITUALITY OF GOD'S LAW—AN INCIDENT—YEARS OF SORROW.

On Friday, April 3rd, 1772, in an obscure corner of the parish of Stoke-upon-Trent, in the county of Stafford, in the lonely habitation of Joseph and Ellen Bourne, of the Ford-Hay farm, Hugh, their third son, and fifth child, was born. Here he first saw the light, and commenced his journey through an eventful life. Children brought up in such solitary situations from early infancy, often acquire a natural shyness and timidity ; and perhaps no man ever displayed a greater portion of bashfulness than Hugh Bourne : nor was he able in any measure to conquer this propensity, until he was more than thirty years of age ; indeed it was discernable in his appearance and person to the latest period of his life.

There is a striking contrast existing even in this enlightened nineteenth century, between the children of the moorlanders, and those of the potters, their next neighbours. In the former you see timidity and bashfulness,—in the latter a boldness and forwardness, and a prying inquisitiveness never seen in the moorland youths. Apparently the faculties of the young potter's mind, are much earlier in life developed ; but if we contrast their physical energy and muscular ability, we shall find the young moorland has considerably the advantage over his neighbour the potter, being accustomed from childhood to plain and homely food, early rising, the labour and toil of the field, exposed to heat and cold, wet and dry, frost and snow, the cutting blast of winter, and the sweet and pleasant mountain air, these moorland swains " Can bear the extremities of the weather without injury ;" their exposure to out-door labour and toil braces the nerves, and increases in the muscle strength, elasticity, and power of endurance. But the mental faculties appear at a first glance to be very feeble, and to require time,—like the wide spreading oak of old England, to grow to solidity and firmness—before they can be capable of development in the various branches of art and science. Besides, there is a great difference in what we call constitutional character, both among the sons of the mountain and the sons of populous cities and towns. Happily for young Bourne, and for thousands that owe their status in the church to his labours and energies, he was blest with a prudent, God-fearing preceptor—a pious mother. The formation of the character of the founder of the English camp meetings, &c., was the work of this excellent woman : his earliest thoughts, at the first dawnings of reason in the infant mind, were THOUGHTS OF GOD, and heaven, the dwelling-place of his dread Majesty. These were the first impressions on a mind which became imbued with principles of the first magnitude ; and here we see a model of the order in which a child's education should be arranged ; indeed, we consider these the first link in the chain of causes that produced such great and powerful effects as are seen in H. Bourne's life, and the Primitive Methodist Connexion,—these, undoubtedly, arose in the child's mind from the pious daily lessons given by the mother to her elder children. Who can read or calculate the amount of good such mothers have produced by such praiseworthy conduct ?

Just picture to your mind, reader, the pious mother seated at the wheel ! the spinning wheel ! her hands and feet busily employed in the industrious art of spinning flax, or wool, to clothe her family. Five children are listening to the words of sweetness as they flow from the mother's lips to her infant charge ; words of the richest value to an immortal mind ; words that contain the first principles of the child's duty to its Maker. " Thou shalt love the Lord thy God with all thine heart, and with all thy soul, and with all thy might.—And these words which I command thee this day, shall be in thine heart, and thou shalt teach them diligently unto thy children, and shalt talk of them when thou sittest in thine house, and when thou walkest by the way, and when thou liest down, and when thou risest up ; and thou shalt bind them for a sign upon thine hand, and they shall be as frontlets between thine eyes, and thou shalt write them upon the posts of thy house, and on thy gates."—Deut. vi. 5-9. These great principles and duties laid down by Moses, and enjoined upon all the Israel of God, were written upon the mind and memory, and engraven upon the heart of Mrs. Bourne, and she daily taught them to her children ; and among the infant group or cluster of five, little Hugh was often listening, with the ardour of an enquiring mind, to the gracious words which fell from his mother's lips. Can we be surprised or astonished to hear him say in after life, " My first thoughts were thoughts of God, maker of heaven and earth! "

We will now trace the footsteps of the child Hugh, and jot down, as we pass along, the various effects produced on his infant mind by his first and lasting impression, *thoughts of God!*

Some extracts from a letter written by him, dated Bemersley, August 17, 1800, will shew the experience of his infant mind :—

" When I was four or five years old, I had as clear ideas of God as it was possible for any one to have at that age. My thoughts were, that God was an everlasting and eternal being ; that he dwelt above the skies ; that he created heaven and earth, and all things seen and unseen ; that he was able to destroy all things, or to alter the form of everything ; that he was present everywhere ; that he knew the thoughts of every one. I thought that heaven was a place of happiness, and that those who were righteous, and kept God's commandments, were admitted thither, and could see God,—which I thought the greatest happiness—and were happy for ever and ever : and that hell was a place of torments, and all that did wickedly, and broke God's commandments, were sent thither to be tormented by the devil and his angels, in blue flaming brimstone, for ever and ever. These views made me very intent upon keeping what I thought to be God's commandments ; I was diligent to know his will, I delighted in his name, I was eager to know how to please him, and was surprised to see people so careless and indifferent about things on which so great a concern depended ; for I thought that if the commandments were ever so hard, it was better to keep them and go to heaven, than to break them and go to hell ; and it was a great grief to me to know anybody swear, or do anything that was wicked. I soon learned to read,—instructed by my mother—and greatly delighted to read the bible, and religious books; and having in one of them —Watts' Hymns—this line,—

> " Jehovah rides upon a cloud,
> And thunders through the world,"—

I thought I should see him when it thundered, and accordingly I would be out of doors at such times, and my mother could not keep me in the house; having looked many times, and could not see him, I asked my mother about it, and she told me he was invisible; however, I still got out of doors when it thundered, for I thought that the LORD was there, and I would be as near him as possible, for my soul was filled with love—love to him—and I thought I was greatly beloved by him also. . . . I desired nothing so much as to know his will, and I thought I would do it if it were ever so hard. This I look upon as an extraordinary work of grace; but whether I should have obtained the new birth at that time, if any one had taught me the nature and necessity of it, I cannot tell; but, however, there passed a few years that I can look back upon with pleasure."

We think as Hugh Bourne thought, in 1800, when he penned the above,—that this was certainly an extraordinary work of grace upon his young and tender mind. He that was well acquainted with the future, perfectly cognitive of what was in the distance, waiting this child's arrival at manhood, when he was to be called to perform the mind and will of the great head of the church, in acts and deeds that should benefit thousands of the poor outcasts among the human family, and prepare them for the better world, was now moulding and fashioning the intellectual and moral capacities of this child's mind. When the boy Hugh had nearly completed the first seven years of his eventful life, he began by constant reading and studying God's holy word, to understand in some measure the nature and spirituality of the commandments, or law of God—a high attainment this for a child so young—for how few, comparatively, of those of maturer years, attain the full knowledge of the spirituality of God's law; many, very many, we fear, pass through life altogether ignorant of what was now known by this child.

But a new scene is opened—he writes as follows :—" I was not
able to keep the law, so I fell under the curse of a broken law ; I
now felt the terrors of the Lord come upon me, and I saw myself
in danger of falling into hell every moment. I found that I was
already under the condemnation, and subject to the wrath of God,
and the curse of the law, for I found that I not only had broken
the law, but that I, as it were, broke all the commandments every
hour and every minute ; I now experienced the truth of Solomon's
words,—" The spirit of a man will sustain his infirmity, but a
wounded spirit who can bear ? "

We shall lay before the reader a circumstance, apparently
small in itself, but which was lasting in its effects, and gave a
colouring to his after life ; the matter was this :—The farm his
parents occupied, being inconvenient for roads, they on one occasion by favour brought several loads of coals down a neighbour's
field, and laid them down at the bottom of it near a brook. A
piece of wood was then laid over for a bridge, and the coals had to
be carried over the brook into their own field, then re-loaded and
taken home ; and as children love to be aiming at what they are
hardly able to perform, young Hugh pressed to have a basket,
and carry coals over the brook as well as the rest ; but it was objected, he was too little, he might fall into the brook, or he
might get into the mire which lay near the way in which they
passed : but as in such cases, the ardour of an active child is not
easily repressed, he was at length accommodated with a basket,
and he succeeded beyond expectation. He had been in the habit, in
any little work he had to do, of applying to the Lord to help him,
but in this instance he had gone farther than to ask the Lord to
help him to carry the coals,—he had made a great promise to the
Lord ; he had promised if the Lord would but help him this time,
all the family should worship him,* and even this was hardly the
whole extent of his promise. And when the spectators were com-
mending him, he said within himself—" They little think the

* We would remark,—the *worship* the child Hugh had in his mind when
he promised the Lord "the whole family should worship him," was the
worship of sacrifice according to the law of Moses, of which he had read
in the bible ; such were his infant thoughts on worship ; but what part of
his father's stock he intended to offer, wether sheep or oxen, we have no
means of ascertaining.

Lord is helping me,"—and he wondered in his infant mind that they did not ask the Lord to help them.—He succeeded entirely in carrying the coals, made no false step, did not tire even to the last, was much commended, and was glad to think how wonderfully the Lord had helped him. But when all was over, he began to think of his promise ; but behold, it was strangely beyond his power to perform. He strove for a day or two to put it off, but it still kept coming into his mind : at length he attempted to make it out that he had not promised so much, and was immediately struck with the thought that he was trying to tell a lie to the Lord,—his heart sunk within him, and a foundation was laid for upwards of twenty years' sorrow.

Tender as were his years at that important moment, his sorrows were heavy—his distress was great; but as soon as his infant mind came to steady thought, he set himself to examine whether there was yet any remedy, or any prospect of his escaping the lake of fire and brimstone, which is the second death ; and this was, more or less, a constant subject of thought and enquiry with him for upwards of twenty sorrowful years. Had there been any one to guide his steps and to direct his infant mind to the Saviour, and to a full, free, and present salvation, in and by HIM, things might have been different ; but on this subject he had none to converse with, no one to instruct him,—not even his mother, who feared the Lord above many, could afford him help. She herself was yet ignorant of the scriptural plan of salvation,—" Justification by faith,"—she was altogether wedded to salvation by works. " Do this and live "—was the foundation on which she grounded her own hopes of salvation ; hence, she enjoined upon herself and children the strictest rules of morality, and was rigorous in having the duties performed by her children, as she herself had been taught from her earliest childhood, they should be ; nor did she find out the true way into the sheepfold of Christ until twenty years of sorrow had been endured by her son Hugh, and he had received the manifestation of Jesus Christ's love and mercy : besides, her child's sorrows were unknown to her ; he kept them to himself, not daring to open his mind to any one, not even his beloved mother ; and for this very reason he firmly believed the people and his mother knew whether the Lord was with him. There is no doubt, had Mrs.

Bourne known the state of her child's mind, she would have felt all the feelings of maternal tenderness, and would have sympathised with him in his sufferings, and afforded him all the comfort and help in her power; but the child Hugh covered his sorrow in the best manner he could, and continued his search after relief, as *hope* was not altogether extinct. This hope was weak and feeble, nevertheless it buoyed up the spirit of this extraordinary child, and excited in him an anxious desire after good, and a diligent application to the Holy Scriptures, in order to ascertain whether any possibility remained of his getting to heaven. He was thus addicted to thoughtful reading, but instead of its producing immediate ease, it produced the contrary, for he soon began to be sensible, that the spirituality of the law of God extended to his very thoughts, as well as his words and actions. Thus conviction, like a sharp-pointed arrow, pierced his inmost soul, and embittered the daily kindness he received from the hand of his mother. He found he had not power over evil thoughts and desires, but he sinned and broke the ·law of God continually, and thereby exposed himself every moment to the danger of hell fire.

For twenty years he could say,—" The good that I would I do not; but the evil which I would not, that I do. . . . O wretched man that I am ! who shall deliver me from the body of this death ? "—Rom. vii, 19-24. And during those twenty years he seldom went to bed at night without a dread of awaking in hell before morning ; and in the morning he awoke to fresh terrors.

We make no doubt the reader will think with us, that this was a long period of mental suffering, terror, agony, and distress of mind ;—all these years he cried to God in secret prayer and agony for a dispensation of mercy through Jesus Christ. He was a strict churchman, and outwardly moral, but he was sensible that in the inner man he broke the law of God every moment. On one occasion, however, he felt some sense of the favour of God, and for a few days had rest ; and in another instance, in the year 1794, he had a peculiar answer to prayer, and his mind was easier for some time ; but with these two exceptions he might in language similar to that of JOB, say—" Let those *twenty years* perish."

We believe every candid reader will think that Hugh Bourne in early life underwent a severe training for the work of the ministry, which he in after life was so fully engaged in, and that the twenty years of gall and wormwood were not without fruit. As results of this discipline, we may say, first—he acquired a knowledge of the purity of God, the extent of his holy law, and the sinfulness of sin; second, by this means, in some measure, he was led to refrain from the free use of strong drink, and to be outwardly moral, and what was then considered *righteous*; indeed it was the general opinion of the neighbours that Hugh Bourne was a religious and righteous young man, but they had no conception of his own feelings on the subject; third, this distress caused him to be more diligent in study and the acquirement of knowledge, which in after life was of the utmost importance to the infant society which he was instrumental in bringing into being.

CHAPTER III.

The subject that now claims our attention is Hugh Bourne's
education, in connection with several circumstances that transpired
while he was ardently searching after religious, general, and scientific knowledge.   The lonely situation of the Ford-Hay farm, the
badness of the roads about, and its great distance from any school,
linked with the economical plan Mrs. Bourne had formed in her
own mind, as a counterpoise to her husband's expensive habit of
tippling, led her to take upon herself the important charge of.
educating the children ; and in carrying out this laudable design,
with none of the juveniles was she so successful as with Hugh ;
he learned the alphabet perfectly in a week, and after this she
had very little trouble in teaching him to read : such were his
ardour of soul and quickness of apprehension, that he soon accomplished the tasks assigned him, and took great delight in
reading, especially the historical parts of the bible, often interro-
gating his mother on any difficult passage that caught his attention while so employed : his mother also taught him to write,
and under her care he made some progress in the first rules of arithmetic.   Being so quick a learner, his father sent him to school
at Werrington, in Caverswall parish, to a Mr. Samuel Cooper, who
was a self-taught scholar.   This gentleman appears to have paid
some regard to morals and the external duties of religion, as he
regularly prayed with his pupils at the close of each day's school

labour,—an excellent and praiseworthy practice, especially in those days, when the practice was considered derogatory to the character of a teacher, and too methodistical by school-masters in general.

The distance from Ford-Hay to Werrington school was fully two miles, which was considerable for a boy so young to walk night and morning : " For I well remember," says he, " writing 1779 in my copy book as the year of our Lord, so that I was then only seven years of age." He further writes :—" When my father's expensive habits are considered, his putting me to school may be thought extraordinary ; but the hand of God was in it. An aged man, who was occasionally at my father's house, was very pressing for me to be brought up for a *parson*, and others took up the same notion." This appears to have had influence for the moment with Mr. Bourne respecting his son Hugh ; for he set the boy to commit to memory the morning and evening church prayers ; and such was the boy's memory, that he could repeat the whole order of the church service, Te Deum, Litany, &c. included, and in this he took great delight, and learned to pronounce like the clergyman the family were in the habit of hearing at Bucknall church,—then called a chapel of ease :—the church catechism, many of Watts' psalms and hymns, with portions of scripture, were all committed to memory by him. We question the purity of the father's motives in chiming in with the views others had formed of his son Hugh's being brought up for a parson :—had not pride a hand in this ? did it not foster the idea, and induce him to send him to school to realize it—viz : that of making his son a parson ? Thanks and praise to an overruling providence : the all-seeing eye of Omniscience was on the lad ; the Lord knew what was in the womb of futurity ; the great head of the church designed him for a larger cure than the circumscribed one of a parochial clergyman ; and subsequent circumstances shattered to atoms the parson-making notions of the father, and to our satisfaction prove the insincerity of the father's motives in sending his son to school for such a purpose. Young Hugh, in consequence of the notions of his father, was removed from under the care of Mr. Cooper, and sent to Bucknall endowed school, in Stoke parish, connected with the church at that place. To this he had to trudge about the same distance as when at Mr Cooper's school. Here he found a preceptor of a different stamp to that of his former master, in the person of Mr. Thomas Harrison,—a great scholar, but not quite a capital teacher, (says H. B.) neither does the boy appear to have had so high an esteem for him as he had for Mr. Cooper. We may here remark, that master Hugh was not allowed to enjoy the benefit of Mr. Harrison's tutorship very regularly, for the father soon began to shift from the purpose of having his son brought up for a parson.   In a morning he would frequently say, " Hugh, thou must stop at home to-day, we are very busy, and cannot do without thee ; thou shalt go to school to-morrow."

Thus the time passed between work and study alternately. To become an adept in book learning, young Bourne aspired, and every spare minute of time was by him bought up for study and deep thinking. We find him next under the tuition of Mr. W. Bennison, who had succeeded Mr. Harrison, the great scholar, and master of Bucknall endowed school.   In this gentleman the pupil found the excellency of good teaching ; he made rapid progress, and was soon in the proud position of head scholar in the school. Of the good teaching and superintendence of Mr. William Bennison, he always spoke with grateful remembrance, and in the highest terms of esteem.

The studies through which master Hugh went at school are very soon told, and the books soon enumerated :—reading, English grammar, arithmetic, and the first part of mensuration, with the rudiments of latin, were his studies.   His books consisted of the bible, Fisher's grammar, and a pocket dictionary, in which last he greatly delighted, as it assisted him in compassing the English language.   But we soon come to a period when a full stop is put to his school labours and studies.   His father's patience is exhausted, his parson-making notions evaporate into the air, and young Hugh has now to learn the science of his father's callings upon the farm and in the wheelwright's shop ;—different schools to what he had found at Werrington and Bucknall,—farming, building carts and waggons, making ploughs and harrows, and other implements requisite for a farmer's use, such is to be his future employment ; strange contrast between this and the polite accomplishments requisite in a clergyman of the established church.

Had he been designed for a back-wood's man, or a farmer in the forests of America, the father could not have done better than teach his son his own trade ; however, we now find him under his father's tutorship, and we can assure the reader Mr. Bourne was no gentle teacher ; the violence of his temper often caused the son to sigh in secret and pray for deliverance. He could not now be more than twelve or thirteen years of age, as he learned the wheelwrighting before the family left Ford-Hay farm. From a document before us we find the family removed to Bemersley in the year 1788, at which time Hugh would be sixteen years of age, he being born April 3rd, 1772, and the time of removal for farmers in North Staffordshire was then old May day, so that he would have spent one month and nine days of his seventeenth year at Ford-Hay, before removing to Bemersley. Notwithstanding his youth while at Ford-Hay, he toiled upon the farm or in the wheelwright's shop according to his father's calls, and the state of the weather and time of the year. Hard work was his daily lot ; he from his infancy knew not what it was to eat the bread of idleness. Industry, self-denial, and frugal care marked his footsteps all his youthful years ; and well it was for thousands then unborn that he was thus exercised, and accustomed to hardship, toil, and self-denial.

We must now enquire how, amidst all this labour and toil, young Bourne spent his leisure hours; what method he took to allay the ardent thirst for knowledge that possessed his mind. By some it might be thought that his intellectual improvement was at an end when he was taken from school, to break clods upon the farm, or toil in the wheelwright's shop. Let us hear what he himself says on the subject:—" When I was taken from school, my zeal for reading and study was intense. I went through the arithmetic afresh, and also geometry ; I also paid attention to astronomy, and natural philosophy, and made progress in history and geography : but my chief study was the bible, and religion ; often redeeming a few minutes from meal-times, and frequently after a hard day's work, I continued reading till midnight, when the family were in bed : so with hard work and hard study I was quite a slave, and the zeal for reading has accompanied me through life."

This we think may have been a dispensation of divine providence, for had it not been so, he might not have been able duly
to fill up the station in which the Lord in his mercy saw it good
in after life to place hin.

After Mr. Joseph Bourne had removed from Ford-Hay to the
larger farm at Bemersley, he gave up the wheelwrighting and
timber trades. This very circumstance to master Hugh was like
the refulgent rays of morning light shining in a dark place ;
indeed there were now to be discovered to his aspiring mind
sources from which he might draw supplies in rich abundance to
satiate his intellectual appetite.

This occurred as follows :—Mr. Bourne had a brother-in-law
living at Milton, about three miles from Bemersley, whose name
was Mr. William Sharratt ; he was a celebrated millwright and
engineer ; to this gentleman's establishment young Hugh was
transferred : it was to him a happy release ; it was a joyful morning when he wended his way to his uncle's, at Milton.   There
was a striking contrast between the father and uncle,—the former
was violent, and given to paroxysms of rage,—the latter was kind
and affable ; easy of approach ; and perfectly agreeable to commu-
nicate information to his pupils or apprentices. Besides, engineering
was more congenial to the mind of master Hugh than his father's
trade, for he says, " I never was fond of wheelwrighting, although
I learned it ; it was at my father's instance, not by my own
choice."   The bent and determination of young Bourne now was
to improve himself, and subsequent events have proved the
steadiness of his youthful aspirations.   Dr. Watts tells us, " A
soul inspired with the warmest aspirations after celestial beatitude,
keeps its powers attentive."   This was the case with young
Bourne ˙in his aspirations to high attainments, in scientific and
religious knowledge : close application to the branches of natural
philosophy, to which his mind was now directed by his kind uncle,
distinguished the days and nights of this young tyro. Mechanics,
hydrostatics, hydraulics, pneumatics, and optics, with the various
applications of wind, water, and steam to mills, engines, and machinery in general, were diligently investigated, the various prob-
lems thereof were solved, and a sound   practical knowledge
obtained.   His hard-earned knowledge was to him, in his retired
moments, a source of sacred pleasure and delight,—theories
studied in private were in his business reduced to practice, and

that which would not stand this test was cast aside, so that he soon became a proficient in engineering, and of great assistance to his uncle.

In his father's service his acquaintance with men and things had been contracted and superficial, confined to the locality of the lonely homestead of Ford-Hay farm, where, as he has said, the family seldom saw the face of a stranger. Is it therefore any wonder the boy Hugh grew up a bashful rustic ?

" To all obliging, yet reserved to all : "—

yet he was scrupulously vigilant and cautious in his movements, incessant watchfulness and circumspection marked his every step. But, however, in this new and enlarged sphere, his native rusticity received a polish from his observation of men and things. Henceforward he became a close observer—" Looked vigilantly on persons and things ; he was a close remarker."—

" He reads much ;
He is a great observer; and he looks
Quite through the deeds of men."—SHAKESPEARE.

The circle of Mr. Sharratt's acquaintance and business was large and extensive. This furnished his nephew with an opportunity of seeing different parts of the country, which to him was a new school—a school of progression. It has been said, " In philosophical enquiries, the order of nature should govern, which in all progression is to go from the place one is then in, to that which lies next to it." Master Hugh's philosophical enquiries had previously been confined to the " Geometry of motion, a mathematical science which shows the effects of powers, or moving forces, so far as they are applied to engines, and demonstrates the laws of motion : " but now his uncle's numerous calls to different parts of the nation, bring young Bourne's progressive powers into motion, that is, his legs and feet have to carry him from one place to another,—for there were no rail-roads at that time, so that he had to walk the country through where business called him. But this gave greater scope or enlargement to his intellectual faculties ; he could feast his thoughts on those fresh objects that adorned the landscape, or were met with in the domestic circles in which he from time to time was called to sojourn.

He thus learned much, which in after life was of great service to him. We will relate a circumstance that was printed on his memory, and there remained to the latest period of his life :—

He was remarkably temperate in his habits; the principles of sobriety and virtue had been planted, it has been seen, by his excellent mother; but on two occasions, when a youth, he was caught, as he said, by intoxication. He related to the biographer, perhaps not twelve months before his death, that he well remembered one of these tippling stirs; he said, " I had a golden half guinea in my pocket when intoxicated, and I thought I would freely give it to any one that would make me sober, so disagreeable were my feelings on that sad occasion, that it was a lesson to me through life; " nevertheless he drank a little, though but very little, and his refusing to drink with the mechanics in his uncle's employ gave offence at times, but he was resolute. Happily, Mr. Sharratt was a very temperate man, and this was a shelter to his nephew where he took refuge, and was thus better screened from the opposition of his fellow workmen. The circumstance we wish to relate will be best given perhaps in his own words :—" My uncle," says he, " having to put up a mill in a distant part of Cheshire, to grind or crush bark for a tanner, he took me with him, and we were at the gentleman's house where strong drink was plentiful, and my uncle tasted more freely than usual, which induced me to copy a little after him. But the gentleman of the house had a brother living with him who would not drink at all; this surprised me, as he also was a man of property, and thought of shortly becoming a master tanner. We slept together, and he kneeled down by the bedside and said his prayers, and I connected his saying his prayers with his abstaining from strong drink, and thought if he can do without strong drink I can, and I have had cause to thank God for this deliverance ; but for more than forty years I had to bear the reproach of being, as it was said, like nobody else : but the Lord has caused that strong drink reproach to cease, by raising up teetotalism. To his name be the glory.—At sea, 1844." Thus the reader will perceive, that the example of the tanner's brother lived in the recollection of Hugh Bourne, even when on the bosom of the wide Atlantic, on his way to America, considerably more than half a century after this incident occurred. While under his uncle's roof, his leisure was chiefly occupied with theological readings, and the study of God's word,—this last was a duty he could not on any account forego.

In the fields of divinity he had been a gleaner from early childhood, gathering slowly and laboriously from puritan, episcopal, and other writers, all the information that lay within his reach on the subject of man's salvation—a subject fraught with the most momentous consequences to his own welfare and peace. His sorrow on account of sin, and the fear of the torments of hell, which haunted his mind for the long period of twenty years, drove him to study, and to continual searching after comfort. He himself observes, " While I was absorbed in study and deep thought, my mind was less sensible to the pain and anguish of soul, which at times of retirement I was subject to." He at this period also commenced afresh to study the English language ;—not with a view of using hard words, and becoming versed in elegancies of style,—but that he might be able in good intelligible terms to give to others the ideas existing in his own mind : hence simplicity marks all the compositions that flowed from his pen in after life, so that the understanding of the labouring poor can easily comprehend his sense and sentiments, and for a proof of what we assert, we refer the reader particularly to a treatise " On the origin of language," and on " English Grammar," published by him in the Primitive Methodist Preachers' Magazine some years ago. Historical and geographical research also claimed a portion of his valuable time ; and in this field he gleaned vast stores of useful knowledge, insomuch that he could narrate with ease and dignity the principal events and facts recorded in ancient and modern, as well as church history, and at the same time describe the position of the places where the events transpired. The ecclesiastical history published by him for a series of years in the Primitive Methodist Magazine, of which he was the originator and editor, will illustrate what we say, and tend to show that few men were better versed in this kind of history than Hugh Bourne.

The British constitution, and the principles of jurisprudence, were studied by him with equal success ; hence his aptitude for rule and law-making for the Primitive Methodist Community, for which he was by providence raised up as if to be a legislator and governor. The classics, especially the Hebrew, Greek, and

Latin languages, and also French, obtained a share of his attention ; and like all his studies were pursued amidst difficulties, but still perseveringly pursued. For the present, however, we forbear to dwell any longer on his education and general studies, that we may proceed with his religious experience.

CHAPTER IV.

HEARS THE METHODISTS AT THE ASH—HIS CONVICTION NOT OWING TO
THE METHODISTS—A SMALL SOCIETY AT RIDGWAY—NEVER SAW
MR. WESLEY—A VISIT TO MACCLESFIELD—SEES SOME METHODISTS—HIS
GOOD WORKS—HANLEY WINDMILL—CLERK OF THE WORKS—ARMINIAN
MAGAZINE—MOTHER BORROWS A BOOK—MR. WESLEY'S SERMON—ARMI-
NIANS AND METHODISTS—QUAKERS, AND THEIR BOOKS, AND PERSECUTIONS
—FLETCHER'S LETTERS—CAPTAIN BARNABY AND OLD BOOTY—RESOLU-
TIONS—TEMPTATIONS—NOT ACQUAINTED WITH A PRESENT SALVATION—
OBTAINS DELIVERANCE—COMFORT AND JOY—DESIRES THE SALVATION OF
THE WORLD.

Hugh Bourne heard the methodists preach when he was very
young, and on this matter, subsequently writes as follows:—
" When I was a little boy at Ford-Hay, I was taken to hear
preaching at the Ash, a village not two miles from our place.
The chapel was fitted up by a Mr. Wood, who lived there, and
owned the Ash estates, and was a methodist ; and as the preaching was on the opposite Sunday to the Bucknall chapel service,
some of our people occasionally went and took me with them.
The preachers were zealous, but I could scarcely ever tell what
they said : and after a time Mr. Wood died, and the preaching
was soon discontinued. After this I scarcely knew anything of
the methodists during the time we remained in Stoke parish.
My being convinced of sin had nothing to do with the methodists,
as I did not then know what methodism was : that conviction
was a matter between God and myself ; no human being knew of
it, neither durst I speak of it to any one. I could then work a
little, and it took place between me and the Lord when I was
working in my little way in one of my father's fields. We, as
children, happily grew up without acquiring the habit of cursing
and swearing ; my father himself was a passionate man, and he
would have been severe if any one had been guilty of using such

language.*   When we came to Bemersley, there was a small society of methodists in Ridgway, a small village about half a mile from Bemersley, and they had their preaching in Standley-fields farm house; but having better church accommodation than when we lived at the Ford-Hay, we were what are considered good church-goers.   I never had an opportunity of hearing Mr. Wesley, neither did I ever see him; and through hearing evil reports, I was in my mind prejudiced against him.   Nor do I remember ever seeing any of his writings previous to the year 1799; I was for a number of years in doubt whether there was any really religious person in the world, any one really in the way to heaven : I knew of none who came up to my idea of religion, or to the idea I formed of it, neither had I met with any one more moral than myself, and seldom with any equally moral ; and as I did not myself see any possibility of escaping hell, my thought was,—what will become of them ?—but on one occasion I and another man went over to Macclesfield, and on our return a friend came with us through the town, and on noticing people going down the street, the person with me asked where they were going : the friend said, ' They are going to the methodist chapel ; it is a pretty place, you have not time, or else we would have gone down and have looked at it.'   While this was passing, my eye was upon the people, and it was impressed upon my mind, these have real religion.   This startled me from head to foot ; and I would in my own opinion have given a good deal for an acquaintance with these Macclesfield methodists, but that could not be accomplished.   The impression, however, never left me, and to this day I believe that the impression was from the Holy Ghost. —At sea, 1844."

We may here notice, that Hugh Bourne and his friend were travelling on worldly matters on the Sabbath day, which was highly improper, as he himself afterwards thought and preached. His strict morality, and the notions he had formed of religion, had not at that time sufficient weight with him to deter him from taking unnecessary journeys on the Lord's day.   The grosser acts of immorality, such as swearing, drunkenness, lying, cheating, &c.,

---

* Here is one redeeming trait in the father's character.   No child or servant was allowed by him to use profane language.   We doubt his example fell behind his precepts.

he shunned with the utmost abhorrence. This, and attention to
the established church's mode of worship—saying his prayers
night and morning, giving alms to relieve the distressed, and
striving to act justly toward his fellow men—this was the sum
and substance of Hugh Bourne's religion; but the views he had
of the spirituality of the law of God, and the sorrow that oppres-
sed his mind for so many years on account of his fearful appre-
hensions of the divine displeasure, caused him to be far from
satisfied with himself, or with the attainments of his churchism :
there was an inward monitor that told him he was not right with
the Lord ; and yet so deeply was he wedded to the law of works,
like his excellent mother, who had planted her creed in his heart,
that he could not see " That the great gift of salvation to lost and
fallen man, was not by works, lest any man should boast,—But
to him that worketh not, but believeth on him that justifieth the
ungodly, his faith is counted to him for righteousness."

Some years after this Macclesfield journey, a new windmill was
building at Hanley, in the Staffordshire Potteries. Hugh Bourne
was engaged in the millwrighting department, and understanding
that the clerk of the works was a methodist, he thought this was
a golden opportunity. He said to himself, " Now I shall see in
this man the perfection of methodism." He had occasionally
come into contact with professional methodists, and he bore great
respect to them, because they refrained from swearing ; but as a
whole those specimens of methodism that he had seen, or been
acquainted with, were far from coming up to the idea he had
formed of what religious characters should be. But he thought
in the gentleman appointed to over-look the erection of the
Hanley windmill, he should see an example of real religion, such
as appeared in the Macclesfield methodists. In this he was
doomed to disappointment. This gentleman was a kind, steady,
and respectable man ; but in regard to morality, he was not
equal to Bourne himself ; and this in a great measure tended to
lower in his estimation the example of the Macclesfield methodists : but, as he observes, " It did not quite sweep it away."
The example of the methodist clerk of the works was an injury
instead of a benefit to his mind ; it was a stumbling-block to
him, and caused a relaxation in his moral conduct, and he now
nearly gave up all for lost. Hope that had buoyed up his spirias

for so long a period during the struggles of his soul after
light and truth, now apparently died within him, for he thought
there was not a really righteous person in the world. " On one
occasion, when the Hanley mill was erecting," says he, " I got
a little information, which afterwards came into use. Being one
day in our over-looker's house, I took up a book belonging to his
brother ; it was a volume of the Arminian Magazine, for the year
1795, and I was interested with Bruce's Travels, and also noticed
a religious letter, written by a female, and dated Bristol, October
22nd, 1771 ; this letter took my attention, and caused me to
wonder who the Arminians were, and where they lived."

We shall now conduct the reader to a memorable period of
Hugh Bourne's life, the year of our Lord, 1799 : this was to
him the eventful year of jubilee ; his dungeon flamed with
hallowed light, the chains and fetters of sin were loosened, his
prison doors flew open, and his captive spirit was set free !   In
Isaiah xlii. 16. the Lord says, " I will bring the blind by a way
that they knew not ; I will lead them in paths *that* they have not
known : I will make darkness light before them, and crooked
things straight." This the Almighty, in his abundant mercy,
through the blood of the covenant, graciously fulfilled in H.
Bourne's experience this eventful year ! and in many instances
this same promise was fulfilled in his subsequent life and
labours. He had previously read a variety of the religious
books of different denominations, quakers, and others, and some
few very old ones ; and in particular a large work, entitled " A
child of light walking in darkness," by the Rev. T. Goodwin.
But out of these he could not learn the way to flee from the
wrath to come, the wrath that he saw continually hanging over
his head, and which he daily expected would burst with indigna-
tion and fury upon him, and sink him into hell : neither could he
determine which religious society was right. This latter difficulty
has puzzled many persons beside Hugh Bourne, and has caused
them to defer joining in fellowship with the people of God : but
Psalm cxii. 4. says, " Unto the upright there ariseth light in
darkness." This was verified in the case of our subject : infinite
wisdom saw the sincerity of his heart when panting for the gracious truths of the gospel, and compassion opened upon his dark
and intricate path a blaze of pure and divine light, by which he

was enabled fully to cast his soul, with all the weight of its accumulated sin, at the feet of Jesus, and realize salvation through his death upon the cross.

This was brought about as follows :—Mrs. Bourne, being on family business at Burslem one day, asked a Mr. J. Mayer, a methodist, to lend her a book for her own reading, when he very kindly put into her hands a book as thick as a bible, composed of biographies, treatises, sermons, and tracts, bound up together : it contained the life of the Rev. J. Fletcher, of Madely, in Shropshire ; sermons by Mr. Wesley, Jane Cooper's letters, life of T. Taylor and John Haime, methodist preachers ; Alleine's Alarm, Baxter's call to the unconverted, a treatise on the articles and homilies of the church of England, and other matters. This book contained a body of divinity entirely new to Hugh Bourne ; not one of the publications it contained had ever fallen in his way before, although he had been a reader from early life. On the volume he looked with delight and pleasure ; and when he had run over the title pages of the different pieces it contained, he at once, with zeal and avidity, commenced reading ; and many an hour he stole from sleep and meal-times for the purpose ; he read and thought, and thought again : the light this wonderful book afforded to his enquiring mind, cheered his path, and he was now fully lifted out of the *slough of despond,* in which he had been wallowing for twenty years. A main wish of his heart for years had been to find out which was the right religious society ; and his dissatisfaction on this point was the insurmountable obstacle that stood in the way between him and that christian fellowship he so long and ardently desired. He thought the people among whom he should discover true and vital godliness, should be the very people to whom he would attach himself,—" Their God should be his God."

In this book he found a sermon by Mr. Wesley, founded upon John v. 7 ; this cleared the matter up, and at once removed the thick vail of ignorance, that for so many years of sorrow had covered his mind, and hidden from him the true sense of a subject he was so anxious to understand. Mr. Wesley says, in the sermon referred to, " Whatever the generality of people may think, it is certain that opinion is not religion, no, not right opinion ;—not assent to one or ten thousand truths ;— even right opinion is as distant from religion as the east is from the west. Persons may be quite right in their opinions, and yet have no religion at all ; and on the other hand, persons may be truly religious who hold many wrong opinions." And Mr. Wesley further shows that there have been really religious persons among different denominations. Hugh Bourne writes, "The reading of this sermon opened my mind, and cleared my way for reading the other treatises in the said book ; and this sermon gave me more light and information than any book I had ever before read. And previous to this, I do not know of having received any real spiritual light from any or all the sermons I had ever heard ; but this sermon of Mr. Wesley's, on the Trinity, was to me as a light indeed ; it cleared my way through, and gave me to see that I might join any really religious society, without under-valuing others, and might profit by all, and this has been a blessing to me ever since."

The reader may be ready to ask why he did not forthwith go and join the methodists ? and we may answer, that the Lord in his guiding providence did not so lead him. When the Hanley windmill was building, he was stumbled by the conduct of the clerk of the works, whom he supposed to be a true methodist ; and as regarded externals, his own morals surpassed those of many professors of methodism, even in his unconverted state. Another obstacle which stood in the way of his joining the methodists was, an objection to the house in which the Ridgway class met. This by himself and others was thought unworthy, and made him think the methodists were a fallen people ; and, indeed, at this time he firmly believed it was so. But the promise—"I will bring the blind by a way *that* they know not"—the Lord in his mercy was about to verify, by removing the stumbling block out of his way. The Ridgway preaching had by this time been removed to the house of Mr. John Birchenough, a farmer ; he was a methodist, and his house stood in what are called Standley fields, a short distance from Ridgway, and about a quarter of a mile from Bemersley ; at the services here H. Bourne occasionally attended. It so happened in one of his business journeys, that a person asked him to carry a message to farmer Birchenough's. He says respecting this visit, "While I was conversing with my neighbour Birchenough, my attention was drawn to a book in the window. I took it up, and behold, it was the Arminian magazine for 1795 ; I asked him to lend it me. "O," said the good old man, "you are as welcome as flowers in May; and I have several more volumes, and you shall read them all." Truly for a little time I was a happy man; but how was I surprised to find the Arminians were the methodists! My views were changed,—I then thought the methodists of North Staffordshire were fallen, but that perhaps the others were not." *

" At this time I had a few weeks' work to do for a respectable quaker; and he lent me large volumes, containing the annals of the first race of quakers: and having been delivered from laying stress on opinions, I found that the religion of the heart was alike in all. The first race of quakers were endued largely with the spirit of the martyrs: they exhibited examples of faith, patience, and sufferings, not often equalled ; and a recital of the persecutions they endured is enough to make a person's ears tingle: many went through afflictions and imprisonments to crowns of life, and even in the midst of dreadful persecution, their zeal for open-air worship was great, and could not be conquered. The reading of the quakers' books enabled me to see a little more clearly into the mystery and power of faith,—truly their trials of faith were great. And at home my friend Birchenough lent me the life of Mr. Wesley, by Coke and Moore, and this gave me assistance. I also was much enlightened in reading Mr. Fletcher's "Letters on the spiritual manifestation of the Son of God," which were published in the methodist magazine, for 1793 ; and I was edified also by reading the biographies in the magazines ;—on the whole I got a clearer view of the manifestation of Jesus Christ, of justification by faith, and of being born again, and I felt a degree of satisfaction in contemplating religion. But, alas! such a flood of evil thoughts poured into my mind, that I did not set out for heaven with all my heart. I did not then know that satan had power to suggest evil thoughts ; but so great was their force, that I concluded to put off seeking religion till a future time ; still I was aware of its being happy for those

* It may be recollected he had seen a volume of the Arminian Magazine on a former occasion, and had been particularly struck with a letter it contained; and he had even resolved to go into the west of England in search of these people called Arminians, not knowing they were the same as the methodists ; hence his surprise on making this discovery.

who sought and obtained it: but to the present day the awfulness
of that putting off, almost causes me to tremble."—Thus wrote
Hugh Bourne on the wide Atlantic, in 1844.

We have thus traced the providential dealings of heaven with
this extraordinary man to nearly the dawn of that day when the
sun of righteousness with refulgent rays shone upon his dark and
benighted mind; and as the darkness is generally greater just
before the breaking of day, or the sun rising from beneath the
horizon, so it was with Hugh Bourne immediately before his
conversion to the God and father of our Lord Jesus Christ. The
sable curtain, or veil of moral darkness, was thrown on the path
that lay before him, by the foul fiend of the bottomless
pit, the adversary of mankind, that goes "About like a roaring
lion, seeking whom he may devour;" and if it were possible for
joy to be diffused through the regions of despair, we conceive it
would have been so on this occasion. We could easily imagine
there would be a chuckling of hellish delight at having again
thwarted this son of twenty years' bondage, in his attempt at
escaping the chains and fetters which his satanic majesty had
rivetted upon his mind for so long a period! Behold, the arch
fiend dashes the cup of comfort from his lip when he is about to
taste it, and he is again made to drink at the too often fatal waters
of procrastination, and his soul's salvation is deferred to a future
time. But how great is the mercy of our God, who willeth not
the death of one sinner; and Hugh Bourne might with propriety
have said, "'Great is thy mercy toward me, and thou hast delivered my soul from the lowest hell!'"

A circumstance now turned up that at once settled the matter
between him and the salvation of his soul. The miserable history
of captain Barnaby and old Booty fell in his way. The day after
Hugh Bourne read this strange account, he was working at the
windmill of his friend the quaker, at Werrington. "And in the
noon hour," he says, "I was relating to the men what I had read;
and as I was finishing the account, an impression went through my
mind, it will not do to go after old Booty—it will not do to go
after old Booty! and it kept repeating in my mind with force for
some time; it did not appear to be a voice, but an impression
equal to a voice. I was startled from head to foot, and afraid of

the men perceiving that something was the matter with me ; and, indeed, there, was " No room for mirth or trifling here," for as the impression went through my mind—it will not do to go after old Booty—my conscience replied, it will not do to go into that burning mountain; I must never come out again." His mind was made up in an instant—he at one stroke cut off every thing that hindered, sought the Lord with his whole heart, determining whatever inconvenience it might bring upon him, or whatever loss he might sustain, he would flee from the wrath to come ; his soul's immortal interest was at stake, there was no time to be lost, now was the day of salvation. His soul was humbled in the dust before the Lord ; he acknowledged that in the multiplicity of business calls, he had made over free with the Sabbath, and had not strictly attended to its sanctity; but now at all risks of worldly interests as a business man, he lays the axe " At the root of the tree" of every thing that would lead him to a breach of the holy Sabbath ; and the words of Jesus Christ, " I will love him, and will manifest myself unto him," arrest his attention, and he begins to pray for this manifestation with all his might: but, behold, the old adversary cast at him another fiery dart, and it came suddenly to his mind, that it was too late—that he had sinned against light in not setting out for heaven when he knew the way—that delaying was committing the unpardonable sin, and that he was now worse than Cain and Judas ! This assault from the powers of darkness, threw him into the greatest distress and agony of mind. To think that he from infancy had been striving, according to the light he had, to serve and fear God, and now it had come to this—namely, the committing the unpardonable sin ! The pains of hell gat hold upon him, and the sorrows of death compassed him about. He cried out by reason of the disquietude of his soul, his sleep left him, his appetite failed him, lovers and friends stood aloof, the enemy following up the stroke which had laid him in the dust of despondency, and clothed his soul with sackcloth and ashes, now suggested he must not pray, for this would make the matter still worse. This was a calamity he least expected ; he had been a praying person from the earliest dawn of childhood, and now, must not pray at all ! This quite overcame his reasoning faculties, and sank his spirit within him to the depth of the deepest grief. In this direful state of inbred woe, he had none to confer with him, no man that he knew cared for

his soul ; and he was ignorant that "The prince of the power of
the air" could put bad thoughts into people's minds : " And now,"
says he, " two or three of my days were sorrowful indeed ; but it
came to my mind I had better pray, for if I did not pray Jesus
Christ would not manifest himself unto me, and then I could not
be born again; and if not born again, I should be sure to go to
hell, and I could but go to hell praying!   Certainly here was a
ray from the true light which lighteth every man that cometh into
the world, but my heart felt as hard as a stone.   This too was
very distressing, as I had not been accustomed to feel hardness
of heart; but in a few days I felt a degree of comfort in prayer,
and this enabled me fully to believe that the Lord had not wholly
forsaken me."   The small portion of comfort he felt in prayer
was like the rising light that shines more and more unto the perfect day : still the sorrows of his inmost soul were truly heavy,
and the wrestlings with God in the agony of prayer for mercy
were great.   The time was now with increased diligence redeemed
for exercises in prayer and devotedness to God.   Every moment
was carefully bought up and spent in petitioning heaven for the
great blessings of pardon, and the remission of his sins and trans-
gressions.

The reader must bear in mind, that in the spring of the year
1799, Hugh Bourne was an entire stranger to the doctrine of a
free, full, and present salvation, which in after life became the
great topic of all his sayings and writings in prose and poetry, and
of his public ministrations and private conversations.   " But,"
says he, " I touched upon the great fundamental doctrine of the
blessed gospel of truth, one Sunday morning in my father's house, as
I sat reading in Mr. Fletcher's letters on the spiritual manifestation
of the Son of God, and realized the blessing named in John xiv.
21. where Christ says, ' I will love him, and will manifest myself
to him ; ' and he manifested himself to me ; and I was born again
in an instant! yea, passed from death unto life.   The naughty
was taken out of my heart, and the good put in.   In an instant I
had power over sin, which I had not before; and I was filled with
joy, and love, and glory, which made a full amends for the twenty
years' suffering !   The bible looked new ; creation looked new ;
and I felt a love to all mankind ; and my desire was that friends
and enemies, and all the world, if possible, might be saved."

CHAPTER V.

WILDERNESS OF PAIN—MOUNT SINAI—MOUNT SION—HIGH FLOW OF JOY—
POWER OVER SIN—SUBTLE SUGGESTION—LOSES HIS EVIDENCE—QUAKERS'
MEETING—BUNYAN'S PILGRIM—THE LORD'S WILL RESPECTING HIS BEING
A METHODIST—LOVEFEAST AT BURSLEM—HIS FIRST TICKET—AN EXCUR-
SION—NOTICES ON CLASS MEETINGS—WEARIED AT A PRAYER MEETING—
RELIGIOUS BOOKS—GROWTH IN GRACE—DISSENTING CHAPEL AND SER-
MON—HEARS MR. BRADBURN—A NOTE ON PREACHING AND PRAYING.

We have travelled with Hugh Bourne in the wilderness of pain
and sorrow for twenty years, but now have come from the mount
that burned with fire, and blackness, and tempest, from the glare
and thunders of Sinai, and are come to Mount Sion, and to Jesus,
the mediator of the new covenant, and to the blood of sprinkling,
that speaketh better things than that of Abel, and have witnessed
the joy of his heart at the glorious transition from a life of slavish
fear, to one of praise and thanksgiving. Let us accompany him in
his onward progress, and listen to what he says in the first part
of his journey to the better country :—" When the high flow of
joy had subsided, I still felt myself filled with all joy and peace in
believing : the peace of God which passeth all understanding, kept
my heart and mind through Christ Jesus : being justified by faith,
I had peace with God through our Lord Jesus Christ. Ere long it
came to my mind that all was fancy : and I did not then know that
this was a suggestion of the enemy of souls, to weaken my faith,
or at least to throw me out of faith. This put me to a pause ;
but among other things it struck my mind that I had inward
power ; and I said within myself, I have power over sin now, and
I had not before, and I am sure it is right, and so on I reasoned ;
it being evident the Lord had given me power over sin, and
still continued to bestow that power, I held fast my faith, and
pressed on in the Lord. After a time it came to my mind that I

had done with sorrow, and now I should only have joy. This subtle suggestion of the enemy of souls threw me off my guard, and after some days, by means of a sudden temptation, I lost the evidence of the pardon of my sins,—I then had sorrow indeed : I did not lose the evidence by any outward ·act, but by a giving way in my heart. I mourned deeply ; but after a time I was invited to the Quakers' quarterly meeting, on a week-day at Leek, a market town about seven or eight miles from Bemersley. I went, and while one of. their public friends was speaking on a point touching my experience, I was again led into faith, and the Lord restored me to the joy of his salvation, and I came home thankful to Almighty God ; and after this I learned to hold fast the beginning of my confidence steadfast to the end." There is a great variety in the Lord's dealings with the precious souls of the sons of men. To some he sends guides and brethren, from their first setting out in the journey to the better country, to assist, comfort, and encourage them in the way ; and like kind and gentle shepherds, they carry the lambs in their bosom, leading them that are with young into green pastures, and feeding them beside the still waters : others, like christian, Bunyan's first pilgrim, have to start and make their way alone.

Hugh Bourne was a firm believer in the efficacy and influence of the prayers of the church of God upon earth. He thus expresses himself, " Every one has a part in the prayers of the whole church of Christ upon earth, and in their exercisings of faith ; and in addition to this, christians in fellowship are helped by the immediate exercisings of faith for each other when absent, and with each other when present ; and when they are met together to pray one for another, each helping each to walk humbly before God, strengthening each other patiently to bear the trials of life, and the tribulations of this present world. But like Bunyan's pilgrim, I had to make my way alone. The Lord neither gave me guide nor companion in the way to the cross. I was painfully convinced of sin when I was but a small boy, and this without the aid or knowledge of any man ; and during my twenty ·sorrowful years, I went through much moral and religious readings. In the year 1799, I opened upon methodist readings, useful to me in general ; and Messrs. J. Wesley and J. Fletcher's writings were, by the blessing of God, made

useful to me above any other. This same year I read the books
of the first quakers—great examples of patient suffering, zealous
for open-air worship, mighty in faith. They would exercise faith
even in silence, until they moved whole neighbourhoods by so
doing. I was much edified in reading of the faith, patience, and
sufferings of the primitive quakers; but I met with none in the
like faith and power, nor was their morality superior to what
mine was before the Lord manifested himself to me, and pardoned
my sins; and in my quaker friend's house, at Werrington, I saw
no signs of family worship. Then there were the methodists, who
had a society at Ridgway, and their weekly class-meetings had
been held in one and the same house for some years; and a member of the family living in that house, was of unhappy note in the
neighbourhood, and had been so for years, and people not favoura-
ble to religion, made no scruple of setting forth this person as
being the best methodist among them; and as I knew but little
of the methodists, and never heard this contradicted, it need not
be a wonder that I should think the methodists a fallen people.
Being quite in a dilemma, I made prayer and supplication to
Almighty God to manifest his will, and lead me right in this important matter; and I determined to consult no man, nor to take
any man's advice, but wait until the Lord should make known his
holy will in regard to this very weighty affair, and to attend diligently the means of grace; * for I was sensible it was my duty to
join some religious society; but until I had received direction
from the Lord, no human persuasion could have prevailed with
me to join any religious community. I waited some weeks for an
answer, till the Lord in his mercy manifested his will that I
should be a methodist."

In June, this year, 1799, Hugh Bourne's aged friend, farmer
Birchenough, at the methodist preaching house, told him of a
lovefeast, to be held on Burslem Wake Monday evening, which
would be towards the latter end of the month. This lovefeast, he
said, would be in the methodist chapel, at Burslem, and he dis-

* The usual custom of the Bourne family, from Hugh Bourne's childhood, was to attend the morning service at the established church, two
miles distant from either Ford-Hay or Bemersley, where they resided;
but since H. B's. reading of the methodist magazine, he, his mother, and
brother James, attended the methodist preaching service in the afternoon,
at Mr. J. Birchenough's.

40

tinctly wished Hugh Bourne to attend it, saying, he would attend with him ; and as he (H. B.) had read of lovefeasts in Mr. Wesley's life, the prospect of seeing one was pleasing. "One day," says he, "my aged friend said the preaching at his house on the ensuing Sabbath would be at six o'clock in the evening, as the preacher purposed to make an excursion; and he was to accompany the preacher, and he wished me to be of the party. I agreed, and it happened to be the time of renewing tickets, and I having come over to friend Birchenough's early on the Sunday morning, the preacher, for readiness, was writing the tickets; and on his asking my name, I said I am not one of you. But friend B. said you must take the ticket to go with me to Burslem lovefeast. So I took it, little thinking that receiving the ticket constituted me a member; so my aged friend and his helper made me a member without letting me know that they did so. On the excursion, the preacher spoke at two places; and when we were returning, he spoke to me of helping at the class. My quick answer was that I should not go to that house. He asked me why? and with some reluctance I told him. He said the class must be removed. I was startled, and said, you must not remove your class for me. He said whether you join or not, it must be removed, for it is contrary to the rules for the class to meet in such a house. And he observed he should speak to Mr. Brettell, the superintendent preacher, on the subject. This pacified me; and I was further surprised on being told that the objectionable person at Ridgway was not a member, nor ever had been. At Burslem, on the wake Monday, I was surprised on being told of my being a member of the Methodist Connexion, but as the Lord had not then manifested his will, it seemed easy to withdraw again if needful. I was accompanied by my aged friend to the powerful and lively lovefeast, led by Mr. J. Brettell; and this lovefeast I shall ever remember. In it the Lord manifested to me that it was his will for me to be a methodist; and notwithstanding my timidity, I was near rising up to speak, and at the close, I was heart and hand a methodist. The next Sabbath morning, the Ridgway class having been removed to a suitable house, I was there as a regular member; and my beloved mother joined : our leaders were four Burslem methodists, who were planned to come in turns. The labour was considerable, but the Lord put it into their hearts, and their kind attention to us was great; and we were on Mr. Wesley's preferable plan of having variety in class leading."

Class leading notices.—Variety in class leading was a valuable and essential part in primitive methodism; and in June, 1744, Mr. Wesley, in conference, made various rules and regulations in regard to class leading, some of which are as follow :—

Q. "How may the leaders of classes be made more useful?

A. 1.—Let each of them be diligently examined concerning his method of meeting class. 2.—Let us recommend to all the following directions :—*first*, Let every leader carefully enquire how every soul in his class prospers ; not only how each person observes the outward rules, but how he grows in the knowledge and love of God. *Second*, Let the leaders converse with all the preachers as frequently and as freely as possible.

Q. Can anything further be done, in order to make the meeting of the classes lively and profitable ?

A 1.—Let the leaders frequently meet each other's classes. 2.—Let us observe which leaders are most useful to those under their care ; and let these meet the other classes as often as possible. 3.—Frequently make new leaders."—So far, Mr. Wesley.

"We had due cause to thank God for setting us forth with variety in class leading in our Ridgway class. Our kind-hearted local preachers were planned to preach at our friend Birchenough's every Sunday, at two o'clock in the afternoon. We had no public prayer meetings appointed, or any other public or social means,—I ought to have said of our blessed Lord and Saviour Jesus Christ, ' He hath done all things well,' but instead of that, I gave way to temptation, so as to think our public means were scanty ; but I may well say, ' The Lord pardoned his servant in this thing.' One Sunday morning I went to Burslem, to see a prayer meeting ; but in it I felt wearied, which made me angry

with myself.*   The chief means of grace with me were the
preachings, and when it so happened that a preacher could not
come, I felt it as a loss : but I was taken to a lovefeast held this
same year, 1799, in Tunstall chapel, and to the preaching in
Burslem chapel in the evening; and after this I attended the
Sunday preachings in these two chapels ; and for about three
times, I attended a prayer meeting in a house after preaching.
I was asked to pray ; but if I attempted it, the power of utterance
seemed to forsake me, and I knew not whether I should ever be
able to pray in public ; and in the prayer meetings I always felt
a weariness, which caused me to be angry with myself, thinking
the fault was in me, and I could not account for it.   I attended
from a wish to be acquainted with prayer meetings ; but the
bodily labour was too great for this to be continued.   I grew most
in grace at preachings ; and yet it was almost without the aid of
memory, as at the conclusion I seldom could remember a single
sentence.   At times texts would come into my mind, and I found
myself almost involuntarily planning out sermons, yet hardly ever
so as to satisfy myself.   Tunstall is three miles west from Bemersley, and Burslem is one mile south of Tunstall, and we reckon it
to be about three miles and a half from Bemersley : but the satisfaction of being sure to hear sermons, made all amends.   I may also
notice, that I was present in Tunstall chapel when the Sunday
school was commenced.   On my setting out for heaven in earnest,
my readings and studies were turned very much, though not wholly,
from arts and sciences, and general learning, and fixed more fully
than before on the scriptures of truth, and on christian
experience and doctrines.   The methodist magazines supplied
treasures of experience, and Mr. Wesley's sermons, and his
notes on the new testament, laid down doctrines; and to these
were afterwards added Mr. Fletcher's checks to antinomi-
anism,—these books with others formed a treasury.   I had to
work hard and closely ; still by redeeming the time, and applying my spare hours to earnest prayer, to exercises of faith, and
diligence in study, I, by the good hand of God upon me, got a

* We judge the fault was not in Hugh Bourne's inattention to the voice
of prayer, but in the long winded supplications of the prayer makers. It
is more than probable the Burslem methodists had departed in some
measure from the short and lively exercises strongly recommended by
Mr. Wesley to the methodist societies ; if so, we do not wonder at Hugh
Bourne's being wearied ; as long prayers and sermons, unaccompanied
with a divine unction, are always wearisome.

more clear and extensive knowledge of the scriptures, with clearer
views of christian experience, and a more correct and enlarged
acquaintance with the doctrines of Christ. My daily temptations
and trials were great ; still by the blessing of God, I experienced
a growth in grace, and an enlargement of heart. I was happy in
not undervaluing other religious communities ; and one week-day
evening returning from work, coming through Hanley, I stepped
into a dissenting chapel : the minister spoke from Numbers xxi.
4.—" And the soul of the people was much discouraged because
of the way." I was blest under his preaching, and on my way
home, the words, I will never leave thee nor forsake thee, so came
into my mind, that I turned my head to see who spake, but there
was no body near ; and the word again went through my mind
with a flow of heavenly power. This was strengthening, and my
heavenly father knew that I had need of it, and to him be the
glory and dominion, for ever and ever, amen. I *respected* other
religious communities, but *loved* my own : the travelling preachers
I highly esteemed, and I honoured the local preachers ; and any
one that prayed in public, in prayer meetings, I respected as
greatly superior to myself : I willingly, gladly, and thankfully
took the lowest seat. As my opportunities of attending preachings on week-days were limited, and as I did not pray in public,
nor sustain any part in the circuit management, nor in its
general business affairs, my main work was to attend to my own
growth in grace, and in this, by the blessing of Almighty God,
I was greatly assisted by the various means of grace, and by pious
conversations ; and the connexion by supplying me with these
helps, was, under God, of great service to me, and I valued it
highly. For two years, from June 1799, the time of my joining
the Wesleyans, I was much edified in hearing sermons, and had
great zeal for attending preachings ; but during that time, I
ranked with such as are edified without being able to tell what
the preacher has said : with about one single exception,* I re-
tained scarcely any remembrance of what the preachers said during
those two years, yet I loved the preachers, and had great zeal to
sit under their ministry. What I read would dwell in my

* This exception was as follows :—In July, 1799, Mr. Samuel Bradburn,
then superintendent of Birmingham circuit, being on his way to the Manchester conference, stopped and preached on a week-night at Burslem.
He had been represented to Hugh Bourne as one of the greatest and most

memory; what I heard preached from the pulpit, would for the most part, be gone by the time the service was ended : In some instances, I have remembered a single sentence, and occasionally two or three sentences, but even these in general faded away."

popular preachers in the Wesleyan Connexion; and H. Bourne happening to be over at Burslem on business, had an opportunity of hearing him, and heard him with admiration. His text was, Psalm cxix. 132.   In the course of his sermon, he spoke rather disparagingly of preaching in general; said it was merely talking to our fellow creatures, and seemed to make light of it. But praying, he observed, was great—talking to Almighty God. H. Bourne had looked upon methodist preachers as being little, if any, inferior to the angels, and their preachings as precious gold; but the views given him by this much extolled preacher, began to season his admiration, and had at first a slow and gradual, but after some years, a powerful influence on his mind and conduct. He says, "There was certainly a misleading in the matter; but it may be cleared up by a few remarks on *praying and preaching*. Praying is great,—it is talking to the Almighty; yet by and through the blood of the Lamb it is free to all, even to little children. Preaching is of two kinds or sorts: one sort is mentioned in 1 Peter i. 12. 'Them that have preached the gospel unto you with the Holy Ghost sent down from heaven.' And in 1 Corinthians, ii. 4. "And my speech and my preaching *was* . . . . . in demonstration of the spirit and of power.' This sort of preaching is great and high, yea, 'It is mighty through God to the pulling down of strong holds.' It is a means of turning many to righteousness, and 'They that turn many to righteousness shall shine as the stars for ever and ever.' The other sort of preaching is that which stands only in man's wisdom : it is noticed and spoken against in 1 Corinthians, ii. 4. 'And my speech and my preaching was not with enticing words of man's wisdom,' and in verse 13. 'Not in the words which man's wisdom teacheth;' and 1 Corinthians, i. 17. 'For Christ sent me to preach the gospel, not with wisdom of words, lest the cross of Christ should be made of none effect.'" This latter was unhappily Mr. Bradburn's own sort of preaching, and in it stood his great popularity; and this sort cannot be set too low: but this popular man's words dwelling continually in H. Bourne's mind, induced him at length to look upon preaching as being in general of very little use. Whatever may be thought of Mr. Bradburn's opinion, and the effect that opinion had upon Hugh Bourne's mind, one thing we think is certain,—this circumstance of under-valuing preaching, will be found to have been the first cause which induced him in after years to bring into active service at camp meetings and other means the powerful hosts of pious praying labourers, and foster with parental care and watchfulness the talents of praying men and women, which have been of such signal service in the Primitive Methodist Connexion, and which were so highly valued and esteemed by him to his dying day; indeed, the praying labourers were looked upon by him as the principal instruments in the revival and perpetuation of primitive methodism.

CHAPTER VI.

A NEW CHAPTER OF EVENTS—FIRST HALF OF NINETEENTH CENTURY—
ARCHIMEDES—MAJESTIC RIVERS, THEIR SOURCES—ENGLISH CAMP MEET-
INGS—THE DIAMOND—DALES GREEN AND HARRISEHEAD—MOW COP—
KINGSWOOD COLLIERS AND THOSE OF MOW—THE PAST CONSTRASTED WITH
THE PRESENT TIMES—CHURCHES AND CHAPELS—PROGRESS—ITS CAUSES.

" The first springs of great events, like those of great rivers,
are often small." We must now direct the reader's attention to a
new chapter of events,—events that produced in the first half of
the nineteenth century, a great moral, and spiritual improvement
in the condition of the labouring masses of our countrymen;
indeed, Hugh Bourne, according to our notion, was raised up of
God for the special purpose of benefiting the poor of our father-
land, by providing a useful ministry, adapted to the wants of the
lower grades of society, which had been too much neglected since
the days of Whitfield and Wesley. Of this anon.

" Give me a point of support for my lever, and I will lift the
world," said Archimedes the ancient geometrician, who in
defence of his country, when besieged by Marcellus the Roman
general, contrived means to raise the enemy's vessels of war
into the air, to dash them upon the sea, and set them on
fire with burning mirrors. Hugh Bourne was honoured to
employ an instrument as powerful as the lever of Archimedes,
namely, a plain, simple, and devoted ministry of the gospel,
which having the bible for its fulcrum, and faith as its motive
power, lifted tens of thousands up out of an horrible pit, and
out of the miry clay, and raised them from the deepest moral
and spiritual degradation, to a position of worldly respectability,
personal happiness, and general usefulness.

Look, gentle reader, at the majestic rivers that carry on the
face of their broad channels the ships of war, and the vessels
which carry the flags of all nations, and are laden with the rich

productions of the earth, and ask yourself from whence flow these mighty waters, by the traffic on which our giant merchants and lords of commerce are aggrandized : the answer to the question will be found to have reference to some remote mountain, or elevated table land ; there you will find the fountain-heads or starting-places of those powerful streams or rivers, which are of such vast importance to the cities of opulence, by whose towers and banks they roll in majesty to their termination, there to commingle with the waters of the mighty deep. And if we turn our thoughts to the ENGLISH CAMP MEETINGS, and the great and powerful revival of primitive methodism that followed their introduction, the question arises, with whom, and on what part of the British Isles did they originate ? Come with us, gentle reader, and we will show you an uncultivated mountain,—a moral wilderness, where the people are wholly given up to the imaginations of their own evil hearts, no man caring for their souls, as the scene where heaven designed the mighty movement referred to to commence, and where the blessed lever was first planted. Hugh Bourne was in the year 1800 in his native rusticity, like the precious gem encased in earth, or encrusted with concrete matter ; but the rude concretion lessons not the intrinsic value of the diamond ; it only prevents the light and lustre thereof from bursting forth. The hand of the lapidary removes the surrounding particles that mar its appearance, and brings out the brilliancy inherent in it.   " It will seem a hard matter to shadow a gem, or well paint a diamond that hath many sides, and give the lustre where it ought ; " and we can assure the reader it is a difficult matter to show forth all the rays of light that dart across our path, as we journey with the subject of this memoir, before we arrive at the point where the blaze of evangelical light, clear as the sun, bursts upon our astonished vision, and the spirit of Almighty God is poured out upon the *mountaineers* of Mow Cop, and the inhabitants of the surrounding neighbourhood, who are thereby aroused from their spiritual lethargy, and have their faces turned towards the zion of God, while they are enquiring their way thither.

> " So man, who here seems principal, alone,
>   Perhaps acts second to some power unknown ;
>   Touches some wheel, or verges to some goal,—
>   'Tis but a part we see, and not a whole."

Temptations, sufferings, and severe trials beset the path of Hugh
Bourne ; business calls multiply, and daily labours increase ; so
that he is cut off from the week-night ministrations of the travelling preachers, as well as prayer meetings, and other social means
held on the week-nights, for the edification of the church.   This
debarring by business calls from a participation in social and
religious intercourse with the people of God, to a young and
zealous convert was distressing ; and to a mind so well convinced
as was Hugh Bourne's of the good arising from christian fellowship, must have been so grievous, that we do not wonder that in
this part of his pilgrimage he manifests some degree of impatience, instead of resting in the Lord till the tide of opportunities
and privileges shall return in his favour.

Early in the year 1800, he purchased a quantity of oak timber,
growing on a farm at Dales Green, between Harrisehead and
Mow Cop.   This very circumstance brought him into contact with
the colliers, and others of the inhabitants of this mountainous
part of North Staffordshire.   Mow Cop—anciently called Mole
Cop—is a rough, craggy mountain, running nearly north and
south , ranging between Staffordshire and Cheshire, and is situate
in both counties.   The southern end is nearly two miles from the
vale of Kidsgrove colliery, in Staffordshire, and the northern end
runs within about three miles of the town of Congleton, in
Cheshire ; and is about three miles north-west from Bemersley,
the homestead of the Bourne family.   Harrisehead, the scene of
Hugh Bourne's early labours in the cause of truth and piety, is
half a mile east from Mow Cop : it is a somewhat lower range of
country running parallel with Mow Cop to a considerable extent.
This lower range is elevated perhaps some hundreds of feet
above the level of the flat parts of Cheshire,—this we gather from
the elevation of Mow Cop, which is said to be one thousand feet
above the level of the sea.   The land on Mow Cop and its neighbourhood, was, in 1800, to a considerable degree, unproductive ;
indeed, the greater part of the moorlands of North Staffordshire
resembles the bleak and barren parts of North Wales.   Prior to
Hugh Bourne's speculation in the oak timber, at Dales Green, he
had regretted the scantiness of the means of grace at Ridgway,
where he met in society : but here he found things considerably
worse,—the whole of the inhabitants, apparently, were destitute

of religion and religious feelings, and given up to the grosser acts
of immorality and ungodliness, insomuch that at times it was
difficult for a stranger to pass over Harrisehead without being
insulted or injured. Mr. Wesley gives an appalling account of
the character of the Kingswood colliers, when the gospel was first
introduced among them by Mr. Whitfield had himself; and in
the mountainous district of Mow Cop, the Kingswood colliers
were resembled by the colliers of North Staffordshire; and we
question very much whether the latter did not exceed the former
in ignorance and crime. Among the mountains and barren rocks
of Mow Cop and its vicinity, providence led Hugh Bourne to fix
the lever of gospel truth, by which the rustics were lifted from the
depths of ignorance, blind stupidity, and sin, into the light of
God's countenance, as manifested in the Lord Jesus Christ.
Hugh Bourne is no sooner in possession of his Dales Green pur-
chase, than he begins to think how he can get away from such a
moral desert; for such was the general character of the people,
that he greatly feared for his own religious safety : and his mind
was not a little pained with the idea that haunted him in the
intercourse with these characters, which his business calls compelled him to practice, that one day or another he should fall by
the hand of the enemy, through the agency of these ungodly
colliers, and so make shipwreck of faith and a good conscience.
But the providence that guides the helm of human affairs, permitted him not to realize his wishes as to leaving the place, but
contrariwise he was detained, and as it were, chained for a time in
this uncultivated wilderness. His business engagements increase
on his hands,—he is employed to execute the carpenter's work at
a mountain farm—the manager of the Stonetrough colliery en-
gages him to do the wood work connected with the working of
that coal mine, so that all prospect of leaving is for the present
out of the question. The reader will pardon our tarrying a little
longer on this celebrated spot, as we cannot pass it over without
a few remarks.

We will, by the reader's permission, accompany him to the top
of Mow Cop, and when we have gained the summit, and quietly
seated ourselves, we will suppose some companions interesting
themselves in surveying the uneven declivity of this mountain
range, and the romantic scenery that meets the eye at the
southern end of the mountain. There is a striking contrast,

however, between the sights and scenes of 1800, and the pleasing
and interesting objects of the present period. We will now direct
the attention of our kind attendants, whom we will suppose still seated near the ruins of an ancient observatory or tower, on the heights
of Mow :—first, to the past, or the opening of the nineteenth century. The scene, on retrospection, will be anything but pleasing.
The craggy rocks, unsightly knobs, holes, sharp slopes, &c., on which
here and there stood the rough, irregular, stone-built huts of the
rustic colliers, who inhabited this hilly country, first meet the eye.
The ignorance, indolence, and dissipated habits of the people,
linked with the unproductive nature of the soil, gave to the scene
a desolate and desert-like appearance, which had so existed from
time immemorial. The moral aspect of the place was still worse
than the physical. The soul-withering and pestilential blast of
immorality had put its mark on the habits of the people in nearly
every mountain-hut and home—the genius of sin and ungodliness
every where reigned predominant—midnight marauders prowled
about in search of plunder—blasphemy, profane mirth, cock-fight-
ing, bull-baiting, and other scenes revolting to the feelings of
humanity every where prevailed through the district—not a
sanctuary, with the exception of one solitary chapel of ease, to be
seen within miles of the southern and eastern declivities of Mow
Cop—all was desolation and confusion, the people following the
imagination of their own evil hearts, and no man caring for their
souls' welfare; but let us turn from the revolting scenes of the
past, and, secondly, contemplate the present. The picturesque
views that now meet the eye are delightful—the pleasing trans-
formation which has taken place in the landscape is every where
seen from this commanding eminence—the numerous churches,
chapels, and Sunday schools, that now stand out in bold relief in
this thickly populated district, speak with greater force than
words can command, as to the present state of religious feeling
among these mountaineers—the clean and well behaved children
seen on the Lord's day morning going to the Sabbath schools, and
the well-clad congregations that regularly attend the different
places of worship, present a pleasing sight. The former rude
huts have nearly all disappeared from the sides of Mow,—the
rough stone walls have given place to the hawthorn and holly;
many of the natives have become freeholders and owners of
modern-built cottages, and neatly laid out gardens, where the

honeysuckle and other sweet smelling flowers are tastefully trained, and grow luxuriantly, perfuming the mountain air with a fragrance both pleasing and refreshing to those who seek the pleasure and benefit of the summer breezes of Mow Cop. The little enclosures are well cleared and laid down ; and the green herbage is irrigated with water from the mountain springs, or artificial pools, made to receive the surplus water in the rainy seasons. Here, also, that useful appendage to a labouring man's establishment, a small Welsh cow, is to be seen grazing and ruminating, returning to the hand of kind and gentle treatment, full remuneration for the trouble and kindness bestowed on it. On the southern declivity, and the Staffordshire part of Mow Cop, near to the highest part of the mountain, stands a new and modern-built village, a district church, an elegant, newly-erected Wesleyan chapel, which has a very fine and commanding appearance, and the Primitive Methodists' chapel of less dimensions,— these, together with the week and Sabbath school buildings, ornament the heights of Mow. Truly it might be said of this mountain range of country, " The wilderness and the solitary place shall be glad for them ; and the desert shall rejoice, and blossom as the rose. It shall blossom abundantly, and rejoice even with joy and singing : the glory of Lebanon shall be given unto it, the excellency of Carmel and Sharon, they shall see the glory of the LORD, *and* the excellency of our God."—Isaiah xxxv. 1, 2. If we from the summit throw a glance towards the south and east, we shall see newly-raised hamlets, or clusters of well-built houses, here and there continued for two or three miles, diverging to the level or valleys, where the mountain range commences ; and in one of our recent excursions, we counted sixteen churches and chapels, all erected, with one exception, (that of Newchapel,) within the present century, and schools are attached to the greater part of them. Hugh Bourne was found in 1801, erecting the first of these sacred sanctuaries. The primary cause of these great improvements in the moral and social condition of this district, was the introduction of gospel truths in simplicity of style among the people at the beginning of the present century. Sabbath school tuition, and other religious agencies, such as bible and tract societies, have lent their aid in disseminating better principles, and fostering better habits among the population. Teetotalism has achieved success, by rescuing drunkards from destruction, and bettering their condition in society. Education

in week-day schools has also had a hand in this good work. In considering other causes, we may name science, which has made
gigantic strides here, as elsewhere, especially in the application of
steam to machinery and railroads. This has given, within the
last half century, a great impetus to the iron and coal trades of
these parts, while the rich iron and coal mines are found to be to
the increasing population an invaluable benefit. Down in one of
the dingles between Golden Hill and Mow Cop, you may see the
glare and hear the roar of a blast furnace, the thunder of
huge forge hammers, the noise of rolling mills, and the clatter
of boiler makers, which together form a strange and startling
combination to a visitor standing on the heights of Mow, particularly when the sable curtain of night has fallen on the horizon.
The small and the monster engines are lifting water, coal, and
iron-stone from the bowels of the earth ; and, indeed, the whole
district is alive with the din and hum of bustling crowds of men
and boys, all actively engaged in their various callings. The
great increase in the staple trade of this locality, without doubt,
has bettered the temporal condition of the people ; but this, with
out the aid of the higher and better motives and principles that
flow from the gospel, has a tendency in many instances to de-
moralize rather than improve the morals and habits of men.
Happily for these natives and residents of the mountain, the day-
star from on high had visited them : Hugh Bourne had lifted
aloft the blazing torch of divine revelation among them in the
open air, so that when providence turned the tide of prosperity
upon the neighbourhood, they were prepared to receive the abundance of wealth poured upon them. The good seed sown in the
first seven years of the nineteenth century, fortunately, had taken
root,—it grew and flourished, and has yielded an abundant harvest, in the extension of houses for religious worship, and insti-
tutions connected therewith, all tending to the spiritual and moral
inprovement of the inhabitants. There are other causes which
might be specified, as having contributed to the great improvement of Mow Cop, but these for the present must suffice : and
we must now respectfully take leave of the friends who have
tarried with us so long on this favoured spot, and hasten to the
next chapter, to continue the thread of our narrative, which will
show the connection between Hugh Bourne and this part of
North Staffordshire, and the religious and moral bearing that
connection had on the people.

CHAPTER VII.

LOSS OF MEANS—BASHFULNESS—T. MAXFIELD—A WRITTEN STATEMENT OF
HIS CONVERSION—DANIEL SHUBOTHAM—A CAROUSAL—DANIEL REPROVED
FOR SWEARING—"ONCE IN GRACE ALWAYS IN GRACE"—DANIEL'S PA-
ROXYSMS—MAXFIELD'S SMITHY—A SCENE—"A SAFE MAN"—NO SINIS-
TER MOTIVE—CARPENTER, SMITH, AND COLLIER—LABOURS FOR SOULS
ARE SUCCESSFUL.

Hugh Bourne it has been seen, in consequence of the increase
in his business calls, was tied to this dark and benighted part of
the country, and all fellowship (except on the Sabbath) with ministers and religious people was apparently cut off. His natural
bashfulness was such that there was no prospect of even social
intercourse with the mountaineers. There was, however, one
man among the natives, namely, Mr. Thomas Maxfield, of Mow
Cop, farrier and blacksmith, with whom he could trust himself to
hold converse. This man had his smithy or workshop at Harrisehead; and H. B. having occasion for iron work in his business as
a carpenter, had frequently to call at the smithy, and with Mr. M.
he would talk with all the zeal of a new convert; and having a
written statement or account of his own conversion and experience,
with trepidation he put the writing one day into the blacksmith's
hands, little thinking that this document was designed by a higher
power to be the first link in the chain of causes, which should
produce a mighty revival of PRIMITIVE METHODISM, that should
extend its beneficial influence to thousands then unborn, and
perhaps to the utmost bounds of the habitable globe. Let us
carefully watch associated events as they turn up in our onward
progress through the life of Hugh Bourne.

There was then, in the year 1800, living at Harrisehead, a man of the name of Daniel Shubotham, who was a relation to H. B.—their fathers were own or first cousins. Daniel's father was a large farmer, a coal master, and a man of property. He gave Daniel a good education, and left him a handsome independency, in land and houses ; but after his father's death, his wildness had been such, that he had made all away—except perhaps two dwelling houses, with their gardens—and had become a working collier. He was a man of a vehement turn of mind, a great fighter, and a sort of leading man among the rough people. He was married, and had two children. He was ungodly and dissipated, bold and talented as a poacher, and had acquired the bad habit of much swearing. In Swift's ' Polite conversation,' we have the following :—" It is the opinion of our most refined *swearers* that the same oath or curse cannot, consistently with true politeness, be repeated above nine times in the same company." But Daniel's politeness could outstrip this, for he would not stop at ninety and nine times for all the polite people in the world : however, a circumstance transpired about this time, or a little before it, that curbed his tongue in the exercise of this profane practice. A mountain farmer, one of his own kind for wickedness, invited Daniel and other colliers, of what we call the rough fleet, to a feast or strong drink carousal,—

" Where the ungoverned appetite and brutish vice engender folly,
And brooding ignorance hatches crime."

In the course of the evening when their potations had excited their passions, Daniel let loose his tongue in his old practice, until the wicked farmer became alarmed or annoyed, and turned upon him with, " Thou art the worst curser and swearer Dan I ever heard in my life,—I am quite ashamed of thee ; "—and he poured out reproof upon him with vehemence. Daniel did not think himself a worse swearer than the farmer, but he was confused, stood self-condemned, and could not say a word in reply to his pot companion's accusation ; but he afterwards observed, that from that time his swearing habit almost entirely left him.*

* This is somewhat like John Bunyan being successfully reproved by an ungodly woman.

Daniel at times had convictions of sin: but there had lived at
Harrisehead a drunken shoemaker, who sometimes preached, and
who held what he himself called, "once in grace always in grace;"
and this man had built Daniel up in his own way, and had prejudiced his mind against the methodists, and taught him to be a
talker on religion. Hugh Bourne was a stranger to all this, and
almost altogether unacquainted with Daniel: he had seen him
when they were boys, but since that period he had had little or
no intercourse with him.

In the spring of the year 1800, when Hugh Bourne was working at the Ash farm, his cousin Daniel came to see him. He
(H. B.) knew nothing of his relative's character and conduct, and
hearing him talk of religion he received him kindly, but spoke
very little to him, and that little was with great care and fear;
but he held a hope that Daniel was in the way for heaven: as to
his talk—"once in grace always in grace"—it had little weight with
H Bourne, as he had been put right with regard to opinions by
reading Mr. Wesley's sermon before named. After this for
some months their interviews were few and far between; he still
thinking Daniel in the way to heaven. On one occasion, however,
when H. Bourne was working at the Stonetrough colliery, on his
contract, Daniel Shubotham was employed at the same place as a
collier, consequently, they saw each other more frequently; but
"He paid little attention to me," says H. B. "until a peculiar
circumstance changed his views."

To this circumstance we wish particularly to draw the attention
of the reader. Daniel's conviction of sin, it appears, so agonized
him, as at times to render him incapable of following his daily
employment. During such paroxysms, no man could pacify him
but T. Maxfield; and he would sit on the blacksmith's smithy
hearth the day over. And on one of these occasions, when the
moody fit was on, and he was in his usual place, the smithy
hearth, he let loose his tongue against his relation, saying, "What
a timid, bashful fellow he was; no company for any one, and he had
no comfort of his life;" and he went on till T. Maxfield, being
rather irritated, said in his own peculiar way, and moorland dialect,
"Aye lad! but he's a safe mon." From that moment the decree
went forth as to Daniel. Nor should we over-look the fact that

the silent harbinger, the written statement of Hugh Bourne's experience, had done its work, and fulfilled its mission on T. Maxfield's mind, who was greatly prepossessed in favour of the writer; and when he heard Daniel's remarks, he could not help speaking, and on the spur of the moment he spoke from the sincerity of his heart. No sooner are the memorable words uttered by the blacksmith, than that very instant Daniel springs upon his feet, and vaults from the hearth to the floor of the smithy, and cries with vehemence, "I'll be a safe man, for I'll go and join him." The sudden and unexpected movements of Daniel came like an electric shock upon the blacksmith,—he stood aghast! amazed! and astonished! at the effect that short sentence—"he's a safe mon"—had produced on his friend Daniel. Reflection threw his thoughts on the consequences,—if Dan should do as he said, join H. Bourne, there would be an end of their companionship, in which they heretofore had been so strongly united, joining in the leadership of the nefarious practices of card-playing, night-poaching, and other wicked and demoralizing diversions, degrading to their own character, and pernicious to the juvenile and the better disposed part of society.

The courteous reader will, we charitably hope, pardon us for making a pause for a short period at this part of our journey, as we have now arrived at one of the peculiar turns in the life of Hugh Bourne. At this one point or turn in the good man's path, which is as the shining light, a number of ideas crowd the impartial and candid mind with all the force and demonstration of indubitable truth, stripping the origin of the great revival of primitive methodism of all sinister motives whatever. Here three men pass in review before us,—one is as opposite in principle and character from the other two as the north from the south; for there is no connection between the renewed and carnal minds,—the one bears the impress of the moral image of Deity: the others are of their father the devil, whose works they do. The remote causes preceding the bringing out of any great and important movement in the religious world are generally hid from the inquisitive and prying thoughts and minds of men. They have no conception or idea of the way and method by which the providence of God will achieve the object by HIM especially designed. Indeed, to a finite mind it is incomprehensible, far surpassing the utmost stretch of our powers of intellect. If Hugh Bourne, when he was conversing with T. Maxfield in his smithy on religious topics, and when he put the written statement of his own conversion and experience* into the blacksmith's hands, had been interrogated thus,—Have you any conception of what will be the result of this blacksmith's reading your written statement of your personal feelings and experience?—do you think, candid reader, he would not have smiled at such a question, or have doubted the sanity of the questioner? We firmly believe that every unprejudiced reader will agree with us, when we say that beyond the desire of doing his new acquaintance good, by leading him to true repentance, and a new birth unto righteousness, he had neither motive nor design of any kind. We can assure the reader that we questioned father Bourne, not a long time before he left the world, respecting the design he had as to a separate connexion; his answer was worthy of the man,—"Such a thing never entered our heads, until necessity forced it upon us,—the Lord himself was the founder of the work." So we believe; and it will be our endeavour, as we journey onward, to give to every man that may cross our path, or appear in the field of activity and labour, his meed of praise according to the time of his labours, and the part he took in the commencement and carrying out the great work that followed the circumstance of lending the written statement to Mr. Thomas Maxfield, and the subsequent contest in the smithy, which induced Daniel Shubotham to seek and join his relative, Hugh Bourne.

* We have the written statement in our possession; and we can assure the reader we highly value it. It is dated, Bemersley, August 17th, 1800.

CHAPTER VIII.

RESULT OF THE CONVERSATION BETWEEN THE BLACKSMITH AND THE
COLLIER—A NEW COURSE—H. BOURNE'S TRAVAIL OF SOUL FOR DANIEL'S
SALVATION—EXTRACT FROM HIS DIARY—CHRISTMAS DAY, 1800—ATTACKS
ON DANIEL'S STEADFASTNESS—RUMOURS IN THE COUNTRY—RESULTS OF
DANIEL'S CONVERSION—HUGH BOURNE'S REMARKS THEREON—MATTHIAS
BAYLEY.

Our first business in this chapter is to enquire what followed
the sudden and vehement declaration of the collier in the blacksmith's shop? Was the effect that had been produced upon him
transitory? Was it like the early dew in soon passing away? or
as a dream that is told, soon forgot? No! It was like a "nail
fastened in a sure place by the master of assemblies." It lives in
his recollection; he stands in the light of truth a convicted and
condemned sinner. The thought returns with redoubled force;
the impression is rivetted on his mind and memory—"Hugh
Bourne's a safe man"—" I'll go and join him"—"And I'll be a
safe man!" And he forthwith sought an interview with H.
Bourne, who was ignorant of the feelings and determination of
his kinsman. The smith, when the heat of the contest was over,
and his zeal for Bourne had cooled down, tried his best to undo
what he had done. Yes, he laboured with all his might to remove
the impression he had so unintentionally made on the collier's
mind, by telling him Hugh Bourne was a safe man; but all to
no purpose,—the knot was cut,—the tie of folly's friendship
between the smith and the collier was at once and for ever severed :
this was doubtless so much the more distressing, that Daniel was
the most ingenious and expert poacher of all the gang that lived
about Mow Cop, although the number was by no means small.

A new course is now struck out for the development of the active mind and talent of Daniel. Whenever his labour would allow him, instead of sitting on the smithy hearth chatting with the smith, and planning fresh schemes for plundering the neighbouring gentlemen's game preserves, you might have seen him sitting in the grotesque style of a miner, on his heels, beside his kinsman, listening with ardour to the words of truth and soberness which fell with force and sweetness from his lips, on topics as opposite as light from darkness to what he had been accustomed to hear in the smithy.   Zeal for Christ, and the salvation of Daniel's soul, burned in H. Bourne's heart; for he had found out to his great grief that his kinsman was not born again, or as yet in the right way to the better world.   He, therefore, laid down before him the plan of salvation with rustic simplicity, and with all the earnestness of a new convert, or one that had recently found the " pearl of great price."   An impression of deep sorrow and travail took hold of his soul while conversing with Daniel and another collier, on Wednesday afternoon, December 24th, 1800. This distress first fell upon him when he discovered that his cousin, instead of being in the way to heaven, as he had charitably thought, was still in the broad way to death and hell.   And as soon as they were alone, he threw away his timidity, and in all seriousness, and in the sincerity of his heart, spoke to him on the necessity and importance of getting religion, and making a good start for the kingdom of heaven.   Daniel, with eager earnestness, gave ear to the words of Bourne ; but the day being nearly worn away, and the approach of night at hand, Bourne engaged to pay Daniel a friendly visit at his own cottage the next day, which would be a holiday.   He went home in sorrow; but we will turn to his diary, and hear what he himself says on this important matter.

" Christmas day, *Thursday, December* 25*th*, 1800.   Last night I lay down in sorrow, and this morning I arose in sorrow ; the main cause of my grief was my kinsman not being born again of God.   My natural timidity pressed upon me, so that to me it was a task to go ; but my mouth had been opened before the Lord, and to have drawn back would have been awful: so off I set, taking with me a book written by R. Barclay, the quaker ; and I took the written account of my own conversion and experience.   It was a sorrowful journey ;

but I found Daniel waiting for me, so my introduction was easy. Having never prayed in public, and judging myself not capable of it, I did not pray with the family; but knowing him to be hindered by an erroneous notion, I read him a piece out of Barclay, with which he declared himself satisfied; so the way was open. Next followed a little general conversation. I then rose up to go, requesting him to accompany me a little way. I was full of sorrow; but so soon as we were in a suitable place, I set to preaching the gospel to him with all my might; and taking up John xiv. 21. where the words of Jesus Christ are, " I will love him, and will manifest myself to him; "—I told him that Jesus Christ must be manifested to him, or else he would never be born again, and then he could not go to heaven : and being all the time in deep sorrow, I laid open the gospel of Jesus Christ, showing him of being justified by faith, and having peace with God, through our Lord Jesus Christ : and I dwelt very fully on the manifestation of Jesus Christ unto him. At parting, I put into his hands the full account of my own conversion and experience. I then took leave ; but parted from him in sorrow, fearing he did not take sufficient notice, and I passed the day in sorrow: but God's thoughts were not as my thoughts, for Daniel afterwards told me, that when I was talking to him that morning, every word went through him."

We will now return with the collier from this open-air service to his mountain home, and jot down what awaited his arrival. Temptation and persecution, the common lot of all them "that will live Godly in Christ Jesus," were the poor collier's portion the moment he entered his cottage : for the adversary of souls, and the accuser of the brethren, had marshalled his forces ready to pour a volley of taunting indignities upon him as soon as he returned. There sat the blacksmith and several others, who had come to try the collier's sincerity and fortitude in the cause of truth he had so recently espoused. Daniel's practice hitherto on christmas days had been to spend the greater part of his time with the smith and their companions in playing at cards, and the smith well knew Daniel's fondness for this amusement, and therefore, on his coming into his cottage, he saluted him thus :— " Come, Dan, let's have a game at cards ! " and his partners in iniquity seconded the proposition, one of them adding, " I'll have

Dan for a partner," &c. This was a trial of no common character; the assault came from former friends with all the subtlety of hellish malice, but apparent friendship. Truly, the collier's position under this sudden attack was painfully alarming, and nothing short of the mercy and restraining grace of God could have preserved him : but nobly he withstood the poison-pointed arrows that flew about him on every side ; for " The name of the LORD *is* as a strong tower : the righteous runneth into it, and is safe."—Prov. xviii. 10. " I will call upon the LORD, *who is worthy* to be praised : so shall I be saved from mine enemies."—Psalm xviii. 3. This was the stonghold in which Daniel took shelter ; he found the word of God, which he had heard so effectually delivered by H. Bourne that blessed morning, was a " refuge from the storm, and a covert from the wind and tempest," that now raged about him in fury. The mercy of the Lord held him up ; and he could say in confidence, " The LORD is my defence ; and my God *is* the rock of my refuge."—Psalm xciv. 22. The collier stood as firm as an iron pillar, and as a champion before his enemy ; and boldly facing them, said, " If you will not go with me to heaven, I will not go with you to hell." This to the smith and his fellows was new and strange ; and to make the confusion complete, the collier forthwith seized the bible, and began to read—as the carpenter had been preaching to him—with all his might. This made the foe draw back,—while the collier maintained his ground, still reading the word of God, and sounding it out in his old companions' ears.—

> " How pregnant, sometimes, his replies are, —
> A happiness that often madness hits on,"--

thought they, and sat confused : but anon they rose up ; and when leaving the house, and bidding the collier adieu, in despair they said, HUGH BOURNE has driven him MAD ! Here they touched the string of conjugal affection,—the collier's wife became alarmed—the scene changes—the enemy shifts his position. and directs his attack on the weakest part of the collier's citadel, a very tender point to touch. The devil aims a deadly blow at the collier by exciting the fears of his wife :—" What will become of me and the children, if my husband be taken to the lunatic asylum ? "—instantly darted into the woman's mind, when they said Hugh Bourne had driven her husband mad; and she felt prejudiced against the carpenter, and determined to try to prevent her husband in future from company-keeping with him; but against this the collier set his face as flint, and the Lord greatly supported him. And this man's conversion produced an *extraordinary* stir among the colliers of this mountain district, from Mow Cop to the dingle, or vale of Kidsgrove: the collier's altered conduct was the subject of general remark among the pitmen; and Hugh Bourne's turning him mad was talked over in the delf, and on the coal pit banks, and in other places; and many wondered how these things would end. On this subject Hugh Bourne writes thus :—:" I went through much sorrow on the occasion,—but the Lord in his mercy caused light to rise in darkness; and he caused this sorrowful dispensation to open out in one of the most impor tant movements in my whole life. To him be glory and dominion, for ever and ever, amen.—

" 1.—Daniel Shubotham was one of the first I ever prevailed with fully to set out for heaven, and fully to press on till he obtained the knowledge of salvation by the remission of sins: and in addition to this, the Lord soon raised him up to be a colleague for me in carrying on the work of religion; and for some years he was a colleague indeed.

" 2.—In repentance, a person feels his sins a burden at times almost intolerable, or as the church of England says, *quite so :* and such persons, if well directed, seek to obtain the pardon of all their sins through the blood of Christ. They seek till they obtain, through faith in Jesus Christ, the knowledge of salvation by the remission of sins; and if their faith be weak, they pray and labour, constantly trying more fully to believe : and thus they go on until their faith is increased, and they are enabled to believe with their hearts unto righteousness. I myself was brought into liberty in this way, and so are thousands. The veil is taken away, and they are convinced of sin, and see and are sensible of their lost state : and feeling that they have not inward power over sin—over bad thoughts and desires,—they pray for mercy, and for the pardon of their sins through the blood of Christ; and they go on with it, and their faith increases, and increases until they fully believe, obtain the manifestation of Jesus Christ, and. have forthwith power over sin, and peace with God, and rejoice in the Lord's pardoning grace.

" 3.—Praying mourners into liberty is heavenly: but this requires labour and exertion of mind, and in some instances great labour of mind, and great exertions of faith. The praying labourers have like Jacob to wrestle with God.

" 4.—Bringing persons into repentance, and bringing seeking mourners into liberty in conversations,—these things require exertions of mind, and exertions of faith.

" 5.—Exercisings of faith in silence,—this requires exertion and labour of mind.

" Daniel Shubotham set out for heaven with all his might; and his so doing was attended with mighty consequences. He proved a champion in the way : no difficulties could hinder him, neither could opposition stop him: and he took the same course with others as the Lord directed me to take with him. He in conversations preached Jesus and him crucified, and he did this with a greater zeal than I had ever witnessed. I myself was kept back through timidity, except on Christmas day morning, when my zeal flamed out in conversing with him. My keeping back thereafter Daniel would not allow, for said he, ' You have been useful to me, and you must be useful to others.' And really, in a short time, we were like two flames of fire. I had never in my life noticed anything that equalled this,—it really was primitive methodism indeed!

" At Dales Green, between Mow Cop and Harrisehead, lived Matthias Bayley, another collier, who had started for heaven a few weeks before. He set out through hearing an open-air preacher—the only one in Burslem circuit—and Matthias fell in with me and Daniel, and soon became a champion indeed. Our chapels were the coal pit banks or any other place; and in our conversation way, we preached the gospel to all, good or bad, rough or smooth. People were obliged to hear; and we soon had four other colliers in deep distress, deeply awakened. I then applied to Burslem, the head of the circuit, for assistance, and laid the case before one of the travelling preachers, but could get no help. I may here observe, that I advised Daniel to attend public worship: but not aware of any methodist preaching near, and knowing his prejudice against the methodists, I advised him to attend the church of England service at a village called New Chapel,* about a mile distant, but this he declined. The Lord then opened the way. There was preaching planned for once a fortnight at the house of old Joseph Pointon, on the Cheshire side of Mow; and Matthias had joined good old Joseph Pointon's class. And with some pressing, I prevailed with Daniel to visit Matthias, and in doing this he was so edified, that he for some time visited him two nights a week; and one Sunday, Matthias took him to hear a local preacher. Daniel despised the preacher ! But before the sermon was concluded, he was blest, and even believed that God had pardoned his sins : but sinking again into unbelief, he sought the Lord afresh, and obtained a glorious manifestation when he was just finishing a day's work ; and he set off to the next house, and told the people that God had pardoned his sins, and that they must obtain the same, or they would go to hell. His first impulse was to go to all the houses round ; but on leaving the first house, it came to his mind that the people would not believe him; so he went no further : but in a day or two he rallied again, and was as if in a new world. All his vehemence of mind was employed in making known what the Lord had done for his soul, and that they to whom he was speaking must obtain the same, or else they would go to hell : yet there was such a kindness in his way of speaking, and the unction from the holy one so powerfully attended his words, that he hardly ever gave offence, and his words frequently reached people's hearts ; and he pressed on me to come out with him in this pious work, pleading, that as I had talked effectually to him, I ought to talk to others the same."

* There was then no other sanctuary on the Staffordshire side of Mow for miles.

CHAPTER IX.

HUGH BOURNE'S FEARS AND TIMIDITY—NEW IN THE CONVERTING WORK—
MR. BURGESS—NO HELP FROM BURSLEM—THE PRAYER BOOK—OLD
JANE HALL'S HOUSE OFFERED—PRAYER MEETINGS APPOINTED—H. B.
PRAYS IN PUBLIC—NOISY MEETINGS—A WOMAN CONVERTED REMARKABLY
—A LUNATIC CURED BY FAITH AND PRAYER—A DAY'S PRAYING ON MOW
COP—A NOTE—ORIGINAL PRAYER MEETING RULES.

Hugh Bourne was, by the collier's persuasion, induced to cast
his fears and timidity to the winds, and at once to enter with him
into the great and good work of getting people converted to the
Lord. And he says, "The Lord owned our labours,—four
mourners were in great distress; but the blame of their not getting liberty was laid to my charge. This grieved me very much.
I was quite new in bringing forward the converting work; but I
thought a prayer meeting might do good, and help us through the
difficulty; and I was willing to give a weekly sum for a Burslem
methodist to come and hold a weekly prayer meeting. I applied
to Mr. Burgess, one of the travelling preachers, but could not
obtain any help from any quarter. My trial of mind was severe,
but 'The Lord hath his way in the whirlwind;' and the way was
preparing. I have noticed Daniel's visiting Matthias two nights
a week; and on one of these occasions the two were in a low
state of mind. They talked of praying, but having only prayed
in private, they thought themselves unable to do more. Matthias
produced the church prayer book, he having been a church singer,
but they found no suitable prayer. They were then at a stand:
but Matthias with zeal noticed their praying had succeeded in
their getting their sins pardoned, and he said it would do again;
so they set to it; and Daniel afterwards observed that, ' If the
people had heard their praying, they would have thought it strange :

but the Lord owned it,—he brought them into liberty;' and after that they prayed together at every visit. I had thought if a Burslem prayer-maker attended, he would do the thing aright; but the Lord had chosen otherwise. He put it in the minds of Daniel and Matthias to have a prayer meeting, and old Jane Hall, with her husband's consent, offered her house, and a prayer meeting was given out; and it was determined that I should pray at the meeting: this to me was trying. On the Sunday morning, at the Ridgway class, I broke through, but was far from satisfying myself. When I applied to the travelling preacher for a person to come to Harrisehead to manage the holding of a prayer meeting, I was not aware of the preachers and people being almost totally out of the converting work. I afterwards learned that the Burslem circuit that year was in a forlorn state,—it sunk sixty members,—so there was cause to thank God that my wish for help from that source was frustrated; and it was of the Lord that I had been so much kept from the prayer meetings, and other means of grace in the circuit, otherwise I might have settled down in lukewarmness. 'Help is from the Lord.' I had to grieve before the Lord; and he moved upon Daniel and Matthias to resolve on a prayer meeting, and old Jane Hall to offer her house.*

"At the first prayer meeting at Harrisehead, it so turned out that none of the four convinced colliers could attend. Matthias opened the meeting; and I thought his the best praying I ever heard. Those held at Burslem might have been called talking meetings. The people while on their knees apparently spent as much time in talking as in praying, and at times seemed to spend more. But Matthias filled his time up with praying, with scarcely any talking; and the Lord enabled me to see the excellency of this. We then sang, and I followed; and the instant I began, heaven opened in my soul, and my course throughout was glorious,—grace and glory rested on me all the time I prayed. I may say that the Lord on this occasion 'anointed me with the oil of gladness,' and fitted me to be a public praying labourer. Daniel followed; and then another who had fallen in from a distance, and we gave it out for another meeting on Tuesday in the following week. Next morning I told Daniel what a blessing I

* I believe she had long been the only methodist on Harrisehead.—H.B.

had received at the meeting; and also spoke of Matthias' praying.
'Why,' said Daniel, 'he is for praying no more, because he
could not pray as you did!' But when he came to hear what I
had said, he replied, 'Well, if Hugh Bourne was blest, I will try
again;' and our prayer meetings went on regularly on Tuesday
evenings for some time, and then we changed them to Wednesdays. Ere long one of our seekers got his soul set at liberty;
and next we had a cry out at a meeting, and two were prayed into
liberty; and the other, being at work under ground in a coal pit,
was there set at liberty, and he is now (in 1850) a Wesleyan local
preacher, and has been for many years. Our new converts were
famous talkers for the Lord,—they preached, or set forth the
gospel in conversations, without ceremony, and that part of the
country was soon moralized; and the converting work opened out
among the Kidsgrove colliers, and on a large part of Mow Cop
God was glorified, and sinners were saved. Our situation was
important. We had to establish discipline, maintain order, keep
up the converting work, and promote piety. The prayer meetings
soon claimed our attention. At the time of Congleton May fair,
1801, our meeting was small, but so powerful, that it shook the
country round, and the work began to break out in almost all
directions; and we had a great weight on our hands. Daniel,
Matthias, and myself had often to confer together, and they looked
up to me to supply information; and as my information had been
mainly acquired by reading, it was chiefly primitive,—I may say
unknowingly, primitive,—but Harrisehead, Kidsgrove, and Mow
Cop were moved, and the work was great. The people got to be
in a great degree Israelitish. David says, 'As for me I will call
upon God, and the Lord shall save me: evening, and morning,
and at noon will I pray and cry aloud, and he shall hear my voice.'
And in the Harrisehead prayer meetings the people prayed and
cried aloud, and the Lord heard their voice; and the converting
work went on in a primitive methodist strain,—souls were saved,
and God was glorified; and that most ungodly neighbourhood was
greatly moralized: and the people in their prayer meetings were
so Israelitish, as in a degree to follow the directions in Psalm xlvii.
1. 'O clap your hands, all ye people; shout unto God with the
voice of triumph.' Also Ezra iii. 11-13. says, 'And all the peo
ple shouted with a great shout . . . . . And the noise was heard
afar off.' And one evening at a prayer meeting, the door of the

house happening to stand open, the noise was heard at Mow Cop; and Elizabeth Baddeley, a collier's wife, who lived on that mountain, and who had been grievously addicted to cursing and swearing, heard the noise of prayer and praise even to Mow Cop, and was convinced of sin, and set out for heaven, and became a woman of the first order of piety, and so continued till the Lord took her hence! Matthias usually opened the meeting,—he was one of the most extraordinary men in prayer I ever knew. A second hymn was then sung, and another commenced praying, and in less than a quarter of a minute another would dash off, and so on, till the whole were exercising with all their faith, hearts, and minds, and with all their voices, and the noise might be heard to a considerable distance; yet our rules were strict,—every one must keep out of sin, and none were allowed to use improper expressions, and then they were allowed to go on as they chose. It was the best school I ever knew for training up new beginners; any of these could try their voices, and pray longer or shorter as they thought proper; and any one that could distinguish his or her own voice must have had a pretty good ear; so a new beginner might try his voice without hesitation, and might keep on for half an hour, less or more, at his own choice; and during the great course of united praying, the exercise of faith moved all hearts present, and often some at a distance: also some would be greatly exercised, and feel great trial of mind, and for this we could not then account; but it was the 'Trial of faith,' 1 Peter i. 7. The 'Travail in birth,' Galatians iv. 19. It was no proof of their not growing in grace, but rather, a proof of a greater growth in grace than otherwise."

An instance of Primitive Methodist zeal.—" Samuel Harding being turned out of a lunatic hospital as incurable, was chained in his brother's parlour, on Mow Cop. Daniel, Matthias, and others, with the women, set off one Saturday afternoon to visit him: and before they came in sight, he named them all over, with a ludicrous remark after every name. The family wondered; but the people came in just in the order in which he had named them: and when they prayed, his neck and face reddened, and he rushed with fury to the end of his chain; but on their getting up in faith, he fell like an ox; when they slackened he rose up again in fury; but when they again rose in faith down he fell, and they went on, till at length he began to praise the Lord : he was truly thankful to God and to them. After this he did not live many days ; but he held fast his confidence, and died in the Lord. He was truly a brand plucked out of the fire."

" A day's praying on Mow Cop.—Our rules did not allow over lengthy meetings, still in some instances to close the meeting was not easy ; for when faith was in exercise, and the power was flowing mightily, some were zealous to go on to still greater lengths : and in one of these instances, Daniel zealously said, 'You shall have a meeting upon Mow Cop some Sunday, and have a whole day's praying, and then you will be satisfied.'* This made a pause. In a short time a similar course took place, and he spoke as before ; and some of the people began to think it would do, and occasionally they would talk of it. But I am not sure whether it would not at that time have been premature ; and I never heard Daniel speak of it after his second time of mentioning it,—his main failing was a want of perseverance ; but as the people bore it in mind, I, some years after, made some move toward bringing it forward : but the preachers had so turned Daniel against open-air worship, that the attempt seemed for a time hopeless."

It may be interesting at the close of this chapter, to lay before the reader the already-referred-to regulations for conducting prayer meetings : they are as follow. Rules for prayer meetings. "L—

---

* In a zeal for prayer, it can hardly be too much noticed, the appointment of a meeting on Mow originated : neither D. Shubotham, however, nor any of those by whom his impromptu prophetical promise was heard, had the most distant idea that the English Camp Meetings, and the Primitive Methodist Connexion, would spring from this zeal, and the promise thus elicited ; but God's " ways are not our ways, nor his thoughts our thoughts." We may here briefly indicate the chain of events by which the origination of the P. M. Connexion was brought about. 1.—The conversion of H. Bourne. 2.—His labours at Harrisehead. 3.—The conversion of Shubotham and others through his labours. 4.—Appointing and conducting prayer Meetings. 5.—Zeal for protracted meetings. 6.—The promise of Daniel that a day's meeting on Mow should be held. 7.—The subsequent holding thereof, and of other similar meetings. 8.—The opposition to, and final exclusion of, H. Bourne by the Wesleyans, on account of open-air meetings. 9.—The extensive establishment of Camp-meeting worship ; and 10.—The formation of a class at Standley, near Leek.

The commandment says, 'six days shalt thou labour:' if, by holding long meetings, we render ourselves unfit for properly discharging the duties of our callings, there will be a clash, and our proceedings will not harmonize with the commandment." From this the time for holding the prayer meeting was fixed for one hour, and not to exceed one hour and a quarter.

" 2.—To be careful not to use improper expressions in prayer ; " and it got to be well established among us, (says H. B.) all learnt it, more or less, and the effect was excellent.

" 3.—Attention to these regulations, and keeping out of sin, entitles any one to his or her free liberty in prayer meetings."

CHAPTER X.

We have seen as we have passed along, the colliers of the mountain agitated, an enquiry after truth excited, and a revival of
primitive methodism commence among them.   Let us examine
in our onward course the means of carrying on this great work.
Harrisehead was the place appointed by the guiding hand of providence at which this powerful REVIVAL of primitive methodism
should commence, take root, and flourish, and from which it
should extend its benign and soul-saving influence to tens of
thousands living without God and without hope in the world, and
to myriads as yet unborn.   This great revival was carried on for
a considerable time, and to a pretty large extent, without the aid of
either travelling or local preachers, for this very reason,—Hugh
Bourne could not procure their help at any price.   Assistance
from such source being unattainable, he and his converts had to
shift for themselves as best they could.   If any of them wished to
attend a preaching service, they had to climb over Mow, and go
down to old Joseph Pointon's house, on the Cheshire side of the
mountain, where the preachers were planned to attend once a
fortnight ; but it frequently happened that there was but one sermon a month.   Of this place it might be said, ' The word of the
LORD was precious in those days ; *there was* no open vision.'—1
Samuel iii. 1.   How naturally the question arises in the mind,
in what way did Hugh Bourne and his collier colleagues carry on

the revival without the aid and counsel of ministers or elders ?
The answer is at hand,—they went forth in a way marked out by
providence, by the course of events, as they daily turned up.
This to some appeared quite strange ; hence the stir that was
raised amongst the rustics of the mountain and elsewhere about
the carpenter and his companions. The alarm, as to the novelty
of their proceedings, was groundless ; for the plan pursued by
these heroes for truth was as old or primitive as the Apostles'
days. We said before, the Lord put dignity and honour on the
conversation preachers, and crowned their labours with success.
The carpenter and colliers talked salvation sermons to many, as
the former talked to Daniel Shubotham on Christmas day ; and
although their orations were not accordant with the laws of
rhetoric, and were delivered in the moorland dialect, yet their
gospel-preaching was accompanied with the Holy Ghost sent
down from heaven, and great and powerful effects followed such
preaching. One of the four colliers that were the first of this
talking or conversation ministry, had been connected with a newly-
formed gang of highwaymen, who failed in their first attempt;
and when the Lord, by the agency of Hugh Bourne, introduced
religion among them, the revival scattered the gang, and those
that were not brought to God by repentance, were ere long
brought to condign punishment in prison, or were transported for
felony. When the four colliers were brought into the light and
liberty of the gospel of Jesus Christ, they walked in the steps of
the carpenter and his brethren : they talked salvation sermons,
and signs and wonders followed ; insomuch that men, women, and
children became lowly followers of the crucified one, and were
added to the company of them that believed : and these conversation-preachers followed the apostolic plan,—as recorded in Acts v.
42. " And daily in the temple, and in every house, they ceased not
to teach and preach Jesus Christ,"—with this difference, the colliers'
temples were the coal pit banks, and hovels, and even the bowels
of the earth, where at meal times they preached Jesus and the
resurrection.*

* We are satisfied that the apostolic preaching in the temple was not on
the system in general use in England; for had the apostles' sermons been
previously planned and published, the officers would have been ready to
interrupt them, and on their attempting to deliver a pulpit sermon, they
would have forthwith taken them to prison. The apostles in the temple

Primitive Methodism in Wesley's days rose much, and increased in strength by means of open-air worship, or what was then called field-preaching. Mr. Wesley's rules on this subject are as follow:—

" *Q.* Is field-preaching, then, unlawful?

A. We conceive not. We do not know that it is contrary to any law of either God or man.

Q. Have we not used it too sparingly?

A. It seems we have. 1.—Because our call is to save that which is lost. Now we cannot expect such to seek us; therefore, we should go and seek them. 2.—Because we are particularly called, by going into the highways and hedges (which none else will do) to compel them to come in. 3.—Because that reason against it is not good, 'the house will hold all that come,' it may hold all that come to the house, but not all that come to the field."

" The greatest hindrance to this you may expect from the rich, or cowardly, or lazy methodists; but regard them not, neither stewards, leaders, nor people. Whenever the weather will permit, go out in God's name into the most public places, and tell all ' to repent and believe the gospel.' Every assistant (superintendent) at least, in every circuit, should endeavour to preach abroad every Sunday, especially in the old societies, lest they settle on their lees."

evidently preached Christ on the spur of the moment. Peter's sermon in Solomon's porch, Acts iii. 12-24. can be read over in five minutes; that in Cornelius' house, in Acts x. in two minutes; Paul's sermon at Antioch, in Pisidia, Acts xiii. 16-41. can be read in five minutes; and that at Athens, Acts xvii. 22-31. can be read in two minutes: and as nearly as circumstances would admit, these useful colliers took a similar course. If an opportunity offered, they were ready at a moment's notice to deliver a short discourse. Their conversation sermons were frequently given to only one person; but even then their skill, zeal, experience, and faith were put in full requisition, that if possible they might win that one person to the faith of the gospel of Christ Jesus; and in many instances the exercise of faith was so great, and the unction of the Holy One so attended their speaking, that their words instantaneously went to the heart of the person or persons to whom they spoke.

" These open-air or field-preaching rules," says H. Bourne, " were made by Mr. Wesley and his assistants in conference, and first published June 28th, 1744; and not being repealed, they still stood in force at this time, 1801. And I am of opinion now (1844)that the Lord had, and still hath, a controversy with the Wes-leyans for their neglect of duty in regard to open-air worship; but through reading Mr. Wesley's writings, and other primitive records of methodism, with the writings of the first quakers, the desire for open-air worship was so implanted in me, that nothing could shake it."

The Lord induced the covenanters and others in Scotland, and the first quakers and some in other communities in England, to practice open-air worship; and when it had ceased among these, the Lord renewed it again by Messrs. Whitfield and Wesley, and the first race of methodists; and when the more modern methodists had in a great measure relinquished it, the great head of the church caused *a dispensation of open-air worship* to open out upon the celebrated mountain called Mow Cop, and honoured the subject of this memoir with a distinguished agency in the great and noble work. On July 12th, 1801, he was enabled to commence these labours, and in after years to carry out the design of heaven by disseminating gospel truths among people in the humble walks of life, by means of camp meetings, and other religious services conducted in the open air. To show how he and his collier con-verts followed the openings of providence to enlarge and per-petuate this great revival of primitive methodism, we will furnish the reader with a few extracts from his diary :—

" Religion rapidly increasing, the work on our hands was weighty and important; but in Daniel Shubotham and Matthias Bayley the Lord had favoured me with two excellent colleagues. Daniel was talented,—had been favoured with a good education,* was naturally of a vehement turn; and if his diligence and perse-verence had equalled his zeal and vehemence, he would have been great. He had a good notion of the faith that worketh by love, and of getting into an exercise of faith in meetings and conversa-tion, and a considerable fulness of the divine power usually attended

---

* His father having the means, had him educated rather above the common standard of people moving in a similar sphere.

his exercisings. Matthias was acknowledged by professors and profane : he was firm and persevering; his faith was strong, and his religious exercisings were weighty : a powerful unction attended him, and he had a great talent for praying mourners into liberty,—the Lord was much with him, and he was a firm pillar in our rising work. It was my part to bring forward scripture knowledge and historical information on religious subjects, derived from extensive readings and diligent study. In this practice I had abounded for years ; yet I possessed great timidity, and was fearful of leaning too much to my own understanding. But it was our way to constantly confer together ; and when we had consulted on a matter, and examined it in every point and bearing, and found it suitable, we took measures to give it effect. Daniel at that time was not a member of the methodist society, nor any of the new converts,—Matthias expected,—nor had I been able to prevail with our Burslem circuit authorities to take them in ; so we were left to shape our own course."

"As new converts were constantly multiplying, I was anxious for them to meet in class ; but the circuit authorities neglected us, which caused me much distress of mind. There was a small class which met on Sunday mornings, at old Joseph Pointon's, not more than a mile and a half distant from Harrisehead, only to get to it they had to climb over the mountain. Old Joseph was the leader ; and when any of our people attended, he held it as a prayer meeting, and the class was not led for a number of weeks. This was painful to my mind. I thought every thing made against me. I applied to one of the travelling preachers, and he said the class ought to be led, but nothing was done. The reason the good old man gave for not leading the class was, that the Harrisehead people were stronger in grace than he was ; but at length Daniel and Matthias prevailed with him to resume the leading, and he soon became a champion."

KIDSGROVE.—The mountain colliers talked of religion with a zeal and unction that made an impression wherever they went. The spring of gospel truth, the fountain of living waters, in this hilly country, now burst forth as a mountain cataract upon the adjacent country, and was like—

"Torrents and loud impetuous cataracts,
Which through roads abrupt, and rude unfashioned tracts,
Run down the lofty mountain's channel'd side,
And to the vale convey their foaming tide."

Yes, the vale of Kidsgrove and its colliers were inundated with a flood of light, and felt the fertilizing influence of the mountain streams that flowed through the rough channel of the colliers' conversation preaching. There had been in time past a few methodists at Kidsgrove, but it was, in 1801, (when the revival broke out on the mountain) a forsaken place; but now the primitive revivalists rushed down from their mountain fastnesses, aroused their fellow miners from the deadly lethargy that had held them so long in the sleep of carnality, and several souls were soon converted to God. Hugh Bourne now went three miles on a Sunday morning to lead the Kidsgrove new converts as a class, at the house of Joshua Bayley, brother of Matthias; and this was Hugh Bourne's first class. He continued in this office until he prevailed with Matthias to undertake it, as he had other calls to attend to; and when the Burslem circuit authorities took up the place, they confirmed this appointment, and Matthias led the same class for many years; and that class formed the nucleus of the present powerful establishments of the Wesleyan and the Primitive Methodists at Kidsgrove; for the second class raised at that place was scattered like chaff before the wind, and not a vestige remains to be seen.

CHAPTER XI.

HUGH BOURNE'S FIRST ATTEMPT AT PULPIT PREACHING—MUCH AND MIGHTY
PRAYING—OLD JOSEPH POINTON IS WILLING TO HAVE OPEN-AIR WORSHIP—
THE TEXT AND SERVICE—FIELD PREACHING—A BROADER FOUNDATION—A
SORT OF MODEL SERVICE—PASSING REMARKS—LARGE CONGREGATION—
HOW IT MAY BE ACCOUNTED FOR—IT IS AGREED TO BUILD A CHAPEL—
H. BOURNE HAS THE WORK DEVOLVED UPON HIM—GOLDENHILL POTTERS
—TROUBLES—CESSATION OF THE CONVERTING WORK—H. BOURNE'S HEAD-
SHIP—MODERN METHODISM.

As the preaching at good old Joseph Pointon's, on the Cheshire
side of Mow Cop, was only planned for once a fortnight, and as
the colliers had got it into their heads that Hugh Bourne could
preach, they determined that if they could prevail with him he
should try on a Sunday, when no preacher was planned ; and according to their wishes, an appointment was made for him on Sunday,
July 12th, 1801 ; and it was published for the service to be at
two o'clock in the afternoon.   He writes as follows :—

" This was to be my first attempt ; and I felt much trial of
mind, for I had never even stood up to exhort, except once at a
class meeting, and then my performance was far from being satis-
factory to myself ; still, being at Mow a few days before the time,
I spoke of the preaching being in the open-air ; but good old
Joseph could not bear the thought of it, as like the rest of the
circuit (T. Allen excepted) his zeal against open-air worship was
great ; so I gave up all further thought of it.   There was much
praying on account of this appointment,—very much indeed ; and
on the former part of that Sabbath there was mighty praying :
yet, while climbing up the Staffordshire side of the mountain, I

was in deep sorrow,—I went forth with weeping of soul, being in fear lest my attempt to preach should injure the cause of God; and for my own part I did not expect more than ten or twelve of a congregation. But the Lord's thoughts were not as my thoughts. There had been mighty prayings, and the Lord's arm was made bare. He favoured us with fine weather, and the Lord so moved the neighbourhoods, that people flocked in from all sides. Old Joseph's house was soon filled, and a great number could not get in. We had fixed for preaching in the house, but when the good old man saw the multitude, he said, ' It is like to be out of doors.' It was in settled fine weather,—the ground was warm and pleasant, and people lined the rising mountain like a gallery, and the whole made a fine and imposing appearance. I stood up at the end of the house ; the service opened well, and I read for a text, ' By faith Noah, being warned of God of things not seen as yet, moved with fear, prepared an ark to the saving of his house ; by the which he condemned the world, and became heir of the righteousness which *is* by faith.'—Hebrews xi. 7. I preached with my hand over my face all the time, and I was soon at a loss; but it came to my mind to preach as if speaking to one person, and this opened me a track to which I was accustomed; and the Lord gave me liberty, and one person started for heaven under the sermon. I also related my own experience ; but having joined much in praying and labouring during the previous week, and on this Sabbath morning at the mighty prayer meeting, I felt unwell, and retired into the house to rest me, and left my brother or any one else, to give out a hymn, and conclude ; but instead of forthwith closing the meeting, the brethren and sisters present opened out a course of mighty prayer and labour, with occasional exhortations. The whole may be called a camp meeting."

" To me this proceeding of the praying people was quite unexpected, but it gave me uncommon satisfaction. I soon joined in their valuable labours ; and by the blessing of God, I saw into the excellency of their proceedings, and afterwards was diligent to accompany preachings with extended praying services. Mr. Whitfield, Mr. Wesley, and others practised field preaching ; but here on Mow Cop the Lord caused open-air worship to be commenced on a broader foundation. Truly the Lord was at the head,—the mountain was that day consecrated to the Most High, and the day was gloriously crowned ; and by the blessing of God we may say,—

> ' On the great mountain call'd Mow Cop,
> God did his majesty display ;
> A cloud of glory then rose up,
> To shine unto the perfect day.'

Our conversation preachings, both in doors and in the open air, had been mighty through God to the ' pulling down of strong holds, —numbers having been converted to God ; and on this day, July 12th, 1801, the Lord enlarged our ideas. He in his mercy opened out a dispensation of sacred and divine worship, consisting of a text and sermon, accompanied with a camp meeting movement, performed or carried on by more persons than one ; and this order of proceeding exhibited a newness or enlargement in methodism. In the union of preaching and praying services, the Lord in his divine providence set forth an example for holding future camp meetings. On this system they have been great and useful,—on an opposite method they have been injurious. Also, the accompanying of preachings with praying services, both in-door and out, still continues, and is likely to continue to the end of time ; and this under God, I believe to be the true providential order of the Primitive Methodist Connexion. To God be the praise."

We are here led to make a few passing remarks on the open-air service on Sunday, July 12th, 1801, held upon the celebrated mountain of camp meeting notoriety.

1.—The disappointment at not being able to procure the preachers' assistance from the Burslem circuit, singularly proved a means of facilitating the prime object of the people's wishes— the spread of the work. They were compelled to try their abilities for public prayer making, and succeeded to the glory of God, and the conversion of many ; and the revival increasing, and opening out in such a powerful manner, with the want of an orderly administration of the word according to established custom, no doubt led them to turn their attention to H. Bourne, which eventually led him to the trial of his ministerial talents.

2.—The nature of the influence that moved the country round, causing the people, professors and profane, to flock in such numbers to hear the new beginner, does not appear at first sight perhaps to a superficial observer. It requires an inquiring mind to comprehend it. (1) It could not be the popularity of his preaching abilities that caused the people to come in such numbers on that Sunday to hear the word more than on another, (as the regular congregation had not averaged more than a dozen,) for this very plain reason, he had never before tried at pulpit preaching. (2) We think the loveliness of the road to good old Joseph's, could have had no influence in the matter, as climbing over the rough, broken, irregular steeps of Mow Cop, from the Staffordshire to the Cheshire side, was no very easy task; but this the greater part of the people had to accomplish, as they came from Biddulph Moor, in the Leek circuit, and other places in the moorlands for several miles round. (3) Perhaps the generally-received notions of the irreligious respecting the preacher's character and manner of proceeding, might in some measure influence the attendance, for it was thought by many he was rather odd; and it was also thought his religious frenzy was contagious, for it was spreading in the neighbourhood, and many had taken from him the infection,—hence Mr. Maxfield said he had driven DANIEL SHUBOTHAM crazy. This we think, along with the novelty of the thing, would have some influence on public attention. (4) But there were excited in the minds of the pious, higher motives and holier influences: in the closet, at the family altar, and in public prayer meetings, the souls of the newly-raised-up praying labourers had been poured out before God in incessant prayer and supplications, that heaven might be propitious to the efforts of his servant in his first attempt at preaching God's word to the people according to established custom. Strong cries pierced the eternal portals, and faith that "staggered not," grasped in wrestling agony the promises of Diety, in his behalf, and in behalf of the perishing souls of the people. The pious labourers pleaded that the Lord would stamp with dignity, and crown with honour and success, the labours of the day. These prayers were heard, and numbers, saints and sinners, were doubtless moved on to attend in answer thereto. Here, then, we see, whatever else might operate, some reasons for the large attendance; many of the pious were anxious to see the glory of the Lord in answer to their prayers; and others, both saints and sinners, were influenced from on high through the efficacy of these prayers.

3.—Answers of mercy came down upon the meeting like the dew upon the hill of Hermon, according to the promise of the Lord to his ancient people by the prophet Hosea,—" I will be as the dew unto Israel : he shall grow as the lily, and cast forth his roots as Lebanon. His branches shall spread, and his beauty shall be as the olive tree, and his smell as Lebanon. They that dwell under his shadow shall return ; they shall revive *as* the corn, and grow as the vine : the scent thereof *shall be* as the wine of Lebanon."—Hosea xiv. 5-7. " Like a cloud of dew in the heat of harvest " the heavenly graces of God's Holy Spirit came down upon the people, and shed forth their benign influence upon their hearts. *Jehovah nissi* (the Lord my banner) might have been in-scribed upon their private, family, and public altars. No sooner does the standard-bearer plant upon the mountain the ensigns of the world's redeemer, and the banner of the cross wave in the heavenly and devotional breezes, than the people flock in crowds to participate in the rich and precious benefits bestowed by the preaching of a free, full, and present salvation.

" Lastly, the text selected was appropriate for the occasion, as the effects produced, and the events that have followed, have amply proved. A door, an effectual door, was now opened for open-air worship, by which thousands of precious souls have since found refuge in the ark of the covenant of Christ's atonement from the impending wrath of God which will assuredly be poured out upon the impenitent.

" The camp meeting course on this great Sabbath, upon Mow Cop," says H Bourne, " by the good hand of God upon us, in-creased our faith in the Lord, added vigour to our zeal, and caused our labours to be, in general, more powerful,—new converts in-creased, and the country was more and more moralized : but I was pained at not being able to get the people taken into the Wesleyan society. Still so had the pious labourers abounded, and the new converts increased, that on Friday, July 31st, 1801, the colliers waited on me to say that they had agreed to have a chapel, and Daniel Shubotham would give a piece of his garden as a site on which to build it. This was an undertaking indeed ; but believ-ing it would forward the cause of God, I promised to give the timber. As I had been brought up to hard labour, and had

through sobriety and frugality saved some money, it was in my
power, and the Lord gave me a heart to do it, although the timber
would cost about thirty pounds. In a few days they waited on
me again, and said they might dig the foundation, but could do
nothing further in it, and they wished me to take the matter up;
but having never been connected with chapel building, I was
reluctant. Some may wonder why they did not apply to the
circuit authorities: the answer is very plain,—they had none
(Matthias excepted) to look to but me, and I myself was a newly-
raised preacher, altogether ignorant of chapel management; so I
was completely taken by surprise, and was quite in a dilemma.
The cause of God was rising so powerfully as to make it evident
that a chapel would be needed; and the circuit authorities turned
a deaf ear to all I could say in behalf of the place: and the previous ungodly conduct of the inhabitants had filled that part to a
considerable degree with poverty; but a zeal for the Lord had
implanted in me a strong desire for promoting and keeping up the
cause of God. This turned the scale, and caused me at once to
take the matter in hand, to build a chapel on what had been the
profane Harrisehead; and I was soon involved from head to foot.
Materials had to be brought from a great distance, and the roads in
general were not good, and in some parts very bad; and there was
no one to lay on a hand, or advance a single pound, and it was
difficult at times to get materials carried. The chapel was built
of brick, and slated; and it was large enough to accommodate
about two hundred persons. It was not too large for the population; but before I could get the roof covered, one of the gables
was blown down, and the roof fell in. I hope the Lord will have
mercy on any one who has to pass through such scenes of trouble."

"At Goldenhill the society was very low, moving in modern
methodism. One of the members of that society, a working potter, who was born at Harrisehead, where his parents still lived, in
1801, coming over to see them, came to our Wednesday night
prayer meeting, and there let loose the tongue of flattery. To me
he was a perfect stranger, and I had an impression he would be
mischievous; but I was thankful next morning to hear he had
left the neighbourhood: but my impression was not wrong, for he
had set it out that he was an 'old standard' in methodism, and
that we were in a new way, a new course, and in new proceedings,

and that we should ruin all. I was thankful he was gone : but he and another potter were soon again at our prayer meeting, and they continued to attend as often as the weather suited them. Now Goldenhill and Latebrook were two large adjoining villages, and we could not learn that a single soul had been converted there for years; and modern methodism had had its chance at this place, Harrisehead, but all was a blank,—it lay in a ruinous state: but now the Lord had brought in by his providence primitive methodism to raise it up, and many had been converted, and a chapel was being erected, and the work was going on with power. Modern methodism, by these two potters, said we were all wrong, and should soon ruin all by our proceedings. I gave notice to Daniel Shubotham and Matthias Bayley, that if these men were suffered to go on as they were going on, the converting work would cease ; but they hoped not; and Daniel said they had known one of them from a boy. These two colliers and I had been in the way of conferring together on every matter, and when we three agreed in opinion, we had always proved right ; and up to this time we had uniformly agreed : but now my opinion was as different from theirs as the east is from the west; and being involved in the chapel building, the main weight lay upon me. Had these potters been honourable and intelligent, they would have seen it right to take the chapel off my hands, and set me at liberty ; and the more so, as if they were suffered to go on, the likelihood was that no chapel would be needed. I was under one of the greatest trials I ever was under within my whole life."

"Ere long what I had foreseen came to pass. Religious strictness was not kept up—faith was weakened—tatlings took the place of sound religious conversations—the spirit of God was grieved, and his glory in a great measure departed. The converting work ceased, and week after week passed without a single soul being brought to God. Complainings abounded ; and at length Daniel and Matthias waking up laid hands on the potters. And they told me that they were not to come any more to Harrisehead as they had done, but they had allowed them to take Newchapel village, where they soon ruined the cause, and then forsook the place ; and one of them fell foully; and Daniel and Matthias learned a lesson which for years they did not forget. It was now evident the two Goldenhill potters aimed their shafts at me, for they did what they could to stir up the young converts and the people against me. It might have been considered that it was upon what these two modern Wesleyans ridiculed as a new way, that the colliers had induced me to undertake to build them a chapel; but had not the chapel building matter been a tie upon me, I should have employed my labours elsewhere. There may have been something wanting in me; as the Lord had placed me in a religious headship, and had given me two or three valuable colleagues, I ought to have taken up without hesitation, whatever self-denial was required of me, and even then to have said, as in Luke xvii. 10. "We are unprofitable servants." And perhaps my unwillingness to be at the head in religious management, grieved the spirit of the Lord, and caused the trouble to come upon me: however, I was thrust out of the management, and my honours were laid in the dust; and the religious cause was cut down, the conversion of sinners stopped, and the prospects of good in a measure were closed. The whole case illustrates Job v. 7. 'Man is born to trouble as the sparks fly upwards.'"

Attempts were made to recover what had been lost, and though the revival for a time was checked, and the people's faith was below the converting power, yet through the mercy of God none fell away, and this was a cause of thankfulness. The people had to humble themselves before God, and almost the whole of them learned a lesson which was a blessing for years; and by the mercy of God the spirit of revival was not wholly lost, although for a time the exercises of faith were too weak to bring up the converting work, and restore it again. The people at Mow and Harrisehead made a valulable discovery. The Lord had trained them up in his work, and they really knew more of revival work than most of the people in England; yet they had strangely yielded to the guidance of the two potters, who, in regard to promoting the work of God, were as ignorant as two children; and indeed we may almost say, more so: and by so giving themselves up to these two modern methodists, they had grieved the holy spirit, and caused the glory of the Lord in a measure to depart; but by the blessing of God, the lesson they learned led them to abide by what the Lord in his mercy had taught them; and for years they were considered as ranking among the firmest people in England: so although they suffered deeply, their sufferings turned to good.

CHAPTER XII.

" Having noticed the unhappy proceedings of the two Goldenhill
potters, as individuals, it may be asked, were they a fair sample
of the Burslem circuit; and if they were, why did that circuit
stand so high in my estimation? Why, being hardly ever among
the people, except on Sundays, and not taking any public part,
the business affairs of the circuit were scarcely known to me;
neither was I aware of its deadness, nor its decreases. My main
business was to attend to my own growth in grace, and the public
means and pious conversations gave me much assistance; and the
circuit, by furnishing these helps, was of service to me, and caused
me to value it highly : but still it did not enter into my mind that
the two potters were a fair sample of the circuit, There were, however, some things which did not look as they might have looked.

1.—T. Allen, a local brother, was occasionally a field preacher,
but this was not the case with any other preacher, travelling or
local, in the circuit.
" 2.—In three years, from July, 1797, to July, 1800, the circuit sank or decreased one hundred and ten members. In 1785-6,
Mr. Thomas Warwick was stationed in Burslem circuit, and
under his ministry the converting work went on famously; and in
July, 1794, Mr. George Marsden was stationed in Burslem circuit,
as the third preacher, and I often heard of a glorious revival under
his ministry; and hearing this so greatly spoken of, had occasionally raised in me a wish to see something of the kind: but

Burslem circuit was become a stranger to such things, as well as to field-preaching.

" 3.—Again, my acquaintance with methodism was obtained in a great measure by reading; and as Mr. Wesley, John Nelson, and others of the first race, were in the way both of field-preaching and getting souls converted to God, I had taken these as sound proceedings of methodism. And when there was at Harrisehead, and Mow Cop, a continuous course of saving souls, of turning sinners from darkness to light, and from the power of satan unto God, I judged it right for such course to continue; and I considered this to be pure methodism, and it was agreeable to methodism in its primitive state. Still as I did not know of the decreases, the conduct of the two potters did not lower my high estimate of the circuit; and I long wished the circuit authorities to take the Harrisehead, Mow Cop, and Kidsgrove converts into Society. And perhaps as they were weary of my applications, they at length put a class paper into my hands, and told me to take them into the society myself. This was rather a knockdown blow; but in the fear of the Lord I undertook it: so I was forced into a kind of headship point blank against my own inclination, and the cross was heavy; still, all things considered, my knowledge of the people may have induced them to think me a proper person to accomplish the task."

" The people for some time had wished to meet in class. I put in Daniel Shubotham as leader,—myself, Matthias, and T. Cotton agreeing to lead it in turn; for unless we would do this, Daniel was not willing to undertake it. The new converts who lived upon Mow Cop, I joined in old Joseph Pointon's class, which met on Sunday mornings,—the other class was to meet in Daniel's house till the chapel was ready, and then it was to meet in the chapel. It was fixed to meet on Monday nights, so any of the members of the Mow Cop class were at liberty to attend when they chose. I never in my life knew a class have more variety in its leading. It was not confined to the four, for others of the colliers occasionally led it, and they were to a certain degree originals. They also were accustomed to despatch,—if they had twenty, or thirty, or more, they would quickly go through the leading. They were generally all in powerful exercises of faith during the leading, and indeed in every part; and the praying course was mighty. The class was long remarkable for the converting power,—many were brought to a knowledge of salvation by the remission of sins, and

I never knew a class more owned of God. Mr. Wesley established variety in class leading, but it did not continue very long;
but as far as I have seen, it is much the best system. Harrisehead and Kidsgrove, with the new converts on Mow Cop, were
now taken into the Burslem Wesleyan circuit: and at the next
conference, held in July, 1802, the circuit reported 850 members,
the increase for the year being 84. Sinners were saved, and God
was glorified. The travelling preachers stationed in the Burslem
circuit, in July, 1802, were Messrs. Joseph Taylor, W. Palmer,
and John Grant; and Mr. Grant was the first travelling preacher
who visited Harrisehead chapel. He came on a Wednesday
evening. He observed that he had expected to have about thirty
to preach to; but, said he, when I came in and saw the congregation, I was surprised! I was amazed! I was astonished! There
were about two hundred. Now this shows the excellency of following out a primitive methodist course, similar to that laid
down by Mr. Wesley and his early helpers. All this great work
had been raised up with very little or scarce any pulpit preaching.
The nearest society was in the house of good old Joseph Pointon,
on the Cheshire side of Mow Cop. The new work was raised up
(a mile and a half distant from old Joseph's, on the Staffordshire
side) in one of the most ignorant, profane, and ungodly parts of
the nation. A young man set out for heaven under Mr. Grant's
sermon, and Mr. Grant ranked high as a preacher. He conversed
well on almost every subject, scientific, religious, or literary. I
was favoured with his conversation several times, and it was a
blessing to me: also, he bought me Parkhurst's Greek Lexicon,
Bell's Greek and English Grammar, and Parkhurst's Hebrew
Lexicon, and Bayley's entrance into the Hebrew language, and
he gave me lessons in Greek and Hebrew; but through family
affliction, he was obliged to leave the circuit, and this was a trial
to me,—but of course the Lord's will is best. Mr. Joseph Taylor
was an extraordinary man, and I profited much by his conversations,—I have cause to thank God for bringing me into the
acquaintance of these two eminent men. I highly respected the
circuit, and the preachers; but in regard to travelling preachers'
duties, we did not think alike. Mr. Wesley required grace, gifts,
and fruit,—the fruit I took to be the conversion of sinners to
God,—and he made field-preaching obligatory: and he and his
brother Charles, J. Nelson, J. Haime, and others, got many
converted; and in reading preachers' experiences in the early

magazines, we find they were both field-preachers and converters. So we have now before us the right and true course of primitive methodism."

"Our travelling preachers in the Burslem Wesleyan circuit set themselves forth as ' *Builders up.*' This was the title they assumed; yet they allowed, if conversions happened, it was well; otherwise, the conversion of sinners to God, some of them said, was no part of their charge,—was not included in their undertaking; and I never knew a Burslem circuit travelling preacher perform what Mr. Wesley calls 'field-preaching,' all the time I was a member, and that was from June, 1799, to June 27th, 1808. This then was, and is, *modern* (not primitive) methodism; and I think there is a broad line of difference between the two. And again, for the most part the converters are better builders up than the others. It was very long before Harrisehead, Kidsgrove, and the Staffordshire part of Mow Cop were taken into the Burslem circuit: but it appears this was of the Lord to make manifest the difference between primitive and modern methodism; and there issued a contest between the two; and primitive methodism actually brought the circuit up, in opposition to all obstacles thrown in the way by modern methodism, as the following tables of yearly conference reports will show:—

MODERN.				PRIMITIVE.				MODERN.			
Dates.	Members.	Decrease.		Dates.	Members.	Increase.		Dates.	Members.	Increase.	Decrease.
1797	860			1801	766	16		1807	1050		
1798	810	50		1802	850	84		1808	1060	10	
1799	810			1803	950	100		1809	1100	40	
1800	750	60		1804	1080	130		1810	1090		10
Decrease...		110		1805	900*	279		1811	980		110
				1806	1000	100					120
				1807	1050	50					50
				Increase...		759		Decrease in 4 years...			70

* The report in July, 1805, was 1359,—the increase for the year being 279. But 459 members were taken off to form Newcastle-under-Lyne circuit.

It will be seen that primitive methodism began to revive, and the decreasing was stopped; and the circuit kept rising to two hundred and seventy nine in one year. And then measures being taken to drive primitive methodism out, the circuit gradually sunk, until it had only ten increase for the year, and then it went down grievously,—yes, it sunk one hundred and ten in one year."

"Before the chapel was completed, Daniel Shubotham consulted me relative to leaving the Wesleyans, and joining another community. He rather took me by surprise: but my reply was to this effect,—you are able to judge for yourselves, and I shall not influence you, but shall do you any favour in my power: but if you join that community, I shall not come among you, for I shall not leave the Wesleyans. He replied, you may come among us nevertheless: but my answer was, I should not, neither would it be proper. In a few days after he told me they had agreed to continue among the Wesleyans. When the Wesleyans were taken into the new chapel at Harrisehead, they evidently showed a preference for modern methodism; for they planned the chapel preaching to be at ten, and two o'clock every Sunday. Now the work having been raised almost without preaching, it would have been more primitive to have had only one sermon each Sunday, and have taken up Newchapel village, or elsewhere, the other part of the day. However, before they came in, the improved method of holding preaching services was established; so soon as the preacher came to a close, the praying started with full force. This was new in the circuit; but there was no stopping it; and the congregation seemed to like it better that the sermon, and at length the preachers seemed all to like it. It was rare to hear of a soul being converted under a sermon. The people looked to themselves and to God for the conversion of precious souls, and the Lord granted them in this respect the desire of their heart. Our people were as keen as fire in reproof; and the preachers not always paying attention to that strictness in which the Harrisehead people had been trained up, they met with keen reproofs: and to reprove preachers was like a new thing upon earth, and it caused some stir at quarter days; and more than once it was said, that restraining motions had been passed; but no one was hardy enough to deliver such a motion, as it would have been like facing a drawn sword. The spirit of reproof in the people, and their firmness in it, had by degrees a sensible effect upon the circuit: and under God, it was ultimately a blessing,—many of the people were firm as iron pillars, and gradually the spirit of revival moved on the circuit generally."

"Having so many calls and so much on my hands, and having a desire to be acquainted with the Hebrew and Greek languages, I undertook to teach a school (a thing much needed) in the chapel. I taught about twelve months, during which I gained an acquaintance with Greek and Hebrew; but unawares I became nervous: this was distressing; but in reading in a publication written by Mr. Wesley, I found that this was caused by too much sitting; but it was troublesome,—hard labour suited me best. What time I could spare from work and study, was spent in prayer meetings and exhortations; and in preachings I generally managed to get into the open air, with a few pious praying labourers. This system the Lord in his providence taught me on Sunday, July 12th, 1801, upon Mow Cop; and I was so satisfied in my own mind of its excellency, that I laboured with my whole strength of mind and body to establish it practically wherever I was called to labour in after life."

In the beginning of the year 1801, the Lord raised up another collier colleague for H. Bourne in the person of Thomas Cotton, who became a most valuable open-air preacher, and laboured successfully in the infancy of the rising cause, and died happy in the Lord.*

There is a striking coincidence between the origin of the English and the American camp meetings, which may here be noticed. The very same year in which they began in America, they may be said to have commenced in England, but without the name in each country. Thus, while Hugh Bourne and the colliers were labouring, and commencing upon Mow Cop, July 12th, 1801, a new course of open-air worship, the same spirit of primitive zeal was manifest in America. On page 522 of the Wesleyan Methodist Magazine, for 1802, we read, in a letter dated May 11th, 1802.—"On the 12th of August, 1801, I laboured inces-

* See the history of the Primitive Methodists, by Hugh Bourne.

santly for four days together, and often till the sun went down."
And in page 523, the same writer says, "About this time I
received the joyful news of the work breaking out in the upper
part of Georgia, and running like fire in dry stubble, since which
most of the circuits in the district have caught the fire, which has
continued to spread. What cannot the methodists do through
grace? Glory be to God, primitive methodism shines in this
country, and through America." The camp meeting accounts in
the Wesleyan magazines would fill volumes; but these short
extracts will shew the reader that they were carried on, though
without the name of camp meetings, in the year 1801. "But I
do not find," says Hugh Bourne, "*the name* till a later period."
And it would appear that primitive methodism requires open-air
worship, and the converting work; and it would be well if primitive methodism shone in every part of England, as in 1801 it did
in America. The flaming accounts in the Wesleyan magazines
roused the mountain colliers, so that they wished to have their
day's praying upon Mow Cop this summer, 1802, which Daniel
Shubotham had promised them in 1801. In T. Cotton and H.
Bourne the colliers found zealous supporters of their wishes on
this important subject: but strange to tell, Daniel, the very man
that first broached the idea, and said in 1801, you shall have a
day's praying on Mow some Sunday, had suffered himself to be
led into strong opposition to open-air worship now in 1802; and
when his fellow colliers and Hugh Bourne wished to have the
day's praying upon Mow, he opposed the proposition being carried
out, and so far succeeded as to put aside the meeting at that time.
Hugh Bourne writes thus:—"Had a day's praying been attempted before they were joined to the Burslem circuit, it might have
succeeded, but not after; still had the Wesleyan ministers
allowed it to be tried, the attempt might have been a means of
doing away with all further thought of open-air worship on a large
scale; but by hindering the attempt, they caused the way to be
left open for camp meeting meditations; and the methodist magazines opened upon us like the light of the morning; and this
caused our petitions to be "*Lord give us a camp meeting!*" and
though clouds and darkness were round about HIM, we had to
believe, or try to believe, against hope; and we continued thus
praying until the month of September, 1804, when the Lord for
a season caused us to be otherwise engaged."

We find no Journals and but few notes by H. Bourne for the year 1802. This year he was a school master in the new chapel at Harrisehead, and he fully and zealously devoted his time and talents to studying the Hebrew and Greek languages. He not only taught a week-day school, but also a Sabbath School was commenced, in which he was a teacher, labouring to promote the moral and religious improvement of the rising generation in that once profane, Sabbath-desecrating district; and in this respect the Lord greatly owned the labours of himself and his collier coadjutors. The Harrisehead Sunday school may with propriety be said to have been the parent of all the other Sabbath schools in the neighbourhood, whether under the law Church, Wesleyan Methodist Conference, or Primitive Methodist management : and now this part of the moorlands of North Staffordshire abounds with buildings appropriated for the teaching of the rising generation on both Sabbath and week-days; and we are happy to say that these seminaries are on the increase. The progress Hugh Bourne made in learning Greek and Hebrew we must leave to conjecture and incidental hints : but in his journals the reader may find in very plain English something about his method of study, when he shut himself up in Harrisehead chapel, and pinned himself down to teach children, as well as school himself. He always joined a considerable portion of faith and prayer with his classical studies ; and when it is understood that in the early part of his pilgrimage, he was considerably influenced by the views of the "friends," or quakers, as they are called, and strove in all matters to be led by the Spirit of God ; and that he firmly believed that in answer to prayer the Lord in a great measure inspired him with his Holy Spirit to enable him to learn Greek and Hebrew, it will be believed that his studies were both earnest and devotional, and that he had an eye to the glory of God in all things. Indeed in all the multifarious toils, both mental and physical, in which he engaged, he was of the same spirit, a man of single purpose and sincere piety. Perhaps no man ever watched with greater thought and clearer perception of mind than H. Bourne did, what he considered to be the openings of divine providence, with regard to visiting or labouring on new ground. If he did not perceive as he thought a call to any locality, he very soon left it, or never went to it, and turned his attention elsewhere : but when a call by the providence of God was manifest, the place

and people from that moment shared his affection, assiduity, and
care.   In his mind they found a resting place, and were continually borne agonizingly to the throne of grace, and God's
mercy was incessantly supplicated through Christ for aid and
assistance, to plant successfully the standard of the gospel there.
And as far as our own knowledge of the man extends, aided by
the access we have had to his papers, we have seldom found his
judgment at fault in such cases, or his labours unsuccessful ; but
it is remarkable that in many of the places which shared his early
labours, such as Kidsgrove, Norton, Brown Edge, Bidduph Moor,
Bradley Green, &c., methodism, both Wesleyan and primitive,
has taken deep root in the minds and habits of the people, and
still grows and flourishes to this day.

CHAPTER XIII.

Early in the year 1803, Mr. Bourne seems to have experienced
conflicts which were of no common character; hence he writes:—
"Feb. 12th, 1803. This week I had greater trials than I ever
had since I set out for heaven." And he then relates a circumstance which afforded him great pleasure:—" On Wednesday, my
brother William was brought in." *

"*Feb.* 17th, 1803," he writes, " Mr. Butler, a young preacher
that has come in Mr. Grant's stead, came to preach at Harrisehead.
I was with him before preaching ; he seems a zealous young man,
and wishes to be a *revivalist.* At Mr. Handley's, the next morn-

* Mr. William Bourne was a man of giant strength, equal it is said to
that of two or three ordinary men. After his conversion to God he joined
the society of friends, emigrated to America, became a travelling minister,
and for years continued annually to visit the various stations in the different
states of the union, preaching the word of life to his brethren ; and we
think he is now gone to the paradise of God, as the family have not heard
from him for many years.

ing, I said to him that I was not able at all times to take up the
cross in reproving sin,—referring to what he had spoken about it
in his sermon. He replied, if we will be servants of Christ, we
must take up the cross. I said, if Mr. Butler means to keep
clear of the blood of all men, he must take up the cross. He said
he looked for it. I told him he would also be persecuted by the
methodists. This he was unwilling to believe. I told him the
people here (Harrisehead) had been persecuted by, and had stood
it out against both preachers and people, a number of whom had
opposed them, and prevailed so far as to bring the revival to an
end; and it was with great difficulty that a degree of the
revival spirit was regained.   He was struck with surprise; and
said the work had been attended with difficulty and trouble.
I said it had been carried on in the fire. He had before been
admiring the earnestness of spirit seen in the congregation, and
their zeal in singing and prayer. I told him Mr. Lockwood had
been one who had aided in bringing them into that way,—it being
the way he carried on meetings. He said in his journey hither,
he slept all night with Mr. Lockwood; but observed, that if he
were to exert himself like Mr. Lockwood, there would soon be an
end to his life. I told him we had persons convinced and converted too in the midst of the noise, even when one could scarcely
distinguish a word; but such earnest ways of carrying on meetings
were disliked by the greater part of methodists. We prayed at parting, and had a glorious time. Old Jane Hall was there. Thomas
Hurd wished to get into the revival spirit. I told him if he did
he would meet with great persecution. He wished me to explain.
I told him Snowden used to say, 'Religion is a thing that the
world can never forgive.' He said it is a true saying. I replied,
a revival spirit is what we methodists, in some places, cannot forgive. O, said he, you have given me the hint. At night we had
a very lively time at Norton."

Hugh Bourne's manner of conversing with the preachers was
not always very agreeable to their feelings, as a few extracts from
his diary will shew.

"*Monday, Feb. 21st*, 1803.—At night, Daniel Shubotham told
me that the preachers were offended at my using freedoms with
them, and that I had set Mr. Butler a reasoning to such a degree,

that he could scarcely preach. I was rather tempted for a short time, but was soon delivered."

"*Wednesday, Feb. 23rd.*—Daniel informed me that there was a great charge laid against me at Burslem among the preachers. He blamed my conduct, but old Selby* and another defended me; and at prayer my mind was stayed on God.—Glory, glory. In the afternoon I could scarcely keep out of reasoning. I thought it was hard that I should continually be a man of strife. At night I went to the meeting, where I was blessed beyond any former time. On Monday last I felt in my soul a great washing; but to-night I was anointed with the oil of gladness. I have thought before that nothing could exceed the blessings I enjoyed; but this was a *glory* and *gladness*, which exceeded everything I had ever known or thought of. I found myself willing to be anything or nothing, to do or suffer for the Lord! O, that my heart and soul may always be given up to the living God! that I may serve him continually, and deal plainly with every one."

"*Monday, Feb. 28th.*—In the morning I was convinced of giving way to worldly desires, but was set at liberty in private prayer:—found that I must be given up to the will of the Lord at all times, and in every thing. Praise the Lord, O my soul! I was particularly struck with the earnestness of the people while hearing those, who but a little time back had been greater sinners than most, were now praising him that had 'loved them, and washed them in his own blood,' and declaring they would rather be cut in pieces than sin against him again."

"*Thursday, March 17th.*—I have for some time had a great backwardness to self-denial, through which I find the enemy has got some advantage over me. I find self-denial easy to be talked of, but hard to be practised. For some days I have read the journals of Mr. Wesley. Equally surprising on whatever side we view this great man,—whether we consider his unbounded zeal, his deep penetration, his steady perseverence, his moderation of spirit, his faithfulness in reproving, or his wisdom in managing;

---

* Old Selby was a man of slender ability, but a great converter and revivalist.

and one cannot but admire how wonderfully the Lord supported
him in all his difficulties, and enabled him to surmount every
obstacle, and wrought such a work by him as the world has not
seen since the apostles' days." Such was Hugh Bourne's opinion
of Mr. Wesley.

" *Thursday, March* 31*st.*—This day I found temptations more
strong and powerful than at any time this week before, and the
Lord shewed me many things in my· heart with which I was not
before acquainted.   I had been seeking an easier way than the Lord
had laid out for us.   I before concluded that I had a full sense of
my own unworthiness ; but now I found if blessings, either temporal
or spiritual, were withheld, my' sense of unworthiness was swept
away, and I could not help repining.   At night I was at Norton,
and began again to have the usual power and liberty."

" *Friday, April* 1*st.*—To-day I reviewed and examined my
conduct through the late temptations.   I also read in Mr. Wesley's
writings, and made the following resolutions.   1.—To put away
all trifling talk, and follow after godly seriousness.   2.—To put
away all slothfulness, and to be always (if possible) diligently
employed.   3.—To put away all softness and indulgence, and endeavour to endure hardness.   4.—To avoid sitting as much as
possible, as I have already been weakened by it.   5.—To pay more
attention to health and cleanliness, which I have of late foolishly
neglected.   6.—To endeavour to fast every Wednesday and Friday,
as was the custom in the primitive church, and has been with some
methodists.   7.—To take up every cross, and never flinch at any
self-denial or sufferings for Christ.   All these I know will be
attended with bodily pain : but I have clearly found, that admit-
ting the least sin into my heart, will be attended with greater
pain and torment than all put together.   These have been
clearly laid down before me, and I have deliberately taken my
choice.   8.—To be given up to prayer, and always endeavour to
act faith on the promise for strength to walk perfectly before him.
O Lord help me, and establish me."

" *Sunday, April* 3*rd.*—To-day is my birth-day.   I have
always observed that about this time I have been more stirred
up in religion than usual ; and so it has now almost involuntarily

happened. For sometime past I have been seeking more bodily
ease than is allowed to those that will go to heaven, of which
being now convinced, I find myself determined to take up the
cross."

The foregoing extracts from his diary shew the inward
struggles and conflicts of a mind fully bent on finding the way
to heaven, glorifying God on earth, and striving to be useful
in his day and generation. This year his labours, and his calls
from different places in the neighbourhood, greatly increased ;
and he was diligent in the home mission field, insomuch that he
had now to divide his time, and adopt a more systematic
arrangement with regard to the week-night meetings. Burslem
and Tunstall were generally his Sunday places,—there he regularly attended as a hearer, unless some other appointment
prevented him. Harrisehead, Norton, Brown Edge, Whitfield,
Woodhouse Lane, Ridgway, and other places, were taken on his
own private week-night plan. At each of these places he laboured
with success,—many were converted, and not a few praying
labourers and conversation-preachers raised up and set to work in
the vineyard of his Lord and master. He continued at Harise-
head as a school master part of this year, diligently studying
Hebrew, Greek, &c., and he seems to have made considerable
progress both in the classics, and the composition of the English
language.

The year 1804 apparently was a year of much fruit. The
grace of God was shed more abundantly upon him, and he was
made more fully acquainted with the deep things of God. This
year the American camp meetings were very great, and the
Wesleyan magazines gave such glowing accounts of them, " that
I," says he, " M. Bayley, T. Cotton, and others prayed the
Lord to give us a camp meeting on Mow Cop ; but not being
fully prepared for so great an undertaking, the Lord opened us
out other employment."

Revivalists in Cheshire.—" Cheshire had Wesleyans called
revivalists ; and Mr. J. Clark, blacksmith, at Congleton, at his
own expense, fetched some of them about twenty miles to his
house, to attend the September lovefeast, in the Congleton Wes-

leyan chapel; and a number of us Staffordshire methodists, at
his instance, attended that lovefeast. The Cheshire revivalists
shewed much zeal, and sung a revival hymn; and after the lovefeast they held a meeting in Mr. Clark's house. I thought them
readier in the exercise of faith than we were; but they neither
laid open doctrines, nor explained the mystery of faith: but
Prov. xxvii. 17 says, 'Iron sharpeneth iron; so a man sharpeneth the countenance of his friend.' On our return we conversed
freely, and were lively, and edified one another, and we appeared
to have an increase of faith; and in the evening of the next day,
Monday, I attended the class meeting at Harrisehead chapel,—
the proceedings were more free than usual in the singing, prayers,
and leading. Then followed the main tug of war against the
power of the enemy of souls,—the person who prayed had immediate assistance from the faith of all who were present, the whole
meeting united. The brethren could have exercised faith in
silence, but they laboured with all their heart, and mind, and
voice, and the noise was heard afar off, and all were in a heavenly
uniting faith before the Lord; and in my opinion there was the
greatest out-pouring of the Holy Ghost I had ever known. The
surrounding country was shaken; the veil was taken from many
hearts; and we had so much work in praying for mourners, that
we gave up praying for a camp meeting; and Tunstall, and even
a great part, if not the whole of the Burslem circuit, more or less,
was moved. It was the greatest time of power I had ever known.
To God be glory and dominion, for ever and ever, amen."

On Christmas day, the Stockport revivalists again met the
Staffordshire methodists at a lovefeast in Congleton Wesleyan
chapel. Hugh Bourne writes, "They were stronger in faith than
we. They brought the hymn, 'Glory, glory, glory.' Mr. Shel-
merdine made observations on one of them, who, he thought, did
not speak correctly. One made a strong profession, and added,
that it was the mind of Christ for sinners to be saved, and if this
was not attained, the will of God and the cause of Jesus Christ's
death were not accomplished, and there was something wrong in
the prayer meetings, class leading, exhortations, and preaching.
They returned home the same night,—I was grieved at this.
They spoke of having labouring love; and I thought that this
was labouring love. O, my God, remember them. I was much

established by going among them. Since their first coming, many have obtained clean hearts, and the work has been great among sinners, and it has almost spread through this circuit. It has quite altered the society at Harrisehead, and the Lord has worked powerfully there. I wanted to have sanctification at Norton, and at first I was rather impatient; but seeing this to be a temptation, I readily and easily gave them up to Jesus; and I have since seen the desire of my heart. Before I had some authority at Norton, but this has swept it away, and we discourse level handed. Glory be to God, for ever and ever, amen."

The same Christmas week there followed a lovefeast at Harrisehead. Hear what Hugh Bourne says :—" The mighty out-pouring of the Holy Ghost in the Harrisehead chapel made a heavenly move ; and there was a stir when it was reported that at Christmas, there would be a lovefeast in Harrisehead chapel ; for when the time came, people flocked in from east, west, north, and south. The chapel was loaded,—the people stood on and between the forms ; and Mr. James Steele, of Tunstall, took a part in leading the lovefeast. Twenty souls were prayed into liberty; and Mr. Steele, and others from Tunstall, were converted into revivalists. It was a mighty revivalist move ; and the Lord enabled those from Tunstall to carry an increase of the revival fire and revival work to that place. The mighty out-pouring of the Holy Ghost in Harrisehead chapel, in September, had reached Tunstall, and had made a gracious move; but on this Christmas occasion, it increased to a gracious out-pouring of the Holy Spirit. The Tunstall deadness, which had been proverbial for years, was done away, and Tunstall rose into revival notice, insomuch that shortly after this great lovefeast, William Clowes, Thomas Woodnorth, James Nixon, William Morris, and others, were brought to God, and became useful evangelists. ' Blessed be the everlasting God, the father of our Lord Jesus Christ, who has begotten us again to a lively hope through the resurrection of Jesus Christ from the dead.' Glory be to God ! Glory be to God ! Amen. Thou, Lord, hast filled me with thy love ; thou hast made me glad with thy salvation; my heart rejoices in the living God ; thou hast put my enemies under my feet ; I rejoice, I triumph, my soul rejoices in God, in him is my trust, and he is the horn of my salvation. He hath cleansed my soul from sin ; he hath filled me with love in the Holy Ghost."

" After this I was for a few days rather unwatchful, and was
many times drawn into hastiness of spirit; but, however, I held
fast faith, though it was by main force, for I was determined to
believe. Daniel, one day, asked how I went on. I replied to this
effect,—if ·I must be judged by works, I must be thrown
clear out of sanctification, for my works have been worse for two
or three days than when only in a justified state. He said, I
have compared it to a person bad of a fever; he is very bad and
weak; he has the doctor, and is cured of the fever; but still the
body is weak, and he has the actions of a sickly person ; the fever
is sin, after sin is destroyed we want establishing ; but this does
not prove that we are not cleansed from sin, but that we are weak
and want building up—want establishing, so that we should hold
fast our confidence, and not reason, but apply to the fountain:
and even if we were drawn into sin, 'we have an advocate with
the father, Jesus Christ the righteous.' This helped me to see
through the matter. Another time I for some days thought that
I had sin in my heart, but could not tell ; I thought I felt the
motions of sin, but I resolutely held fast faith. Daniel told me
that it was only the violence of temptation,—that when wrung by
violent temptations, it might seem as if I had sin, when I had
not; and I was told by others not to take temptation for sin : so
I escaped this snare. I have since found that many stumble at
this—they take temptation for sin. I was once very near throwing away my confidence, at a Sunday night's meeting at the
Stonetrough. At prayer, at Daniel's, before we went to the meeting, J. Gidman obtained a clean heart. I was very happy, but
some were more greatly blessed. Satan brought this upon me so
strongly, as to get me into some degree of impatience before we
reached the meeting : by this means I in some measure departed
from the faith,—I rather reasoned. When the meeting began, a
number of temptations came dashing at me on all sides. It ran
through me many times,—what did I think of it now? Had I a
clean heart now? I thought, well, they do not lodge,—I have
no desire for them : then it came this and that lodges; and I
could not say but I had a desire for this and that; and if I had
had a clean heart, it would not have been so. Well, I thought
this sort of work will not do,—if I have not a clean heart I will
have one. I applied immediately to Jesus Christ. I had a sharp
struggle; but directly it came that I was clean through the word

spoken. Then the devil had done. I found little difference, only the noise of the temptation was gone; so that my heart was clean before, only I had reasoned, and had not applied immediately to Jesus Christ. Then it struck through my mind, was not the word always there? Then it came, that it was firmer than heaven and earth; and it was shewed me, that if I always would believe the word of God, I should stand firmer than heaven and earth. Glory be to God! One Tuesday night I had a most absolute liberty, which continued till Thursday in the forenoon; then a temptation came,—I thought I will not have this, and thrust it away. I had not then learned to go straight to Jesus Christ. It seemed to slacken, but in a few minutes it struck through me like a flaming dart. I then found it was time to stir. I strove against it and cried unto the Lord. It was taken away; but it brought me into heaviness, which continued until Sunday morning, when the Lord set me on the rock again. On Sunday, January 7th, 1805, we had a lovefeast at Burslem. Many of the Harrisehead people spoke of full sanctification; but Mr. Jackson shut up the meeting, at which many were hurt; but we afterwards set to prayer, and there was a pretty clamour. It was just like Harrisehead chapel,—prejudices were swept away, four obtained sanctification, and two justification. I was rarely established, and more so on Monday night. This week I was saved continually, and I plainly viewed Christ all the week. I was full of love, peace, and joy, and had as much as the body would bear. I saw all things clearly. It was put to me what I would choose, how I would choose to be, and my heart replied,— just as thou wilt, Lord. I desired no other worldly circumstances, and I thought if I asked any more love, the body would melt away, as at times I could scarcely stand for the weight of glory. On Monday, January 15th, towards noon, I joined in some talk that was not expedient: I did not view Christ so plainly, and I was puzzled all the week, because I had not the same experience as before. The next Monday, at Harrisehead, Daniel Shubotham told me that I was looking to feelings: if I had Christ that was enough; so I obtained deliverance. On the Monday but one after this, Daniel was going to lead the class. Little Joseph Stubbs, of Hall Green, a praying lad and one that was sanctified, began to pray for the Holy Ghost. It came down on me, I discerned it in the spirit, it brought no particular happiness, but

I felt that it joined me to God. I then felt the blood of Jesus Christ go round my heart: well, I thought, this will quench all the fiery darts of satan before they reach my heart: then it shone brightly in my soul,—then it began to burn, and I found it to be a spirit of burning.* This established me, made me more strong and steady in the faith, and enlarged my heart: now I loved the Lord more—my heart was enlarged. I now had union and communion with the Father, the Son, and the Holy Ghost, and thought I could go to the ends of the earth to speak of Jesus Christ."

" *Friday, Feb.* 18*th.*—I have been for some time rather tried and buffeted, and have felt as if my faith had a load upon it; but the Lord has been shewing me my short-comings. I before scarcely understood what was meant by short-comings—I scarcely saw any; but now I see plenty in almost every thing. Satan would have suggested that I was worse than any body, and that I had no faith, but I was determined to hold Christ, come what would, and I found he was with me; and the Lord gave me to know that he was shewing me my short-comings. I had just read in a letter that it was good to be shewn this,—that we should rejoice at every discovery of this nature. I took it this way, and found my confidence strengthen. Now I see that I have nothing of myself, any more than one that is starting, — he is perhaps more vehement, but I have more faith, I believe more, and trust more, and hope more in God, and Jesus helps me. He is now my all. He is all my strength, my portion, and my all; my soul delights in him. I have no self-dependence; all my confidence is in God. All that I can say is, to me who am less than the least of all saints is this grace given, that I should trust in God."

" *Monday, Feb.* 19*th.*—In the morning the Lord sent me to Bradley Green. I explained to Jemima what sanctification was, and how to obtain and hold it,—few can clearly explain it. At

---

* And it shall come to pass, *that he that is* left in Zion, and *he that* remaineth in Jerusalem, shall be called holy, *even* every one that is written among the living in Jerusalem: when the Lord shall have washed away the filth of the daughters of Zion, and shall have purged the blood of Jerusalem from the midst thereof by the spirit of judgment, and by the spirit of burning.—Isaiah iv. 3-4.

night, at Harrisehead; many were there; the work goes on rapidly. After this Daniel spoke of being sealed by the spirit, and of the full assurance of hope. When we have the full assurance of faith, we have and lay claim to all the promises in the bible,—to this we are sealed by the Holy Spirit. As he told me, I thought he spoke of the fulness of the promises contained in the bible respecting this life. It was suggested that if we gained this, we should have nothing more to press after; that there then would be nothing to set before us as a mark. I was quite startled at it, but soon perceived it was the enemy. I stopped with Daniel till nearly one o'clock, when we prayed, and the Lord I believe sealed me with the full assurance of hope, and to the day of redemption. I found I was then stronger in God: I was let into God, and had full room for growing up into him. It appeared a more mighty work than any I had ever known, an extraordinary solidness and weightiness of spirit came upon me. This particular experience was a constant and steady recollection. Glory be to God! Religion gets deep and solid at Harrisehead. Daniel told me that the unction of the holy one was a burning love. He advised me continually to pray for the Lord to shew me my heart more and more, and Christ at the same time; to pray for light and wisdom. It requires much wisdom and care to carry on a revival, to keep free from counterfeits; but it may be carried on for ever."

"*Tuesday, Feb. 19th.*—I led G. Lomas's class, in the vestry, Burslem. I had much talk with Obadiah Mayer. I explained faith to him, and it lifted up his heart. I shewed the difference of seeking by faith and seeking by works,—if by faith, we expect to receive it every moment—if by works, to receive it sometime."

"*Wednesday, Feb, 20th.*—At night I was at Harrisehead preaching. Tregortha preached an uncommon sermon. Two obtained pardon in the middle of the discourse. They have seldom any meeting without some being in distress. I told Daniel the Lord had sealed me. He examined me very closely. There is an uncommon solidness and weightiness of spirit among them at Harrisehead; they begin to get into the deep things of God. When Daniel found that I had the seal, he said I was now got past doubting, or even reasoning. I said I found no inclination, and scarce any ability to it.   Coming home, at the praying place, in Mr. Heath's field, I thought I have scarcely any power or ability to doubt or reason, without I am determined to reason wilfully and forcibly.   I felt as if held by an irresistible power, and I sank down into nothing before it, and every thing died that was contrary to God.   I felt it die away—I gave myself up to God. Immediately came the spirit of burning, and I was made a habitation of God through the spirit.   I wondered at myself : I could scarcely believe what the spirit witnessed.   It testified that the searcher of hearts was present ! that the mighty God was present ! that the creator of heaven and earth was present !

" *Thursday, Feb. 21st.*—I was still the same, and more and more so, I was abased before God,—I was astonished at myself. Working at Stonetrough, I was thinking, shall I speak of this, or shall I keep silence ?   The spirit said, I am with thee, and no man shall set upon thee to hurt thee.   From this I saw that I must speak without ceasing ; * but I wondered at the testimony that no man, &c., for I thought, is there any one about here that will dispute my testimony ?   I spoke to some, and they seemed ripe ; they received the word, and determined to seek the deep things of God."

Hugh Bourne soon found that his intimate and confidential brethren disputed his testimony on this part of the deep things of God, and none more so than his coadjutor, Daniel Shubotham ; and this cost him many a pang of extreme pain of mind ; but at last the Lord in his infinite mercy revealed this extraordinary work of grace to Daniel.   Others gladly received these great truths in all their plenitude and fulness ; more particularly the young converts ; and amongst these, for the first time, we find our old friend, William Clowes, who was then but newly converted, and was zealously seeking after a fuller and deeper work of grace, listening with all the ardour of an enquiring mind to the precious truths of zion, as they fell from the lips of the subject of this memoir.   The reader shall hear what Hugh Bourne says on the subject of an interview which took place between them.

* *His word* was in mine heart as a burning fire shut up in my bones, and I was weary with forbearing, and I could not *stay*.—Jer. xx. 9.

"*Saturday, March 9th*, 1805.—I was at Tunstall. William Clowes told me that last Monday but one I told him to pray for the spirit of burning. He began to pray for it, and the Lord gave it to him, and it burned in his heart. He spoke of it at class, and the leader checked him, and this surprised him; but it burnt so strongly that the leader could not move him. In going home, his leader asked him further about it, and then told him to get more of it. However, Mrs. Wakelam left off praying for it, through what the leader said. O, my God, restore her! God bless her! Richard Cartledge had it also. When I heard these things I was glad, for I had agreed with the brethren to go to Harrisehead to-morrow; and as Daniel Shubotham was prejudiced against this doctrine, I thought he might injure them; but I was rather more reconciled by considering his deep discretion.

"*Sunday, March 10th*, 1805.—Morning, at Ridgway class,— I led it, and strongly pressed the members to get clean hearts. Afternoon, I went by appointment to Harrisehead. I found Daniel Shubotham engaged with William Clowes and Richard Cartledge. I was glad he pressed them much. They spoke much of the spirit of burning, and I talked further with William Clowes. I bade him beware of reasoning and wrangling. He asked me what prejudice was. I told him, and cautioned him against every temper that is contrary to love. He asked why his leader spoke against him. I told him because his leader, although a wise man in scripture, had yet a low experience. He asked how it came to pass. I said because he trifled. He did not understand how he trifled. I said he would talk jesting talk. He said it was true. I said this would not do. He said he supposed it would not. He asked further about the spirit, and many other things. I told him that I had it at nearly all times burning in my heart. He said that his words sometimes seemed to have a very great sound, as if they sounded within him. I said that I had often noticed the same. Before I received the Holy Ghost—the spirit of burning—I had a happiness which almost melted me; and I was at times as if my heart would draw out of the body to God. This agreed with his experience. After many instructions, we parted. God bless him, for the sake of Jesus Christ. I returned to Harrisehead. Through the above-named brethren and old John Hancock talking with Daniel Shubotham, all his prejudices were swept away, and he received the doctrine about the spirit of burning. He had had it, but did not know what it was, yet he fully believed it to be the Holy Ghost. Hannah Shubotham got it at the two o'clock preaching. I spoke with James Farral; he, too, had the Holy Ghost—the spirit of burning. Daniel Shubotham was extremely fond of the Tunstall men; that is, of William Clowes and Richard Cartledge. He desired me to be with them as much as possible. He advised them to have a band again on Saturday nights, especially as the Lord had owned it. Now Daniel Shubotham and I had come together again, I spoke freely about the work. I noticed the flood of . . . . . . introduced by J. L. He said it was getting out again,—we thought it right to use every means to drive it out. J. L. has got quite slack. Holiness must be kept up, or the society will get low. O, my God, make us pure through Christ! I explained to D. S. the intermediate state between having the heart washed, and receiving the fulness of the Holy Ghost, the state in which people generally have a cool, melting happiness. He was in it but a short time—but a few hours, whereas I was in it above a quarter of a year. We talked of some regulations for keeping the people to faith, and promoting holiness. O, my God, instruct us! The work goes on rapidly.

"*Monday, March 11th.*—To-day I was at Whitfield, and with difficulty reached Harrisehead in time for the class. They had begun to sing. I kneeled down, and the power of God came upon me, and the Lord sealed me afresh: I had more of God than I can remember having had at any one time. I had such discoveries that they were past human language. I kneeled all the time of singing. I spoke with E. Mollot and E. Baddeley; they have the spirit of burning, and are sealed also, and so is E. Hargreaves. Glory to God! The sealing I take to be the solid weightiness of the spirit. After sealing, they have power with God in prayer more than ever. After class we discoursed. T. Cotton said he had the solid weightiness, with sorrow, and love for sinners, but not the spirit of burning. I said I had had both the weightiness and burning, but not sorrow. Daniel Shubotham said J. Hancock had both: that himself had only the weightiness. T. C. said that in prayer sometimes his spirit seemed to go out of his body, and ascend to God,—the body meantime was left almost senseless. They said it was the same with T. K., and with old James Selby. Matthias Bayley sometimes groans in an agony for sinners. We are all unanimous in our opinions. It has been very difficult to understand each other when speaking of the deep things of God : these things are so very difficult to be put into human language. D. Shubotham explained to me this :—" ye ask and receive not, because ye ask amiss, and that ye may consume it upon your lusts (desires.) " A man, said he, becomes double-minded ; he then looks in part to the accomplishment of his desires ; by this means he has not a single eye to the glory of God. This I found in some degree struck in with my former experience ; but the Lord has freed me. Glory to God. After some discourse about keeping to faith, and the necessity of promoting holiness, I came home,—D. S. came with me down two fields. One observation made, was, that when asking for a thing we should stick to the point, pray immediately for it, and be determined to have it."

" *Saturday night, March* 16*th.*—I was at Tunstall ; they go on very well there ; a few grow very fast. William Clowes has had the spirit of burning all over his body,—his faith is uncommon. Mrs. Wakelam said she had received great benefit from my letter. We cannot at present have a band at Tunstall."

" *Monday, March* 18*th.*—I wrote a letter to J. Moors : led Harrisehead class,—a very powerful time. Afterwards, in discourse with Daniel, he spoke of being cleansed by the inspiration of the Holy Ghost. I immediately saw the difference between the *inspiration,* and the indwelling of the Holy Ghost. The word inspiration means *breathing in.* By this I am furnished with an answer to the objection of Daniel and many others, who, when advised to pray for the Holy Ghost, the spirit of burning, ask have I not the Holy Ghost ? If I have not, what cleansed my heart, and what keeps it clean ? The inspiration of the Holy Ghost cleanses my heart, and keeps it clean ; but the indwelling of the Holy Ghost is far greater."

" *Tuesday, March* 19*th.*—I had the spirit all day ; was blest with J. Brindley ; and at Sargent's meeting I had the spirit in a manner I never before experienced,—it was a flame of sacred love. J, Sargent said, that awhile ago, in praying, his spirit was

as if going to leave the body, and he was startled, and gave over.
Going home I had an uncommon flame of sacred love, and such
desires after holiness as I never before knew."

" *Wednesday, March 20th.*—This day, at Mrs. David Leak's,
we concluded on the size of a chapel for Norton.   At this
meeting we subscribed £25 5s.   At prayer after I had the spirit
strongly."

" *Saturday, March 23rd.*—At night I went with an intention of
going to Tunstall meeting, but by his desire, and for his company,
I went with James Booth, a collier, to Burslem band.   William
Clowes was there.   We had a rare time.   Samuel Broad said
that he now grew fast in religion ; that being hard tempted on
one occasion, he remembered an expression of brother Bourne's,
(meaning myself,) that when a temptation came he went straight
to God and was delivered.   My God, spread this plan universally.
They are getting lively at Burslem.   I came back with William
Clowes.   He is invited to meetings about Burslem.   He is now
very solid.   He said that last Saturday night, when he reached
home, he prayed to the Lord to seal him, and the weighty power
of God came upon him, and it made him more steady in spirit.
God bless him !   I went to his house and stayed till after midnight : such a man for faith I scarcely ever saw ; he gains any
blessing almost immediately.   He grows up into God and our Lord
Jesus Christ, at a very great rate.   He said he had been a very
wicked man, had spent all, and had punished his wife—they were
fighting constantly.   She had wept for very distress, and he in his
mind had called himself a rascal, but had not power to leave sin.
His wife told me her experience.   She spoke with greater simplicity than any one I ever met with.   She has strong faith, and
grows very fast.   They both have such confident faith that they
gain whatever they ask for.   O, my God, establish them, and seal
them both, that they may grow up into Jesus Christ in all things.
Amen."

" *Sunday, March 24th.*—At Stonetrough, Joseph Hancock was
converted, and others were in distress.   The revival goes on.
Glory to God."

"*Monday, March 25th.*—At Harrisehead class they go on well. Great prospects. Glory to Jehovah. I stayed with Daniel till Matthias Bayley and Samuel Oakes came. They had been at Aaron Lees' class, and had had five converted, and others were very near. Lord carry on thy work at Tunstall. We discoursed of living by faith, and of perfecting holiness. Daniel said it was very difficult to keep the society clear upon the whole, but I myself believe that the greater part grow in grace. They are particularly taught to be diligent in business, which is needful at all times and in all places. This is a strong part of religion; for 'six days shalt thou labour' is a commandment. I had particular faith for Tunstall."

"*Saturday, March 30th.*—At night I was at Tunstall. I was with William Clowes both before and after meeting. Matthias Bayley, Thomas Cotton, and Samuel Oakes were there. We had a powerful time. At William Clowes' were two young men, one a son of T. Lees, the other of W. Lees. They begin to live by faith, though T. L's. son was but converted last Monday, at A. Lees' class. I fully believe they will both be revivalists. My God prosper them. I desired William Clowes to converse with them as often as he had opportunity, and to talk experience. William Clowes grows at a vast rate. Being at play a part of a day, he shut himself up in the chamber, with the bible, to see what the Lord would do for him. He felt the spirit of burning when he went up; but the Lord gave it to him till it filled every part of his body at once, burning to his finger ends, and his eyesight seemed for a time to be taken away. He says that in his work and every thing, he gives up all to God, and he has full and perfect patience, and submission to the will of God in all things; and when he speaks a word which seems to be out of place, or neglects any thing, he immediately goes to God; and if he only says Lord help me! he feels the power of God even as soon as he has spoken once. This man is such an example of living by faith as I scarcely ever met with, and which I am not at present able to follow : but he is uncommonly strict; and if he happens to drink water without asking the Lord to make him truly thankful, it drives him to God for pardon. I encouraged him to reprove sin, and to take a more prominent part in prayer meetings : this he is rather backward at. His wife gets on well. She said they were sorely plagued before. I told them of giving all up to God.

"*Easter Sunday, April 14th.*—I led our class at Norton. Jesus was with us. From there I went to Brown Edge, to the sacrament. The living God was present. Thence to Harrisehead lovefeast. The preaching was over. The chapel was full, and many out of doors,—the chapel would not hold all at the lovefeast. It was an uncommon time ; and at the close the Lord made bare his arm ; and I believe between twenty and thirty were justified, and some were sanctified. The devil may well rage about Harrisehead chapel."

"*Monday, April 15th.*—I was at Harrisehead class. We had two converted—David, a collier, and old Betty Moors. The work goes on rapidly. Jesus is gathering the people."

"*Saturday, April 20th.*—I was at Tunstall. William Clowes has become a labourer, and the Lord owns his work. He is one raised up immediately by God,—a man of uncommonly deep experience, of an unusual growth in grace, deep humility, steady zeal, and flaming love ; such a man I scarcely ever met with. O, God, this I desire, that thou wouldest make me like him. I desire it from my heart : grant it to me, O, my Father, for the sake of Jesus Christ, that I may be conformed to my Saviour's image, that I may grow up into him. My God grant it. I beseech thee to grant it. It seems as if the Lord had raised him up to assist in keeping the revival steady. He had not attended to building up believers in sanctification, and the deep things of God ; this I advised him to do. I stayed advising, instructing, and talking with him till after midnight, when we prayed, and parted by force. They had ordered for a few to hold a band at his house, but they deferred it ; nevertheless we held a meeting, and at it three obtained pardon : this is now become a constant thing, so many obtain pardon. T. Lees said that I exhorted too long. I find much need that Jesus Christ should bear the iniquity of my holy things."

"*Saturday, April 25th.*—To-night I was at Tunstall. They get on vastly,—great numbers are converted, many grow into the deep work. Ride on and prosper, O Jehovah ! "

We could have enlarged considerably the extracts from the private diary of Hugh Bourne, but we hope the foregoing will suffice for this part of the work, as they contain delightful evidence of his growth in christian experience, and practical usefulness ; while a proper comprehension of his piety, zeal, and labours for Christ and souls, could hardly have been obtained, in our opinion, without them.

CHAPTER XIV.

Recently, new and interesting objects have been presented to
our view in our biographical journey, and some of those remarkable
men have crossed our path, that were so pre-eminently useful in
the second revival of primitive methodism, which commenced at
Harrisehead, in September, 1804, and was carried on in strength
and power, until it was injudiciously crushed, in 1806. We think
our readers cannot help but admire the infinite wisdom and
goodness of God so strikingly manifested in the extraordinary
christian experience of Hugh Bourne. We confess that we have
read of but very few, if any, that have surpassed him in an
acquaintance with the deep things of God. We consider the part
of his eventful life now under notice was fraught with evidences
that he possessed such ideas of God and divine things, as were
essentially necessary to qualify him as a christian minister for the
labour and toil he was designed to bear in the field of gospel
enterprise, ' white already to harvest.'

We have now to mention some persons and circumstances, either directly or indirectly connected with this second revival, and to glance at the movements by which the great work was checked, and the conversion of sinners in the neigbourhood brought to a close for a considerable period; and we shall see that the persons who acted a part in stopping the revival, were the means of facilitating the commencement of the English camp meetings! for as soon as the wheels of the revival chariot stood still, Hugh Bourne, Matthias Bayley, T. Cotton, and a few others, began to cry to God to give them a camp meeting. But the modern innovators had crippled the influence and energy of the mighty Daniel, shaken his faith like reeds before the wind, and turned him point blank against such meetings as camp meetings, or field-preaching. Let us hear what H. Bourne himself says on the subject :—

" In this gracious work we had no encouragement from the travelling preachers. Old Mr. Jackson, the superintendent, though a good man, was not a revivalist; and the young man, Mr. W. France, his colleague, was a most determined anti-revivalist; yet notwithstanding all the array of opposition the work went on, and Mr. Jackson said it was the steadiest revival he ever knew. Great as was the revival at Tunstall, it was still more powerful at Harrisehead and in the neighbourhood; and the steadiness of which Mr. Jackson spoke was induced by the established strictness of conduct, and the powerful exercises of faith. Even in meetings, strict decorum was kept up; and the Stonetrough house being large and convenient, Sabbath evening prayer meetings were held in it; and these got to be so powerful, that the pious praying labourers formed themselves into companies, and prayed and rested by turns. Many flocked in, and for a time there scarcely ever came a sinner in but he either fled or fell. There was uncommon strictness of conduct, and for a time the effects attending these Sabbath evening prayer meetings were great. Revivals, to go on well, require great strictness of conduct as well as powerful exercises of faith. The town of Burslem, the head of the circuit, received a great move, and a number were converted; but the force of modern methodism was so great, that the converting work was not so powerful there as in Tunstall, but the circuit in general had a gracious move. The Wesleyan

conference of 1805, removed William France, and stationed W.
E. Miller in Burslem circuit. Expectations were raised ; but he
having lost the revival spirit, scarcely any thing prospered in his
hands : but Mr. Miller could do what no other preacher had been
able to effect. He could talk on revivalism as no other travelling
preacher had been able to do ; and by so doing, he could get hold
of the people's minds, and bend them to his own views."

   "In 1801 I formed the Harrisehead class, and appointed D.
Shubotham leader ; but he was not willing to undertake it unless
I, Matthias, and T. Cotton would lead it in turn : and, in addition
to this, he would occasionally put one or other of the members to
speak round to the class. And when I formed a class at Norton,
it was on the same system, and thus the Lord led me : and some
years after this, in reading Mr. Wesley's ' Minutes of Conference '
for the year 1744, I there found that variety in class leading was
an essential part of methodism, and in particular of primitive
methodism ; and I may say that in Harrisehead chapel it had
been graciously owned of the Lord ; and if Mr. France * had
tried to get it put away, he would have received a sharp answer ;
but Mr. Miller talked with Daniel about revivalism until he had
quite wheedled him ; and then he advised him to suffer no one to
lead the class except himself.   When Daniel informed me of this,
it cut me to the heart : but I was aware that Mr. Miller having
got hold of his mind, there was no remedy.   The preachers gave
a disastrous blow to the cause of God when they turned Daniel
against open-air worship ; and Mr. Miller's proceedings in regard
to the class made a still further disaster ; so we had disaster upon
disaster.   Shortly after this, Daniel told me that they were to have
their prayer meetings put into a different way by Mr. Miller.   I said,
if you suffer him to turn you out of the plain, straight-forward
way in which the Lord hath raised you up, the converting work
among you will cease, as surely as it did when you suffered the
two potters to turn you out of the way in which the Lord raised
you up ; but he had no ears to hear, neither had others : so the

---

   * After a few times Mr. France and the Harrisehead people got to be
social. He managed his preaching in his way, and they managed their
praying in their way ; and they spoke well of him, and he spoke well of
them.

Lord might have said, as in Jer. xii.10, ' Many pastors have destroyed my vineyard.' The Lord's vineyard was so destroyed, that there was not a single conversion at Harrisehead, or Mow Cop, during the next twelve months; and instead of being at the head of the mighty work of the Lord in this part of North Staffordshire, these places were down in the dust. The agonising distress which Mr. Miller and his helpers had brought on the people, caused much thought and prayer. Mr. M. had been the means of some of the Kidsgrove people keeping rather aloof; but Matthias Bayley, the main leader, was as firm as an iron pillar. The camp meeting subject we took up in the year 1804, as a subject of prayer, and the Lord opened us out a mighty revival which lifted the circuit, and converted Mr. James Steele of Tunstall, and others, into revivalists; and during that conferential year, hundreds were added to the society : and now Mr. Miller and his helpers having again plunged the circuit into the slough of despond, it was a question whether a camp meeting might not assist in raising it up again."

On the English camp meeting course.—" As the beginning or commencement of the English camp meetings formed a grand era in my religious life, it may be useful to give a view of the footsteps of divine providence in preparing the way, and in opening out the glorious work. In the year of our Lord 1801, a glorious work in religion opened out at Harrisehead, Mow Cop, and Kidsgrove, which eventually brought in the English camp meetings, and originated the Primitive Methodist Connexion. And in July, 1801, I was prevailed on by the new converts to preach, or try to preach, at good old Joseph Pointon's, on the Cheshire part of Mow Cop. Before this I had not stood up in the pulpit way; but in conversation, with one or more, I had frequently tried my hand at conversation preaching ; and in setting forth the gospel in this way, the Lord had powerfully and effectually blest the word to many hearts. On this extraordinary day, the Lord caused an excellent course of open-air worship to be commenced—a camp meeting course ; and he opened another course, by causing preachings, so called, but what have since been called 'preaching services,' to be, in general, not confined to the labours of one person only, but two or more to officiate in each service. This system I considered to be providentially given or taught me by the Lord, at what may be called a camp meeting without a name.

This meeting took place before I had joined the new converts to the Wesleyan society, and at a time when I and my brother James, and the colliers, carried on meetings in our own way, when all was clear, and there was no opposition; and from the movements of divine providence on that extraordinary occasion, we conceived the idea of attaching extended praying services to every sermon delivered in or out of doors."

COMMENCEMENT OF THE AMERICAN CAMP MEETINGS, IN 1801.

Extracts from Letters in the Wesleyan Magazines.

" *Kentucky, August,* 1801.—One Sunday it was computed that the several congregations amounted to twenty thousand persons. The meeting continued from Saturday to Tuesday, (above seventy hours,) without one minute's intermission."

" *Bambon County, August 7th,* 1801.—They encamp on the ground, and continue praising God for a whole week, day and night, before they break up."

" *Garrison Forest, October 23rd,* 1801 —Twenty thousand meet at once, and continue encamped for ten or twelve days. Some have been so powerfully convinced, that they have been nine or ten hours without any signs of life, while others have been delivered from their distress in a few hours."

The volume from which these extracts are taken, was published in 1802, and from that time the Wesleyan magazines flamed with American camp meeting accounts till late in the year 1807 : so we had mighty stirrings up in regard to camp meetings ; and of course we may suppose that the whole of the methodists in England would be filled with camp meeting readings, and camp meeting information, and with desires to see a camp meeting. And this, in the year 1804, caused us to pray mightily to God to give us a camp meeting. The Lord manifested his will in pouring out his Holy Spirit in such a manner, that we had vast employment in praying with mourners ; the circuit was moved, and at Christmas, 1804, the Lord gave us Mr. James Steele of Tunstall, and others, as converts to revivalism ; but late in 1805 Mr. Miller came in, and he so cut down the converting work

that not one soul was converted to God in twelve months, either
at Harrisehead, or Mow Cop; and he was a means of the
societies at those places being degraded; and it became a serious
inquiry, would not a camp meeting again raise the cause? There
was much praying, and much advising; but the preachers had
made Daniel Shubotham so unprimitive, that he was opposed to
open-air worship, and this and other things caused the trial of
faith to be heavy; difficulties pressed on every side, but 'the
Lord reigneth; he is clothed with majesty.' And the Lord in
his providence so ordered it, that Daniel's influence was lowered,
or rather for a time turned into a better channel. An American
preacher, Lorenzo Dow, came into Cheshire, and Daniel heard
him at Macclesfield. He spoke so much of the American camp
meetings, that Daniel got completely turned round. I had not
seen the American, but one day a messenger came to say, that he
would that day preach in Harrisehead chapel. I and my brother
attended, and we heard him at Burslem the same day, and at
Congleton the next morning; and I purchased a few of his publications. He was about to leave England. For about five years
I had been accustomed to monthly camp meeting readings; yet
there appeared a sort of newness in these, and I read them with
pleasure."

The first English camp meeting, planned by Hugh Bourne,
was intended to counteract the evils of the parish annual feast.
" In the village of Norton," (says H. B.) " we had yearly suffered
loss by the wake, or parish revel, held yearly, about the 23rd of
August. This had given me much concern, and it came into my
mind, that if we could hold a camp meeting for about three days,
it would engage our young members, and preserve them from
being seduced by the wake vanities. And it appeared to me that
I and my brother, and Thomas Cotton of Mow Cop, would be
sufficient for preaching, and I believed I could get a host of
praying labourers from Harrisehead and Mow Cop: so my way
seemed clear. I considered my methodist friends at Burslem and
Tunstall (T. Allen excepted) would be against it; but I conceived
the meeting would be but small, and that it would be over before they
were aware of it: and without speaking to or consulting any one, I,
the next Monday evening, went to the class meeting in Harrisehead chapel, to engage assistance. While on the way my mind
was pained to think of Daniel's opposition; but to my astonish-

ment and surprise, on my arrival I found my old friend turned round again, and I heard with pleasure that others had talked of having a camp meeting: so it was evident the Lord had prepared the way. And so soon as the leader had spoken round to the members of the class, I stood up and made known my intended Norton camp meeting: and they were all in a zeal in an instant; yes, they would help; and the next expression was, we'll have one upon Mow. But, says another, there's preaching here forenoon and after, how can we? Daniel took up the preachers' plan, looked at it, and said, Thomas Cotton is planned in this chapel on Sunday, May 31st, 1807, that's the camp meeting. In an instant we were all on our knees, and every one praying with all their heart, mind, and voice, and the praying went on till every one had faith to believe that the Lord would stand by, and support these two camp meetings; and if that mighty praying and believing had not taken place, I am not sure whether or not these camp meetings would not have failed."

Publishing Mow Cop camp meeting.—" This was the next question considered. One said, it is for ourselves, let us keep it to ourselves, and not publish it at all. Thomas Cotton said, his friends in Congleton circuit had encouraged him much to have one, and it would be hard not to let them know: so I wrote him some notices. In Burslem, it was observed, they are against open-air worship; but the reply was, T. Allen of Burslem, is an open-air preacher, and we must have him. It was thought best to keep it as secret as possible from the opposers of open-air worship; but there was no keeping it secret, for the report flew through the country as if it had gone on the wings of angels."

THE CAMP MEETING, SUNDAY, MAY 31st, 1807.

" The morning was at first rather unfavourable; but numbers flocked in, and the meeting was hopefully begun. We were in old Joseph Pointon's small field, on the Cheshire side of Mow Cop; the field in which the camp meeting without a name was held on Sunday, July 12th, 1801. We had no previous plan. It was like Judges xxi. 25, ' Every man did *that which was* right in his own eyes.' Stands were erected, and each preacher that stood up preached, spoke experience, or gave an historical account as he thought proper. The variety was great, and a powerful unction from the Holy One rested on the meeting throughout the day, and Daniel Shubotham was great: he and his wife had covenanted together to set the converting work agoing. God was with them; and others also set a praying course on foot; and these praying services were much blessed. The work was mighty through the day : we closed about eight in the evening. The satisfaction was immense, and the *anti-methodistic* zeal against open-air worship was so swept away, that a number of my esteemed friends from Burslem and Tunstall were there, and laboured famously in the prayer meetings, and with mourners; even those who previously had been opposed to open-air meetings, and had teased me much, now manifested a zeal rarely seen.*

For our own satisfaction, and that of others, we shall here insert a verbatim copy of Hugh Bourne's pamphlet, published immediately after the first English camp meeting. This will, we trust, give satisfaction to many that never saw the original pamphlet, printed in 1807.

Observations on Camp Meetings, with an Account of a Camp Meeting held on Sunday, May the 31st, 1807, at Mow, near Harrisehead. By HUGH BOURNE. Price One Penny.

OBSERVATIONS, &c.

The first institution of camp meetings, for the solemn worship of Almighty God, appears to have been very ancient. In Leviticus xxiii. 39, to the end of the chapter, we find that the God of Israel commanded his

---

* Before the Mow camp meeting was held, Mr. Riles, superintendent of the Burslem Wesleyan circuit, said, " One meeting will satisfy all people." I said, " Then we will leave it as that meeting leaves it." He said, " Very well." However, I was so impressed with the day's proceedings, that I wrote an account of them for my own edification. But my brother advised me to print the account, which I did; and in it I advertised two others to be held. My view was, that the publishing an account would prevent untrue reports; but others, without my knowledge, printed my account, and it was circulated by thousands. It was like setting the whole country on fire. It was only a penny pamphlet: but I was almost overwhelmed with troubles.—H. B.

people to build them booths of the boughs of trees, of different kinds, and dwell in them seven days. And that this was to be done annually, imme-diately after gathering in the fruits of the land.

And again, in Nehemiah viii. 13, to the close, we find that Israel had for a time lost sight of this command, but on reviving the reading and exposition of the Law, they also renewed this custom in the city, and de-voted seven days to dwell in booths and attend to the reading of the Law, confession of sin, &c.

Matt. xiv. 13—21. Here we find, that a great multitude of men, women, and children collected together out of the cities, &c., into the desert place where Jesus was, and that they continued with him until the evening, and were fed by his interposition. Our Lord, then, was not displeased with such large and promiscuous collections of people.

In the next chapter, viz., Matt. xv. 29—38, we read thus: "And Jesus departed from thence, and came nigh unto the sea of Galilee, and went up into a mountain, and sat down there. And great multitudes came unto him, &c. Then Jesus called his disciples unto him, and said, I have com-passion on the multitude, because they continue with me now three days, and have nothing to eat, &c. And they that did eat were four thousand." In Mark iv. 39, 40, and John vi. 1—14, we have the same facts recorded. It would seem, therefore, that our Lord himself, on finding the multitude willing to receive instruction in the ways of salvation, had no objection to continue with them in the mountain, or desert, even three days together. See a defence of camp meetings, by the Rev. S. K. Jennings, A.M.

America has had the honour and happiness of again reviving the long neglected institution of sacred camp meetings, and they are there become very frequent and respectable.—High and low, rich and poor, chief magis-trates, judges, &c., attend, and hundreds get converted. They were begun in Kentucky, by an opening of Providence about the year 1797, and from thence they were introduced into North Carolina, and afterward into all the United States.

These meetings are held (by preachings, exhortations, prayer, and other godly exercises,) day and night, for three, four, or five days. Families will go above fifty miles to a camp meeting, in covered waggons, carriages, &c. Taking with them several days' provision, with equipage of blankets, sheets, coverlets, &c., for tents to sleep in, &c. Immediately the camp resembles a very populous town, enclosing a large square of ground. And the thousands of people, attentive and solemn, preparing to seek the most high God, strike the mind with a most pious awe; and the vast number of fires, during the night, together with lamps, lanterns, &c., suspended, and burning, in every direction, and illuminating all round, to a great distance, have a grand and pleasing effect.

Letters concerning these extraordinary things being published in the methodist magazines, paved the way for camp meetings in England. And Lorenzo Dow, the celebrated American preacher, (who lately visited this country,) published a defence of camp meetings, by the Rev. S. K. Jennings, A.M., with other remarks on the subject; which, together with the lively and wonderful descriptions of the work which he gave, both in the pulpit, and in conversation, appear to have been the chief means of fully introducing them.

Mow camp meeting was appointed to be held on Sunday, May 31st, 1807. The morning proved rainy and unfavourable, which rather put it back; but about six o'clock, the Lord sent the clouds off, and gave us a very pleasant day.

The meeting was opened by two holy men from Knutsford—Captain Anderson having previously erected a flag on the mountain to direct strangers, and these three, with some pious people from Macclesfield, carried on and sustained the meeting a considerable time, in a most vigorous and lively manner. They conducted it by preaching, prayer, exhortations, relating experiences, &c. The Lord owned their labours, grace descended, and the people of God were greatly quickened. The congregation rapidly increased, and others began to join in holy exercises.

One of the men from Knutsford, a lawyer, and an Irishman, (who had been converted under the ministry of Lorenzo Dow,) related the troubles he had passed through in Ireland. In the late rebellion in that unhappy land, he had been deprived of thousands; from a state of wealth and afflu-

VOL I.   L

ence, in which he had been brought up, and in which he had lived, he
with his family had been reduced. But for this he thanked God, the
taking away his substance had been the cause of his gaining the true
riches; and he had since given up his profession of an attorney, because
he found it too difficult to keep his religion in that profession. This man
exhorted all to pray for our gracious king, who was worthy, because he
granted liberty of conscience; but he himself had seen a time in Ireland
when a protestant knew not at night but his house and family might be
burned before morning.

Another man had been in many parts of the world, had been preferred
in the army, and had left his leg in Africa. He was a great scholar and
philosopher, had renounced christianity and turned to deism, afterwards
to atheism; but being drawn by curiosity to hear Lorenzo preach, heard
him relate the following circumstance:—At a camp meeting in America,
a black was converted, and in the fulness of joy, praised God with a loud
voice. A deist standing by, who with his fellow deists had endeavoured to
believe that blacks have no souls, said; "You black rascal, why do you go
on in this manner? You have no soul to save.' The poor black replied:
" Massa, if black man no soul, religion make body happy."—Hearing this
made such an impression on him, that he began to pray, and the Lord
made him feel the weight of his sins; he cried for mercy, and the Lord
pardoned him. Jesus Christ was manifested to him, and he was born of
God: he soon after obtained full sanctification; and now lived by faith in
the Son of God. He was so overpowered by the love of God, that he was
obliged to be supported while he spoke.

Meanwhile, the people were flocking in from every quarter. The wind
was cold, but a large grove of fir-trees kept the wind off, and made it very
comfortable. So many hundreds now covered the ground that another
preaching-stand was erected in a distant part of the field, under the cover
of a stone wall. Returning over the field, I met a company at a distance
from the first stand, praying for a man in distress. I could not get near:
but I there found such a measure of the power of God, such a weighty
burning of joy and love, that it was beyond description. I should gladly
have stopped there, but other matters called me away. I perceived that

the Lord was beginning to work mightily. Nearer the first stand was another company praying with mourners. Immediately the man in the other company was praising God, and I found that he had obtained the pardon of his sins, and was born again. I believe this man to have been the first that was born of God at this meeting. Many were afterwards born again or converted in the other company; the number I could not ascertain; but from what information I was able to collect, I suppose, about six.

Meantime, preaching went on without intermission at both stands, and, about noon, the congregation was so much increased, that we were obliged to erect a third preaching-stand; we fixed it a distance below the first, by the side of the fir-tree grove. I got upon this stand, after the first preaching, and was extremely surprised at the amazing sight that appeared before me. The people were nearly all under my eye; and I had not before conceived that such a vast multitude were present;* but the thousands hearing with attention as solemn as death, presented a scene of the most sublime and awfully-pleasing grandeur that my eyes ever beheld.

The preachers seemed to be fired with an uncommon zeal, and an extraordinary unction attended their word, while tears were seen flowing, and sinners trembling on every side. Numbers were convinced, and saints were uncommonly quickened. And the extraordinary steadiness and decorum that were maintained during the whole day, (notwithstanding the vast concourse of people who attended,) seemed to make a great impression upon every mind.

Many preachers were now upon the ground, from Knutsford, Congleton, Wheelock, Burslem, Macclesfield, and other places : and a most extraordinary variety appeared. The man who was turned from deism had been in the field of war, when the grandees of the earth drew the sword and bid the battle bleed. He had seen death flying in every direction, and

* The numbers on the camp ground, were estimated by various persons at different times, to be from two to about four thousand. A camp meeting was (unknowingly) appointed to be held at the same time, on the forest of Delamere: this disappointed many, as they could attend but one. But this Delamere meeting did not take place.

men falling slain on every side. He had walked in blood, over fields covered with mountains of dying and dead. He shewed the happiness of our land, and the gratitude we owed to God for being exempted from being the seat of war. Another, who had seen the horrors of rebellion lately in Ireland, persuaded us to turn to righteousness, because we were exempt from these calamities. E. Anderson related the devotion he had beheld in many parts of the world, which we suppose to be in darkness and super-stition, and exhorted us to turn to God, lest they should rise up in judgment against us. All the preachers seemed to be strengthened in the work. Persuasion dwelt upon their tongues, while the multitudes were trembling or rejoicing around.

The congregation increased so rapidly that a fourth preaching-stand was called for. The work now became general, and the scene was most awful and interesting. In this glass, any one might have viewed the worth of souls. To see the thousands of people, all (except a few stragglers) in solemn attention; a company near the first stand wrestling in prayer for mourners; and four preachers dealing out their lives at every stroke. These things made an impression on my mind, not soon to be forgotten; this extraordinary scene continued till about four o'clock, when the people began to retire; and before six, they were confined to one stand.

About seven o'clock in the evening, a work began among children: six of whom were converted, or born again, before the meeting broke up; and the power of God seemed to have a great effect upon the people pre-sent. At about half-past eight o'clock at night, the meeting was finally closed. A meeting, such as our eyes had never beheld! a meeting, for which many will praise God in time and eternity! such a day as this we never before enjoyed! a day spent in the active service of the living God! a Sabbath in which Jesus Christ made glad the hearts of his saints, and sent his arrows to the hearts of sinners. The propriety and great utility of camp meetings appeared to every one; so great was the work, that the people were ready to say, "We have seen strange things to-day." O may the Lord carry on his work, till righteousness cover the earth, for Jesus' sake. Amen.

Second Mow camp meeting.—I have now to inform our friends, that

(God willing) there will be a camp meeting held in the same place, to begin on Saturday, July 18, 1807, at four o'clock in the afternoon, to be held day and night, for two or three days, or more; and also, that a camp meeting is appointed (Providence permitting) to be held at Norton-in-the-Moors, in the county of Stafford, near the chapel, to begin on Saturday, August 22nd, 1807, at four o'clock in the afternoon, to be held day and night as above.

The provision made for strangers at the camp meeting that is past was small, the cause of which was, that such a meeting being a new thing in England, the managers were unacquainted with the proper method of making preparations for it. In those that are now appointed, they intend to follow the advice of their friends, that is :

1. To get the ground regularly licensed under the toleration act, that all interruption, or misbehaviour, in the time of meeting, may be prevented, or else punished as the law directs.

2. To provide a sufficient quantity of stands and seats.

3. To provide tents, &c., sufficient to defend the people from the inclemency of the weather.

4. To provide a large supply of coals, lanterns, candles, &c., to light the camp during the night.

5. To get provision sufficient to supply all distant comers during the Sabbath.

6. To defray these expenses by public collections during the meeting.

An attentive observer will soon perceive some difference between America and England, with regard to camp meetings. There the people are more employed in farming, which enables them with more convenience to bring provisions, and equipage for tents. With regard to tents, the difficulties will be removed, by the managers erecting them; and tradespeople, who are accustomed to buy their provisions, may, when the Sabbath is past, buy them with as much convenience at Harrisehead and Norton, as at other places.

CHAPTER XV.

A CHAPEL BUILT AT NORTON—H. BOURNE AND J. BRINDLEY COLLECT FOR
IT—H. AND J. BOURNE ARE TRUSTEES—H. BOURNE HAD MISSIONED THE
PLACE—LABOURS IN THE NORTON AND HARRISEHEAD SUNDAY SCHOOLS—
PUBLISHES A CATECHISM—A COPY OF THE CATECHISM, CALLED THE
GREAT SCRIPTURE CATECHISM.

In the year of our Lord 1805, a chapel was erected in the
village of Norton, in behalf of which Hugh Bourne took an active
part; for we find him with John Brindley, perambulating the
parish of Norton, soliciting from the parishioners and others,
donations to aid them in accomplishing so praiseworthy an object,
as building a house for the worship of God, He and his brother
James were trustees for this Wesleyan chapel. Hugh Bourne, in
1801, had taken up Norton, when it was forsaken by others, and
preached salvation to the people in the open air. The Lord
crowned his labours by converting a person named Lomas, and
others, so that he was enabled to raise a society; and he tells us
that he formed the Norton class on the same principle as that on
which he formed the one at Harrisehead, namely, variety in the leading. He had a principal hand in commencing a Wesleyan Sunday
school in the Norton new chapel ; and he regularly taught in the
school, till the Lord in his providence called him to labour
elsewhere. And as a proof of the interest he took in the mental
and moral improvement of the children taught in the Norton and
Harrisehead Sunday Schools, we find his active mind and pen, in
the early part of the year 1807, engaged in compiling a scripture
catechism for the use of those schools. Such is our admiration
of the simplicity and solidity of the " Great Scripture Catechism,"
that we cannot persuade ourselves to withhold the first part from
the pages of this memoir ; and we strongly recommend a thoughtful perusal of it to every lover of Sunday schools.

The Great Scripture Catechism, compiled for Norton and Harrise head Sunday Schools, and intended for Sunday Schools in general. By HUGH BOURNE. Part the first, 1807.

ADDRESS.

The scriptures give a greater liveliness, vigour, and strength to the mind than any other writings, however sentimental or moral. This catechism is not intended to supersede others, but to assist in promoting bible knowledge, and rendering it more lasting and effectual. The children are not required to learn by rote, any, except the scripture words; which are illustrated, and connected by the questions. Yet the illustration and connection are not so forcible and striking, but that sufficient room is left to exercise the learner's penetration and ingenuity. The method here used, often extends the questions to a length which might seem burdensome to the teacher, but one of the children may be employed to ask the questions, and this may be done by all the class in rotation; and it tends to promote a pleasing activity and diligence. We require the children, when repeating the catechism, to give the chapter and verse ; and also frequently to learn the answers in the bible itself, which furnishes a variety, gratifies the active disposition of youth, and enables them more easily to select and arrange portions of scripture, and to apply them in a more plain and forcible manner.

Bemersley, April 27th, 1807.

————

THE GREAT SCRIPTURE CATECHISM.

QUESTION I. Whence is the heaven that is stretched out over our heads, and the earth on which we stand ?

ANSWER. In the beginning God created the heaven and the earth. Gen. i. 1.

2. Was the earth then in the beautiful order, and fine arrangement in which we now see it ; or was it without a regular form ?

A. And the earth was without form, and void; and darkness was upon the face of the deep: and the Spirit of God moved upon the face of the waters. Gen. i. 2.

3. Seeing the earth was all dark and dreary, whence is the pleasing and beautiful light?

A. And God said, let there be light: and there was light. And God saw the light, that it was good. Gen. i. 3, 4.

4. * Labour, rest, and vegetation, require a return of day and night: what account do you give of such a happy change of light and darkness?

A. And God divided the light from the darkness, and God called the light day, and the darkness he called night. And the evening and the morning were the first day. Gen. i. 4, 5.

5. We behold the heavens ornamented with many thousands of lights, or luminaries, shining together in beautiful harmony, order and connection: whence are these, and what is their use?

A. And God said, let there be lights in the firmament of the heaven, to divide the day from the night: and let them be for signs, and for seasons, and for days, and years. And let them be for lights in the firmament of heaven, to give light upon the earth; and it was so. Gen. i. 14, 15.

6. The Psalmist calls upon us to give thanks unto the Lord, the God of Gods, and Lord of Lords, for he is good, for his mercy endureth for ever: what does he there say of the formation and rule of the luminaries?

A. To him that made great lights: for his mercy endureth for ever: the sun to rule by day; the moon and stars to rule by night: for his mercy endureth for ever. Psalm cxxxvi. 7, 8, 9.

7. The sun shines to the ends of the world for light, heat, and vegetation, pouring blessings upon all: what does our Lord Jesus Christ say in

* Labour and work, require light and day; rest and sleep, the darkness and stillness of the night; vegetation (that is, the springing and growing up of grass, herbs, trees, plants, fruits and flowers) requires both the vigour and heat of the day, and the moisture and coolness of the night: the moisture and coolness to feed, and the heat and vigour to ripen.

reference to these invaluable, glorious, and universal blessings ?

A. But I say unto you, love your enemies, bless them that curse you, do good to them that hate you, and pray for them which despitefully use you, and persecute you ; that ye may be the children of your Father which is in heaven : for he maketh his sun to rise on the evil and on the good, and sendeth rain on the just and on the unjust. Matt. v. 44, 45.

8. Truly the light is sweet, and a pleasant thing it is for the eyes to behold the sun : but does not the Psalmist speak of another sun ?

A. For the Lord God is a sun and shield : the Lord will give grace and glory : no good thing will he withhold from them that walk uprightly. O Lord of hosts, blessed is the man that trusteth in thee. Psalm lxxxiv. 11, 12.

9. The Psalmist here by the Holy Ghost unfolds things great and glorious. What does the prophet Malachi also say of this most glorious sun ?

A. But unto you that fear my name, shall the sun of righteousness arise with healing in his wings ; and ye shall go forth, and grow up as calves of the stall. Mal. iv. 2.

10. Glorious news! has Jesus Christ given such encouragement to them that fear him ?

A. And he opened his mouth, and taught them, saying, Blessed are the poor in spirit ; for theirs is the kingdom of heaven. Blessed are they that mourn, for they shall be comforted. Matt. v. 2, 3, 4.

11. What are the cause and state of this holy mourning, this godly sorrow, which works repentance unto salvation ?

A. For thine arrows stick fast in me, and thy hand presseth me sore. There is no soundness in my flesh because of thine anger ; neither is there any rest in my bones because of my sin. For mine iniquities are gone over mine head : as a heavy burden they are too heavy for me. My wounds stink and are corrupt because of my foolishness. I am troubled, I am bowed down greatly, I go mourning all the day long. For my loins

VOL I.   M are filled with a loathsome disease : and there is no soundness in my flesh. I am feeble, and sore broken : I have roared by reason of the disquietness of my heart. Psalm xxxviii. 2—8.

12.   Do persons in such a state earnestly desire pardon ?

A.   Lord, all my desire is before thee; and my groaning is not hid from thee. My heart panteth, my strength faileth me : as for the light of mine eyes, it also is gone from me. Psalm xxxviii. 9, 10.

13.   Do they confess and forsake their sin ?

A.   For I will declare mine iniquity ; I will be sorry for my sin. Psalm xxxviii. 18.

14.   What is their prayer ?

A.   Forsake me not, O Lord : O my God, be not far from me. Make haste to help me, O Lord my salvation. Psalm xxxviii. 21, 22.

15.   What does Jesus say to them ?

A.   Come unto me, all ye that labour, and are heavy laden, and I will give you rest. Take my yoke upon you, and learn of me ; for I am meek and lowly in heart : and ye shall find rest unto your souls. For my yoke is easy and my burden is light. Matt. xi. 28, 29, 30.

16.   Does he invite these only; and not the self-righteous ?

A.   When Jesus heard it, he saith unto them, They that are whole have no need of the physician, but they that are sick. I came not to call the righteous, but sinners to repentance. Mark ii. 17.

17.   And will the sun of righteousness, with healing in his wings, arise unto these. Will Jesus manifest himself unto these ? will Jesus manifest himself unto you ?

A.   He that hath my commandments, and keepeth them, he it is that loveth me : and he that loveth me shall be loved of my Father, and I will love him, and will manifest myself unto him. John xiv. 21.

18.   Well, it is great and glorious to think that Jesus Christ, the Lord

of life and glory, will manifest himself unto you : but when will he thus be found of you ?

A. And ye shall seek me, and find me, when ye shall search for me with all your heart. Jer. xxix. 13.

19. You now begin to unfold the mystery of God : but pray which is the way to heaven ?

A. Jesus saith unto him, I am the way, the truth, and the life : no man cometh unto the Father but by me. John xiv. 6.

20. Are we then in Christ when Jesus Christ manifests himself unto us ?

A. At that day ye shall know that I am in my Father, and you in me, and I in you. John xiv. 20.

21. Are we commanded to put on Christ ?

A. But put ye on the Lord Jesus Christ, and make not provision for the flesh to fulfil the desires thereof. Rom. xiii. 14.

22. This is a hard lesson to flesh and blood, but is there no getting to heaven without being in Christ ?

A. Verily, verily, I say unto you, he that entereth not by the door into the sheepfold, but climbeth up some other way, the same is a thief and a robber. John x. 1.

23. Is Jesus Christ himself the door ?

A. Then said Jesus unto them again, Verily, verily, I say unto you, I am the door of the sheep : all that ever came before me are thieves and robbers : but the sheep did not hear them. I am the door : by me if any man enter in he shall be saved, and shall go in and out, and find pasture. John x. 7, 8, 9.

24. Does the Apostle command and exhort us to have boldness to enter in at this door and way ?

A. Having therefore, brethren, boldness to enter into the holiest by the blood of Jesus, by a new and living way which he hath consecrated

for us, through the veil, that is to say, his flesh ; and having an
High Priest over the house of God; let us draw near with a true
heart, in full assurance of faith, having our hearts sprinkled from an
evil conscience, and our bodies washed with pure water. Heb. x. 19—22.

25. Are we commanded to walk in Christ, and be rooted and built up
in him ?

A. As ye have therefore received Christ Jesus the Lord, so walk ye in
him : rooted and built up in him, and stablished in the faith, as ye have
been taught, abounding therein with thanksgiving. Col. ii. 6, 7.

26. Are we to grow up into Christ in all things ?

A. But speaking the truth in love, may grow up into him in all things,
which is the head, even Christ. Ephes. iv. 15.

27. Does our Lord command us to abide in him ?

A. Abide in me, and I in you. As the branch cannot bear fruit of itself, except it abide in the vine, no more can ye except ye abide in me. I
am the vine, ye are the branches ; he that abideth in me, and I in him,
the same bringeth forth much fruit : for without me ye can do nothing.
John xv. 4, 5.

28. What does he say of those who do not abide in him ?

A. If a man abide not in me, he is cast forth as a branch, and is with-
ered : and men gather them, and cast them into the fire, and they are
burned. John xv. 6.

29. Do they commit sin who abide in Christ ?

A. Whosoever abideth in him, sinneth not; whosoever sinneth, hath
not seen him, neither known him. 1 John iii. 6.

30. If a man does not commit sin, then he must fulfil the law, and
love is the fulfilling of the law.—Rom. xiii. 8—10. What do you say to
this?

A. God is love; and he that dwelleth in love, dwelleth in God, and God
in him. Herein is our love made perfect, that we may have boldness in

the day of judgment; because as he is, so are we in this world. 1 John iv. 16,17.

31. How does St. John describe this change, and the state of those who have not obtained this change?

A. We know that we have passed from death unto life, because we love the brethren. He that loveth not his brother, abideth in death. Whosoever hateth his brother, is a murderer; and ye know that no murderer hath eternal life abiding in him. 1 John iii. 14,15.

32. Passing from death unto life must be a great and surprising change: but must we have Christ dwelling in us in order to have this life?

A. And this is the record, that God hath given us eternal life; and this life is in his son. He that hath the son hath life; and he that hath not the son of God hath not life. 1 John v. 11,12.

33. What does St. John say of the commandment, and of knowing that he dwelleth in us?

A. And this is his commandment, that we should believe on the name of his son Jesus Christ, and love one another as he gave us commandment. And he that keepeth his commandments dwelleth in him, and he in him: and hereby we know that he dwelleth in us, by the spirit which he hath given us. 1 John iii. 23,24.

34. Are we exhorted to abide in him?

A. And now, little children, abide in him; that when he shall appear, we may have confidence, and not be ashamed before him. 1 John ii. 28.

35. Well, but we cannot see the kingdom of God, and much less have confidence, except we be born again. Are those, then, born again who are in Christ?

A. Therefore, if any man be in Christ he is a new creature; old things are passed away, behold, all things are become new. 2 Cor. v. 17.

36. Are these then, as being God's workmanship, to walk in good works?

A. For we are his workmanship, created in Christ Jesus unto good works, which God hath before ordained that we should walk in them. Ephes. ii. 10.

37. Is the condemnation or curse of God removed?

A. There is, therefore, now no condemnation to them which are in Christ Jesus, who walk not after the flesh, but after the spirit. Rom. viii. 1.

38. Are these delivered from the body of sin and death, and raised to newness of life, and a well-grounded hope of a joyful resurrection?

A. And if Christ be in you, the body is dead because of sin, but the spirit is life because of righteousness. But if the spirit of him that raised up Jesus from the dead dwell in you, he that raised up Christ from the dead shall also quicken your mortal bodies by his spirit that dwelleth in you. Rom. viii. 10, 11.

39. Pray what do you understand by the mystery of God, and a well-grounded hope?

A. The mystery which hath been hid from ages and from generations, but now is made manifest unto his saints; to whom God would make known what is the riches of the glory of this mystery among the Gentiles; which is Christ in you the hope of glory. Col. i. 25, 27.

40. This is indeed a glorious hope. Did St. Paul desire this for the Galatians?

A. My little children, of whom I travail in birth again, until Christ be formed in you. Gal. iv. 19.

41. Is every one encouraged to seek this hope?

A. Behold, I stand at the door and knock: if any man hear my voice and open the door, I will come in to him, and will sup with him, and he with me. Rev. iii. 20.

42. Does not the Apostle compare this manifestation of Christ to light shining out of darkness?

A. For God who commanded light to shine out of darkness, hath shined in our hearts, to give the light of the knowledge of the glory of God in the face of Jesus Christ. 2 Cor. iv. 6.

43. Did St. Paul desire that the Ephesians might know the glorious hope of the christian calling, Christ's inheritance or dwelling in the saints?

A. Wherefore, I also, after I heard of your faith in the Lord Jesus, and love unto all the saints, cease not to give thanks for you, making mention of you in my prayers; that the God of our Lord Jesus Christ, the Father of glory, may give unto you the spirit of wisdom and revelation in the knowledge of him; that the eyes of your understanding being enlightened; that ye may know what is the hope of his calling, and what the riches of the glory of his inheritance in the saints. Ephes. i. 15—18.

44. Did St. Paul give up worldly riches, honours, and pleasures, that he might gain this glory?

A. But what things were gain to me, those I counted loss for Christ. Yea, doubtless, and I count all things but loss for the excellency of the knowledge of Christ Jesus my Lord; for whom I have suffered the loss of all things, and do count them but dung that I may win Christ, and be found in him. Phil. iii. 7, 8.

45. And did he win Christ so as to be crucified with him, and live in him?

A. I am crucified with Christ: nevertheless I live; yet not I but Christ liveth in me: and the life which I now live in the flesh, I live by the faith of the son of God, who loved me, and gave himself for me. Gal. ii. 20.

46. Did he pray earnestly that the Ephesians might comprehend this glorious love, and even be filled with all the fulness of God?

A. For this cause I bow my knees unto the Father of our Lord Jesus Christ, of whom the whole family in heaven and earth is named, that he would grant you according to the riches of his glory, to be strengthened with might by his spirit in the inner man; that Christ may dwell in your

hearts by faith; that ye being rooted and grounded in love, may be able
to comprehend with all saints, what is the breadth, and length, and depth,
and height, and to know the love of Christ, which passeth knowledge, that
ye may be filled with all the fulness of God.   Ephes. iii. 14—19.

47.   May we have boldness through any promise of Jesus Christ to
hope for such a great salvation?

A.   Jesus answered and said unto him, if a man love me he will keep
my words, and my Father will love him, and we will come unto him, and
make our abode with him.   John xiv. 23.

48.   Did Jesus Christ pray that we might receive this joy unspeakable,
this heaven upon earth?

A.   Neither pray I for these alone, but for them also which shall believe
on me through their word, that they all may be one, as thou, Father, art
in me, and I in thee, that they also may be one in us; that the world may
believe that thou hast sent me.   And the glory which thou gavest me I
have given them, that they may be one, even as we are one; I in them,
and thou in me, that they may be made perfect in one, and that the world
may know that thou hast sent me, and hast loved them, as thou hast
loved me.   John xvii. 20—23.

49.   These are truly blest in life; but what do you say of their death?

A.   And I heard a voice from heaven saying unto me, write, blessed are
the dead which die in the Lord, from henceforth: yea, saith the spirit,
that they may rest from their labours; and their works do follow them.
Rev. xiv. 13.

50.   What do you understand by their works do follow them?

A.   God shall bring every work into judgment, with every secret thing,
whether it be good or bad.   Eccles. xii. 14.

51.   Then God must be before all things; he must be without beginning and without end, that is, from everlasting to everlasting: what do
you say in this respect?

A. Before the mountains were brought forth, or ever thou hadst formed the earth and the world; even from everlasting to everlasting thou art God. Psalm xc. 2.

52. Is not such knowledge too wonderful for me, is it not high that I cannot attain to it?

A. Canst thou by searching find out God? Canst thou find out the Almighty to perfection? It is high as heaven, what canst thou do? Deeper than hell, what canst thou know? The measure thereof is longer than the earth, and broader than the sea. Job xi. 7, 8, 9.

53. St. Paul was caught up into the third heaven, and into paradise, and heard unspeakable words: did he still say it was unsearchable?

A. O the depth of the riches both of the wisdom and knowledge of God! how unsearchable are his judgments, and his ways past finding out! Rom. xi. 33.

54. Is there no secret place wherein we may be hidden?

A. Can any hide himself in secret places that I shall not see him? saith the Lord: do I not fill heaven and earth? saith the Lord. Jer. xxiii. 24.

55. What does God say of Jezebel, in the church of Thyatira, and of them that commit whoredom with her?

A. Behold, I will cast her into a bed, and them that commit adultery with her into great tribulation, except they repent of their deeds. And I will kill her children with death; and all the churches shall know that I am he which searcheth the reins and the hearts: and I will give unto every one of you according to your works. Rev. ii. 22, 23.

56. How dreadful must whoring and all uncleanness be, when God says he will cast them into a bed, into great tribulation: how ought we to abstain from all appearance of evil! Do you understand that the Lord takes notice of all your sins?

A. If I sin, then thou markest me; and thou wilt not acquit me from mine iniquity. If I be wicked, woe unto me. Job x. 14, 15.

57. And does he behold every one?

A. The Lord looketh from heaven ; he beholdeth all the sons of men.
From the place of his habitation, he looketh upon all the inhabitants of
the earth. Psalm xxxiii. 13, 14.

58. What do you say of God's being always present with you, and
knowing your thoughts, your words, and all your ways?

A. O Lord, thou hast searched me, and known me. Thou knowest
my down-sitting, and mine up-rising ; thou understandest my thought afar
off. Thou compassest my path, and my lying-down, and art acquainted
with all my ways. For there is not a word in my tongue, but, lo, O Lord,
thou knowest it altogether. Thou hast beset me behind and before, and
laid thine hand upon me. Such knowledge is too wonderful for me ; it is
high ; I cannot attain unto it. Psalm cxxxix. 1—6.

59. What do you say as to swift flight, distant places, or darkness, hiding
from him?

A. Whither shall I go from thy spirit? or whither shall I flee from thy
presence? If I ascend up into heaven, thou art there : if I make my bed
in hell, behold, thou art there. If I take the wings of the morning, and
dwell in the uttermost parts of the sea, even there shall thy hand lead me,
and thy right hand shall hold me. If I say, surely the darkness shall
cover me, even the night shall be light about me. Yea, the darkness
hideth not from thee ; but the night shineth as the day : the darkness and
the light are both alike to thee, Psalm cxxxix. 7—12.

60. I see it is best to be in Christ, for such are covered from the wrath
of God : they are blest in life, they are blest in death, they are blest in
judgment, and are they not also blest in the resurrection?

A. But I would not have you to be ignorant, brethren, concerning
them which are asleep, that you sorrow not even as others which have no
hope. For if we believe that Jesus died and rose again, even so them also
which sleep in Jesus will God bring with him. For this we say unto you
by the word of the Lord, that we which are alive, and remain until the
coming of the Lord, shall not prevent them which are asleep. For the

Lord himself shall descend from heaven with a shout, with the voice of the archangel, and with the trump of God : and the dead in Christ shall rise first: then we which are alive and remain, shall be caught up together with them in the clouds, to meet the Lord in the air : and so shall we ever be with the Lord. Wherefore, comfort one another with these words. 1 Thess. iv. 13—18.

CHAPTER XVI.

STRIKING INCIDENTS TO BE NOTICED—DELAMERE FOREST—JOSEPH LOWE—
COPPENHALL CHURCH—A REVIVAL—METHODIST MAGIC—VISIONS OR TRAN-
CES—BOURNE AND CLOWES GO TO JAMES CRAWFOOT'S—REDEEMING THE
TIME—A FEMALE PREACHES, AND ANOTHER IS IN A VISION—CAMP MEETING
TRIALS—A CONTEST AND CONQUEST—JOURNEY TO LICHFIELD—VISIT TO
THE CATHEDRAL — IMPRESSIONS — GOES TO STAFFORD AND OBTAINS A
LICENSE—BILLS UP AT MACCLESFIELD *versus* THE MOW CAMP MEETING—
PREPARATIVES FOR THE MEETING—PUBLISHING THE MEETING BY PLACARD
—SHUBOTHAM IS AGAIN TURNED ROUND—THE MEETING HELD—HELP IS
FORTHCOMING—THE PERSECUTOR—PROGRESS AND SUCCESS.

We shall now call the reader's attention to a few striking events
that occurred between the first and second Mow Cop camp meetings,
and to a new field of religious enterprise in a part of Cheshire, in
which we shall find Hugh Bourne for a time busily employed
making careful and minute observations on men and things, as
they pass in review before him. He there formed an intimate
acquaintance with James Crawfoot, and others, residents on the
forest of Delamere, which led him to greater discoveries in the
mystery of faith, and the doctrine of a full, free, and present
salvation,—a theme on which his soul delighted to dwell to the
latest period of his existence upon earth, and which cheered and
animated his spirit in the Jordan of death. In noticing the circumstance that gave rise, in the order of providence, to Hugh
Bourne's visit to the methodists in this part of Cheshire, we shall
find it was connected with the great work set in motion on and
about Mow Cop.

Mr. Joseph Lowe, son of Mrs. Lowe, of the Moss House farm,
in the neighbourhood of Mow Cop, was converted in the great
revival which commenced in Harrisehead chapel, in September,
1804, and he soon became a successful vineyard labourer, and

was highly esteemed by Hugh Bourne, and the people of the mountain. Mr. Lowe put the Moss House farm into the hands of some of his sons, and he, his wife, and his son Joseph, removed to Mrs. Lowe's own farm, at Gresty Green, near Coppenhall, in Cheshire. Coppenhall church was supplied by a curate, and he and Joseph Lowe got up a heavenly work in the church, and this made a great stir in the parish; but as the curate was only engaged for a time, a methodist chapel was built, and a cause established. Joseph made occasional visits in Staffordshire, and early in the year 1807, he pressed Hugh Bourne to visit the methodist society, at Delamere forest, in Cheshire. The report was current that these people used magic, or were in league with satan. This report excited in the mind of Bourne a curiosity to enquire into the grounds of it: hence, when his old friend made his appearance on a visit to the mountaineers, he related to him what he had heard respecting the forest methodists, and expressed a wish to see them; but he said his bashfulness stood in the way, and he saw no way open for the present, by which to gratify his curiosity respecting this wonderful people. Joseph Lowe soon ventilated the matter. He told him the report was false, and that these forest methodists were a holy people; he himself had been amongst them; and what the world ascribed to magic, were visions or trances which frequently occurred among them, and he had seen several in this way: and they had those in society with them that could exercise faith effectively in silence. And, said he, I would have you look into these things. "He gave me (says Hugh Bourne) all the remarks he had made on these points. 'But,' said he, 'I do not understand them; but you must look into them.' And he observed that they held a meeting the last Saturday evening in each month, at the house of James Crawfoot, a local preacher. He also stated that James Spinner, a local preacher, from the forest, had visited Coppenhall, and the Lord had made him useful; and he advised me to talk with him. But the distance being about thirty miles, and I being timid, the way evidently was not open. But in June, 1807, I again saw Mr. J. Lowe, and he said, 'I have opened your way; but you will have to come round by Coppenhall.' This would be several miles round; 'but,' said he, 'you can come to Coppenhall on the Friday, and I have provided a lodging for you there; and on the Saturday, Mr. Wm. Harding, a son of Mrs.

Harding of the Pump-house,* will go with you to Delamere forest. He at times attends their monthly meetings; and his brother Randle Harding lives near the place. And there I have provided board and lodging for you; so now your way is open. It now looked like a providential call."

Having named at Tunstall, my intention of going to the forest, William Clowes wished to accompany me, he having heard of these people, at a lovefeast at Mr. Breese's, Lea hall, near Wybunbury, Cheshire. So on Friday (June 26, 1807,) we set off, and he went to the house of an acquaintance of his, and the next morning he fell in with me and Mr. Harding. Our way from Coppenhall lay through a marling part: and at one house there was a marling feast, and their marling speech was going on; and Wm. Clowes went and spoke to them, and anon overtook us again, and in the evening we arrived at Mr. Randle Harding's, and soon went to James Crawfoot's house, where the meeting was to be held. There were some people present, and a tall aged man sat in a two-armed chair, preaching, as I thought; but it seemed an idle way. Still I thought he spoke good things. But soon the people spoke of beginning; I was then aware the old man was redeeming the time: nevertheless an unfavourable impression at that time crossed my mind respecting him. He now read a few passages of scripture, and a brisk, sharp prayer meeting commenced. And ere long I noticed a woman struggling, as if in distress, and wondered why they did not pray for her. But two women placed her on a chair, and she appeared to have fainted away. I then thought this is their trance-work. And there she was for a length of time without any notice being taken of her; but I occasionally cast my eyes upon her.

The old man stopped the meeting, and put up a Mrs. Prescot, a farmer's wife, from near Great Budworth, to exhort; and she spoke some time with apparent zeal.† At length the woman on

* Mrs. Harding was the grandmother of Mr. Hugh Harding of Balterley, who married the eldest daughter of James Bourne. Mrs. Harding died at the advanced age of ninety-eight.

† I afterwards learned that Mrs. Prescot had never been at any of their meetings before. Her maiden name was Howel; and before her marriage, it is said, she was very useful; but she was known to be now in a backsliding state, and on that account J. Crawfoot was much blamed by some of the forest people for putting her up to speak.

the chair clasped her hands and praised the Lord, and went on speaking occasionally without stopping, or opening her eyes. She spoke of a fine green meadow, and said, "Let me lie down." She then spoke of a fine river ;—these sayings made me think of Psalm xxiii. 2. She spoke of trumpets, and called out, "Blow! blow! blow!" She after a time called on a young woman by name, and said, "Leave it." And shortly after that she awoke up, and came out of her visionary state; I then went up to the woman to enquire, but all in vain; only one of the women said, "These things strengthen our faith!"

Sunday, June 28, 1807.—" I conversed with J. Spinner, and heard James Crawfoot preach, but did not like him. A man from Runcorn gave me an invitation to preach at his house, as soon as I could make it convenient."

Monday, June 29.—" I came home, to undergo trials beyond the common lot."

Camp meeting trials.—" On my return from Delamere forest, when I set my feet again in Staffordshire, my flesh had no rest; but I was troubled on every side—without were fightings, within were fears. 2 Cor. vii. 5. My brother was in the hay-harvest. All assistance seemed cut off, and to what quarter could I look? All seemed dark. And I soon heard that a Mr. Stevenson of Cobridge, near Burslem, would indict our camp meeting, under the conventicle act. And in such case, each preacher would have to pay a penalty of twenty pounds, and each hearer above sixteen years of age, five shillings. I now concluded that the way was not providentially open, and thought to put posting-bills up to say that no meeting would be held; but, in mighty terror, the Lord gave me to know that I must stand by the camp meetings, or take the bottomless pit for my portion."

If ever man stood in need of christian support and sympathy, that man was Hugh Bourne; and if at any time, at this period,— when he stood alone in the contest against the scorn of worldlings, priestly arrogance, and the fears of friends. Doleful calamities fell thick on every side; tempestuous storms gathered in anger round about him! But see! Hugh Bourne comes out of the battle-field *unscarred.* The God of providence has baffled the enemies of open-air worship, frustrated their designs, discomfited

and vanquished every foe, and the father of the English camp
meetings appears on the heights of Mow Cop crowned with victo-
rious wreaths, while assembled multitudes listen to the word of
life under the broad canopy of a summer sky : and the English
camp meetings are established as on a rock.

HUGH BOURNE'S PREPARATIVES FOR THE SECOND GREAT
CAMP MEETING, HELD UPON MOW COP.

Many were looking forward to the coming meeting, designed
to counteract the evils of the parish wake, on the slopes of Mow;
but on Hugh Bourne alone devolved the work of preparation to
meet the array of opposition that was planned in the minds of
many, both religious and profane.   His dreadful exposure to
total ruin seemed to shut up all further camp meeting prospects ;
and he thought to put out a hand-bill to say that no camp
meeting would be held.   At that momentous period, we consider
the destiny of thousands of precious and immortal souls hung in
suspense; but happily for the perishing outcasts, the providence
of Almighty God interfered.   The terrors of the Lord strike with
dread majesty through the mind of Hugh Bourne.   His soul's
salvation is at stake ;—this compels him to remain firm at the
post of duty : he durst not quit the field of action, either to oblige
one or another.   Necessity is laid upon him, and a woe hangs
over him if he cowardly desert the cause in which he has embarked.   His position was critical ; he well knew what was before
him ; it would not do to have the camp meeting in a field ; the
horrid conventicle act of Charles II. would reach them there.
What, then, can be done ?   Hear him : " I fixed on a suitable
place on one of the tops of the mountain, where it was common,
and got a grant of occupation from a freeholder, and I then drew
up a brief."   Aye, and then he takes his staff, and walks thirty-
seven miles to the Bishop's court at Lichfield, to get a license for
the mountain, to shield himself and those that should attend the
camp meeting, from the consequences of the horrid conventicle act.
In this he was doomed to disappointment ; the registrar refused
his application for a license, without there was a building erected
on the mountain : so he had to retrace his steps, loaded with grief
of mind at the disappointment.   There is now lying on the desk

before us, a fragment of an old diary, on which is noted an incident which turned up in Lichfield cathedral, which we think rather racy. We will give it in his own words, which are as follow :—

"I was at Lichfield to get a license for Mow meeting, and I went into the minster. After the service began, it ran through my mind, 'Get thee out of this place, and beware of the woman that has the golden cup in her hand, and those that are with her; their ways are death : sin no more, lest a worse thing come upon thee.' This startled me, as I had before taken delight in their singing of the service. I saw much lightness and sin among the parsons. It seemed like gross idolatry in them to spend their time in such a manner : but then, I thought the words of the service are good. It then struck me, 'These people draweth nigh unto me with their lips,' &c. I prayed to God that if the impression to go out was from him, it might increase, if not, that it might go away : it increased till I was quite miserable. I then thought to go out, and a voice came, 'Escape for thy life,' &c. They were singing the *Te Deum*. I took my hat as soon as they had done the *Te Deum*, and went out, and the burden was removed. It looked as if judgments hung over that place. I stopped all afternoon in Lichfield, and such a travail of soul came upon me as I never before experienced,—it was for the city; I mourned greatly; it seemed as if the people had almost sinned out the day of their visitation. I trembled for the place and people; O, my God, have mercy on them! I asked James Crawfoot at the forest about this. He said it was the sign of the times. It was Jesus Christ travailing in me. I might go twenty times and not have the same travail. I had found myself willing to die for them. He said something would turn up, either the gospel would be introduced,* or afflictions would come upon them."

In our judgment, an ordinary mind would have sunk in despair under the opposition he met with. Not so, Hugh Bourne, he did not sit down brooding over sorrow, and give up the contest as hopeless; no, no, he was up and at it again. This time his mechanical abilities as a carpenter were brought into use,—his purse was unstrung, timber was purchased, and anon carried to

* Lichfield is now the head of a Primitive Methodist circuit.

the top of Mow. To work he went in earnest, and with his own hands he reared a huge fabric of timber, designated by him a tabernacle, capable of holding a goodly number of people; and also three tents for prayer meetings, in imitation of the Americans': and now the registrar of Lichfield, in answer to a second application, sends him by post a license * for his tabernacle, which, perhaps, some of our readers might be ready to say, surely was sufficient protection against the conventicle act, and would place the camp meeting under the strong arm of British law: no, there is another redoubt to be fortified against the besiegers. This done, the camp on the mountain top is sheltered under Old England's constitution against all attacks and disturbances; therefore, without hesitancy, he marched to the county town, on Thursday, July 16th, 1807, and obtained a license to preach: he there made oath in open court at the general quarter sessions, holden in the Shire-hall of the county of Stafford, to the following effect:—" I, Hugh Bourne, do solemnly declare in the presence of Almighty God, that I am a christian and a protestant; and as such, that I believe that the scriptures of the Old and New Testament, as commonly received among the protestant churches, do contain the revealed will of God, and that I do receive the same as the rule of my faith and practice."

We subjoin a copy of the license:—" I do hereby certify, that at the General Quarter Sessions of the Peace of our Lord the King, holden at Stafford, in and for the county of Stafford, upon Thursday, the Sixteenth day of July, in the year of our Lord, One Thousand Eight Hundred and Seven, Hugh Bourne personally appeared in open court, between the hours of nine and twelve in the forenoon of the same day, and did then and there take and subscribe the oaths of allegiance and supremacy, the declaration against Popery, and the declaration by law directed to be made and subscribed by Protestant Dissenting Ministers and Schoolmasters, pursuant to the several Statutes in that behalf made. Witness my hand, the Sixteenth day of July, in the year of our Lord One Thousand Eight Hundred and Seven.†

ARTHUR HINCKLEY,
Clerk of the Peace for the County of Stafford."

---

* Postage and license cost him 14s., and the tabernacle £30.

+ On the same day, and at the same place and hour, James Bourne, his brother, was also licensed in the same manner.

Thus armed, he returned to his tabernacle, and posted up,—
" Take Notice, this meeting-house is licensed for divine worship ;
and all disturbers of the peace will be prosecuted as the law
directs."

We hope the reader will not think us tedious if we crave indulgence to name a few other preparatives which were necessary. A
few more valiant ministers, soldiers clad with the whole armour of
God, were wanted to garrison the mountain camp ; recruits must be
sought for, and there is no time to be lost; the day is fast approaching when the decisive engagement will be fought. Off
father Bourne sets to the town of Macclesfield ; there he finds
the methodistic tribes all in commotion, some for and some against
the Mow meeting. Among the latter are the Wesleyan ministers,
who have posted large bills, disclaiming all connection with the
camp meetings ; and there were not wanting among them some
who gravely hinted that Hugh Bourne was disaffected towards his
Majesty's government, and that these meetings were got up for
political purposes ; and there is no doubt on our minds but there
were some who thought, that ere long the ring-leader would be
brought to condign punishment, hanged, drawn, and quartered,
and his head be exhibited by the executioner, with, " Behold ! the
head of a traitor ! "—Neither daunted nor beaten off his purpose,
however, he displays the colours of Immanuel, and at Macclesfield
and Knutsford he enlisted some valiant warriors, who fought man-
fully under the banner of the cross, and were of signal service in
gaining the conquest over the oppositionists to the primitive mode
of worshipping God in the open air.

Once more : to complete the preparations, it was necessary to
supply the mountain garrison with provisions. No other commis-
sary than father Bourne is found ; but all this he cheerfully
and willingly performed at his own cost and charge, with the
exception of one shilling that was presented to him by some
one, and the part borne by his brother ; and we might add,
that the most menial office, that of "hewer of wood, or
drawer of water," was performed by him with pleasure, so that the
object of his soul's earnest desires, (the conversion of sinners,)
might be accomplished. All was ready : this devoted man of God
had done everything that human forethought and hard labour
could accomplish for the safety and success of the meeting. He

now quietly waited the issue, reposing implicit confidence in the power and providence of God to bring himself and coadjutors off more than conquerors. He calmly surveyed every redoubt, as a skilful general would do before an engagement; and while he was thus employed, the emissaries of persecution were sent out to spy the mountain arrangements for the coming struggle, and to persuade the colliers to desert him and the camp altogether; and they so far succeeded as to prevail with Daniel Shubotham and a few others to promise not to attend the camp meeting. "I met with Daniel," (says H. B.) "quite shaken! quite changed! He seemed disposed to oppose camp meetings with all his might. I reasoned the matter over with him, and he complied at last, and seemed to be as much for camp meetings; but there is no trusting to such changeable persons." And he then adds, "O Daniel, Daniel, the glory is departed." Thus was Daniel fallen from his former greatness and valiant zeal in the cause of truth, so that he now succumbed to the oppositionists. From an old journal we make the following extract:—"Many persecuted, and opposed, especially the head preacher: he rose almost to madness; and the other preacher made strange work,—they put out papers, and sent them to the societies and circuits round."

A report was spread in the Potteries that there would be no camp meeting, and the preachers were too successful in persuading some of Hugh Bourne's intimate friends (whom he highly valued and esteemed as being by far superior to himself as to divine things) to withdraw their labours from the camp meetings, and merely attend to save their word. They had laboured valiantly, and rendered great support in the praying services of the first great camp meeting; but now, too easily, in our judgment, they yielded to prejudiced interference. However, we wish to cast no reflection on the conduct and character of these good men, for in after years they nobly redeemed themselves by boldly preaching the gospel in the open air, and had great success in winning souls to Christ. In reply to the papers and rumours afloat, printed bills were posted up at Burslem and Tunstall, to say that there would be a camp meeting held on Mow Cop at the time stated; and it was signed "Hugh Bourne, James Bourne, Daniel Shubotham, Matthias Bayley, and Thomas Cotton." But before the meeting came on, poor Daniel, like a weather vane, was turned round again, and he finally took his leave of camp meetings altogether, and left the management and consequences to the other camp meeting fathers, who now publicly acknowledged themselves to be in favour of such meetings.

THE CAMP MEETING.

" The Lord so favoured us," says Hugh Bourne, " that we were in the midst of fine weather. On the Saturday evening, July 18th, we had an excellent course of praying. About six o'clock on Sunday morning, July 19th, 1807, the voice of united worship sounded on Mow Cop. The Lord was graciously present, and a holy unction attended the services. Ere long the converting work broke out, and the praying with mourners went on with power ; and I regretted it being stopped for breakfast, but it soon broke out again, and went on with power. However, after breakfast the prayings did not stop for the preachings,—each went on with force; people came flocking in ; we had Wesleyans in abundance. And from Macclesfield we had Independent methodists ; and we had people from Stockport, which is more than twenty miles distant ; from Knutsford in Cheshire ; from Warrington in Lancashire, which is nearly forty miles distant, we had the Quaker methodists. My tabernacle was filled, and we had hosts besides ; but the Lord graciously favoured us,—the sun shone brightly, and the ground was warm, pleasant, and comfortable, and the gracious power of God rested on the meeting throughout the day. The prayings and preachings were going on most of the day, and the praying labourers, when rather exhausted, would go off to the preachings, and wait till again invigorated, and then go back to one of the praying places, or companies, and fall on again ; and this I think was practised considerably, and the extent and continuation of the prayings exceeded all that I had ever witnessed."

A great trial.—In the afternoon, Mr. Stephenson and another master potter came on horse-back, with another man on foot. Hugh Bourne's large tabernacle was filled, and there were crowds in the open air, and the singings, prayings, preachings, mournings, and rejoicings, were going on in full course, and there is no doubt these men heard the noise afar off. Soon this great man, Mr. S., calls out for the heads of the meeting ; but none obey this lord-ling's call. They were not likely ; The Lord Jesus Christ was the head of the great camp meeting, and the people were all engaged in gospel labours.   Still this master potter spurs his horse, and rides into the midst of the camp, vociferating " Where's the head ? " At length some one names Hugh Bourne. Hugh Bourne is called for, but no Hugh Bourne makes his appearance, for it so happened, just before the gentleman arrived, Hugh Bourne had re-tired to the other side of the Cop to rest, and to indulge in silent meditation and fervent prayer.   At length Hugh Bourne is found. Perhaps the great man expected to see a *gentleman*, but how strangely would he be disappointed when Hugh Bourne made his appearance all in dishabille, for he had been so much absorbed with the preparations for the meeting, that he had quite forgotten to dress in his Sunday suit ; so he had to appear before the great man in the working dress of a moorland carpenter.   The great potter in anger demanded his license. This he calmly put into his hands. He next demanded the tabernacle license, but this our friend had left at home.   Now, thought the great man, I have him ; he shall feel the weight and consequences of the conventicle act ; these unlawful assemblings of the people in such multitudes must and shall be put down.   Hugh Bourne was cool and collected, answering with christian meekness the interroga-tions of the great man, who in anger turned from the humble carpenter, and as he rode away, threatened vengeance on the assembled multitude.   Many were alarmed ; and now the carpen-ter is heard ; he raises his voice and cries, " Whoever is fined for attending this meeting, I will pay all cost and charge."   But stop, the great man suddenly reins back his prancing steed. What's the matter now ? Hear what Hugh Bourne says :—" Mr. S. and his fellow in returning, started in a direction different from that in which they came ; and in so doing, they rode past the fuller congregation, and by a pole on which was the board put up to give notice of the license, &c. And as it was the Lord's camp meeting, he wrought for us. The Lord, it is likely, impressed these men with a terror, and I rather think with a fear lest I should take the law on them, under the toleration act, for disturbing the public worship. They stopped their horses and sent for me, but I went with reluctance. Mr. S. was, however, cool and social. He said in an easy way that we were doing hurt ; but I said we were doing no hurt. ' But,' says he, ' it is contrary to the bible.' My reply was, 'If you will put it down in writing where it is contrary, we will notice it, and if we cannot answer it, we will give up such meetings,' and in this agreeable way he went on till (as I suppose) he was satisfied that I should not take the law upon him; and at parting he said, rather loudly, ' God bless you!' and we with heart and mind said, ' God bless him!' and it was like light out of darkness. The Lord turned Mr. Stephenson's coming to good. Both professors and profane had looked to Mr. S. But after this the notion was, if anything could have been effectively done against the camp meetings, Mr. S. would have done it. But in June, 1812, the conventicle act was repealed, and by the mercy of God this opened the way more fully.

" On the Monday, the congregation was smaller; but the devotional exercises were the same, and it was thought about twenty conversions took place, but there were far more on the Sunday. On Tuesday our congregation was still smaller; and in the evening we closed this great and important meeting. It was one of the greatest and most successful camp meetings ever held in England, as during the three days upwards of sixty souls were hopefully converted from sin to holiness in life and conduct. To God be all the praise, amen. The first, held upon Mow Cop, on Sunday, May 31st, 1807, renewed the converting work, and commenced the English camp meetings, or third revival of Primitive methodism. This great Mow Cop camp meeting held July 18—21, 1807, opened out the converting work in a glorious manner, and stemmed the tide of Newchapel wake ungodliness. It must be noted, however, that it was properly Wolstanton wake, that being the name of the parish, and the wake is held in one and the same week throughout the whole parish of Wolstanton, yet it bears different titles; as for instance, if you set out from Wolstanton, the head of the parish, and travel northward a few miles, you come to Tunstall, and there it is called Tunstall wake: a few miles further is the village called Newchapel; and there is a church-chapel in it, and this gives the title of Newchapel wake throughout the northen part of the parish, including Kidsgrove, Harrisehead, and the Staffordshire part of Mow Cop; and for many years the wake there had been proverbial for ungodliness but this year, 1807, the camp meeting, by the blessing of God, kept back the flood of wickedness, and it never rose so high after. It may be noticed that this camp meeting was mightily owned of God, yet my sufferings were great, and my sorrows of mind were heavy."

We think the friends of the Burslem Wesleyan circuit would have been much better employed had they held a camp meeting at Tunstall, instead of creating such an array of opposition to Hugh Bourne's camp meeting upon Mow Cop. Strange to tell, Daniel Shubotham and others received the thanks of the ministers and the quarterly meeting for not attending the Mow Cop camp meeting, whereas Daniel and others came on the Tuesday, and personally opposed the meeting. However, but a very short time elapsed before it came to Daniel's turn to suffer; and he was turned out of the methodist society, and never joined any religious body after; neither did his brothers and friends, the oppositionists, visit him, but in his distress they left him as an outcast, without one word of consolation. But Hugh Bourne acted as the good Samaritan, or spared him as David would have done Absalom,—he visited him in his affliction, and pointed him to the same Jesus, as on Christmas-day morning, 1800 ; and we trust Daniel found his way to heaven, and has now welcomed his spiritual father to the shores of eternal felicity.

Ere we close this chapter, we will notice the *religious processions.* The circumstances that gave rise to processioning in the Primitive Methodist Connexion were as follow :—The reader will recollect the account of the meeting of the Cheshire and Harrisehead revivalists, at the Michaelmas and Christmas lovefeasts, in the town of Congleton, in the year 1804. "In the following spring, 1805, I," says Hugh Bourne, "and others paid them a visit. On the Sabbath I went out with a party, and by the way we had what they called a ' walking prayer meeting.' A hymn was sung as we walked; prayer followed, still walking ; and so on as in any other prayer meeting ; and this was the first time I ever witnessed such an open-air procession, and it was excellent." Another circumstance relating to processions turned up as follows :—The Sabbath after the great camp meeting, held July 19—21, 1807, a lovefeast was held at Burslem; and it being the last Mr. Miller would hold before he left the circuit, a number from Harrisehead and Mow Cop were invited by him to attend. Hugh Bourne remarks :—"And they went, men and women, in a host. Their road lay through Tunstall, which place is one mile from Burslem ;

and they sung through Tunstall, and all the way to Burslem. This was a noble procession, and it had an excellent effect." And we might further add, Hugh Bourne saw such excellency in this system, that he afterwards adopted it on various occasions, and it has been carried out on a large and extensive scale in the Primitive Methodist Connexion. We have witnessed the gracious influence of such processions upon the public mind in many instances. Hugh Bourne was not present in the Burslem love-feast procession, for the same day he preached in the open air at the village of Red-street, in the Newcastle-under-Lyme circuit, and afterwards assisted his brother in holding a lovefeast, at which eight or more souls were hopefully converted to the Lord; but the same evening he received from an eye-witness the account of the procession, and noted it down in his diary.

CHAPTER XVII.

PREPARATIONS FOR NORTON CAMP MEETING—POWERFUL OPPOSITION—AN
EXCURSION — NANCY   FODEN — METHODIST CONFERENCE *versus* CAMP
MEETINGS — WESLEY'S FIELD-PREACHING NOW DISHONOURED — BROWN-
EDGE CAMP MEETING—J. BOURNE WAVERS—HIS DREAMS—H. BOURNE'S
STEADFASTNESS—NORTON MEETING AND ITS EFFECTS—OPENING OF MR.
SMITH'S KITCHEN, AT TUNSTALL.

The whole weight of the preparations for the forth-coming Norton
camp meeting was now upon H. Bourne, and, if possible, a greater
storm of opposition was on the eve of breaking out against him, and
even his own familiar friends were also turned round. But notwithstanding this, he found time to make an excursion in the
interval between the Mow Cop and Norton great camp meetings.
Hear him :—" After the meeting I visited Macclesfield again, and
was at the house of a friend who was a member of the Independent methodists. These methodists had delegates from different
parts, and were holding a first conference ; and one of their main
matters, was arranging for an interchange of preachers, to promote
variety."

"Having had an invitation to visit the Quaker methodists, I
one morning set out for Warrington, and walked all the way,
although the distance was considerably more than thirty miles.
I was much edified among them, and I preached several times.
I also preached at Rizley, among a people raised up by Lorenzo
Dow, and I had much cause to bless God for this journey. From
Warrington I made my way to Runcorn, and preached there ;
and then my way lying over Delamere forest, I called on
J. Spinner, and on asking about the vision work, a person present
advised calling on Nancy Foden, the woman who went in vision
when I was there before. This woman's husband was a methodist,

and a bricklayer by trade, and a part of their family was not grown up. I found her a motherly woman, and she conversed well on religion, but was reserved in regard to the vision work. This rather pained me; but at length she told me of my unwillingness to preach or to be a preacher, and added, ' You will never grow in grace as you ought, unless you take up that cross.' This was a home blow : I certainly had a great reluctance to preaching, although I preached a good deal. But she had witnessed my reluctance in the trance. And in reply to her remark, my observation was, that in preaching I was at times so shut up as to be hardly able to tell what to say next, and this appeared to me to be a proof that the Lord had not called me to preach. Her reply was to this effect, ' your being occasionally shut up in preaching is no proof of your not being called to preach; it is a proof that you are called to preach, and that your preaching is effective.' Truly this was a new lesson ; I had never met with the like before, and her lesson was worth all the labour and expence of going to Warrington, Rizley, Runcorn, and Delamere forest. Truly, of all that I had ever read or heard, I had never met with anything like this; however, it marked one of the most extraordinary events of my whole life, and I went home a different man."

While father Bourne was itinerating in the neighbouring counties of Lancashire and Cheshire, a most formidable opposition sprung up in a quarter where he had not anticipated it : this was the conference of Wesleyan ministers. The conference concerted measures to put down or stop the further progress of camp meetings, and punish the contumacy of Hugh Bourne, or any other person who should disobey its law. Hence, out came the following manifesto :—" *Q.* What is the judgment of the conference concerning what are called camp meetings? *A.* It is our judgment that, even supposing such meetings to be allowable in America, they are highly improper in England, and likely to be productive of much mischief, and we disclaim all connection with them." We think this *manifesto* anything but respectful to the memory and name of that great and good man, John Wesley, to whom the conference owed their all as ministers of the Wesleyan Connexion; for it is evident that Wesley considered field-preaching a vital and essential part of primitive methodism, and he enjoined the practice of it on all his preachers as a duty incumbent. And we would ask, what are camp meetings but field-preaching, accompanied by extended praying services, by which the talents of praying men and women are called into exercise in the public worship of Almighty God? and we should have thought the sixty souls hopefully saved at the second great camp meeting upon Mow Cop would have been a sufficient proof to the conference that the smile and approbation of God rested on these open-air meetings, and would have induced the conference to sanction open-air worship, and extend the practice of it to every circuit in the connexion; but instead of thankfully receiving this dispensation as from God, and cheerfully and unitedly taking the field themselves as their father and founder had done before them, they send forth to their own community and the world at large, a manifesto, pronouncing the camp meetings mischievous, and disclaiming all connection with them. From that hour we believe the decree went forth, " Let there be another community, whose ministers will take up the cross, and lift up the blazing torch of gospel light in the dark corners of the land, and raise up a people to the Lord from the humblest walks of human society ! " And to us it is evident, that Hugh Bourne and the English camp meetings, in the order of divine providence, were appointed to prepare the way for the raising up of the people now called Primitive Methodists.

Before the approaching Norton camp meeting, a small one was held at Brown-edge, on Sunday, August 16th, 1807. We find the following entry in H. Bourne's journal in reference to it :—

"*Sunday, August 16th*, 1807.—We had a small camp meeting at Brown-edge. Many from Harrisehead attended, but no preachers beside Thomas Cotton and I. At two o'clock p.m. we went into the chapel ; W. Skinner preached. We then returned to the common, and continued till about six o'clock. Cotton had uncommon liberty and power,—many came out to hear, who scarcely ever heard the gospel in their lives."

The foregoing is the plain unvarnished entry in the diary of Hugh Bourne ; and from this it would seem his zeal was tempered with discretion, so far that he did not interfere (except on special occasions) with the regular, planned in-door appointments. When the afternoon service commenced in the Wesleyan chapel, the two camp meeting fathers and their followers repaired to that service, and did not re-commence their out-door labours until the appointed preacher had dismissed his congregation.   If the reader had been acquainted with the people and locality of Brown-edge in the year 1807, it would not at all have surprised him that Hugh Bourne should have supposed that some of these Brown-edge people had never heard the gospel in their whole lives, before hearing it that day at the camp meeting.

But we must now hasten to narrate a few of the circumstances that turned up in the path of Hugh Bourne, in making his preparations and arrangements for Norton camp meeting. The opposition to the second meeting upon Mow was great; but we consider the for-midable array of hostility was greater against the camp meeting at Norton than it had been against that.   The superintendent re-turned from conference, prepared to go the full length of con ferential authority in stopping the tide of open-air innovations- The first step he took was that of laying all the leaders and loca.. preachers under interdict in regard to attending camp meetings ; at the same time urging them to use their influence to prevent the members from attending ;—laying especial stress upon the decision of the conference on the subject. And we are sorry to add, that several of the intimate friends and acquaintances of H. Bourne were induced to forsake his company and stand aloof from him, particularly at the Norton camp meeting.

Up to this time Hugh Bourne had found in his brother James a very valuable colleague, and a firm supporter of open-air wor-ship; but now the conference *manifesto*, and the array of oppo-sition in the Burslem and neighbouring circuits, made such resistance to the camp meetings, that this hitherto firm advocate of and believer in the utility of open-air worship, began to waver, and to reason in his own mind as to how these things could be. Happily, he took a wise and christian course; he sought counsel and wisdom from the Lord, by supplication and prayer ; and the Lord, in a very peculiar and striking dream, satisfied his mind, so that he never doubted after.   This dream we long wished to be made acquainted with, but remained in ignorance of it until we had free access to Hugh Bourne's papers ;—we there found it care-fully recorded in an old diary, and now give the reader a copy of what he wrote respecting it.

"*Tuesday, August 17th*, 1807.—This morning, my brother James related the following:—In the course of the night I dreamed that I was praying to God to give me a token if Norton meeting was agreeable to his will. It seemed that I was near Norton, and a large company was present, and I there saw old John Sargeant, of Woodhouse-lane. He looked the same as when alive, only more young, fresh, and blooming. (He, when alive, had a great fondness for me.) I put out my hand as usual to shake hands, and he came up to me and shook hands. I said, "you look very fresh and healthy; I am glad that you are got about. You are now got pretty well again." He then spoke earnestly, and said, "do not you know that I have been dead a good while?" This struck me; and after recollecting, I said, "I do know." I then asked some questions, and he answered them. I then said, "do you know that we are to have a large meeting at Norton?" He said, "I do know of it." I said, "there is much opposition against it; do not you think that it would be the best way to give it up, and have no meeting?" He very earnestly replied, "No; you must not give it up, nor any part of it. You must carry it on, whatever will be." I then thought to ask him whether we should get preachers, and whether any good would be done; but a divine awe and fear struck through my mind, that I was asking for curiosity, which I must not do, but leave it to God. I then asked a few questions, and felt thankful to God for this token.—Old John Sargeant, who had died some time before, was a member of the society; was fond of the cause, and was extremely happy on his death-bed, and left a glorious testimony. James and I used to hold meetings at his house, and he was very fond of us."

"This is not the first vision of the kind that James Bourne has been favoured with. Mr. Jackson, travelling preacher, who died about a year ago in this circuit, when on his death-bed, wanted to see James, but did not see him. Sometime after his death he came to James in a dream, and talked much with him. He said two angels met him when he came out of the body, and conducted him to paradise. That paradise was glorious; that it was worth contending for, &c. James asked him about the body that he appeared in,—whether he would answer him how soon he could move to Jerusalem, or to the moon. He replied, "As soon as you can think of Jerusalem, or the moon, I can go thither."

LABOURS OF HUGH BOURNE.

This was a very critical period in the history of Hugh Bourne's life. His scrupulosity with regard to preaching and his call to the ministry, was in part removed, in the conversation with Mrs. Foden; so that he shunned not the pulpit; but willingly and cheerfully shouldered this cross; proclaiming Jesus and the resurrection, where and whensoever he was called; either in the chapel, tabernacle, or open-air. And this we consider was a great mercy, for at this period of his eventful life, a methodist storm, like

—" Bellowing clouds burst with a stormy sound,
And with an armed winter strewed the ground."

But no opposition could shake Hugh Bourne, so as to cause him to desert the good work. He believed from the first that the camp meetings were of the Lord, and that it was his duty to stand by them. This, in some degree, arose from the following circumstance :—" Shortly after the Norton and Mow Cop first camp meetings were appointed, Hugh Bourne, D. Shubotham, and M. Bailey, were at pious old Joseph Pointon's, and while praying for those camp meetings, it was strongly impressed on H. Bourne's mind, that "they should not die but live." From this it was concluded, that from some quarter severe opposition would arise ; but that the Lord would stand by these two camp meetings. And from that moment H. Bourne believed himself called of God to stand by the camp meetings, and that if he deserted the cause, it would be at the peril of his soul."

There was no personal quarrel between H. Bourne and the superintendent when they met ; but the one talked modern, and the other primitive methodism ; and we believe in these discussions Mr. Bourne was a match for his reverend opponent. But what this gentleman lacked in argument, he seems to have made up in influence ; and in this he did what he could to damage the intended Norton camp meeting.

To his proceedings Hugh Bourne was no stranger, expecting neither favour nor support from this quarter, consequently he had to look out elsewhere, as he had done before for the great Mow Cop camp meeting ; but, lo ! his opponent had been before him, and had so far succeeded as to leaven with an antagonistic spirit the whole staff (with few exceptions) of the local preachers and leaders in the circuit. Well, " the week, (preceding the Norton wake,)" says Hugh Bourne, " I made great preparations for the meeting, and I went to Macclesfield to engage preachers, and I found that some person there had printed an address to the methodist preachers, on account of their opposition to the camp meetings. Before the first meeting upon Mow Cop, the word of faith given me was, that we should live ; this was for both meetings. I did not then see the need of it, as I expected little or no opposition. After the first, and before the second, it was manifested to me that the Lord would glorify himself more in the second than in the first ; which he gave me to see ; although I had heavier trials. And now it was impressed upon my mind, in the prayer meeting, that the Lord would glorify himself in Norton camp meeting ; and that there mine eyes should see his salvation ;— before this, in taking the poles into the field, satan had reasoned with me whether I was asleep or not. But now the impression came further, that those that rose up against us should be as nothing, &c. I had a very sore travail for a great part of Burslem society ; it appeared as if the Lord had a controversy with them, and that Mr. R. had done a sore thing. O my God, pardon him !

" At Norton was held the first camp meeting ever planned out in England. But I then thought of only a little quiet meeting. Before it was held, the sound of it had reached the Wesleyan conference, and from thence had gone into every circuit, if not into every county of England and Wales. And the towns of Hanley, Burslem, and Tunstall, are all within three miles of Norton, and the potters and colliers were greatly moved, as also was the whole surrounding country. But I had made an establishment, and had got a license from the bishop's court ; and this kept the place in quiet, otherwise we should have had trouble. In the order of the Almighty's divine providence, Norton camp meeting was to decide a great question ; a question on which, in the providence of God, depended the welfare and well-being of thousands and ten thousands. The great question was, " shall the English camp meetings be swept away, or shall they be continued ? If Norton camp meeting proved a failure, they would be done away ; but if the Lord graciously caused it to triumph, the camp meetings would be established. My chief reason for making the appointment was, a desire to preserve our young members from being drawn aside by the vanities of Norton wake. This was the main of what I had in my mind; but the Lord meant it to move the country, and move the nation; and the Lord in his providence caused the continuance or discontinuance of the English camp meetings to depend upon the failure or the success of that one to be held at Norton. As so much depended upon this meeting, it is no wonder that the enemy of souls should stir up opposition. One means would be, the cutting off the supplies, by throwing obstructions in the way, and thereby hindering preachers and praying labourers from attending; but if people had seen me and several local preachers walking in the intended camp meeting field eight or ten days before the time, they might have thought that there was every likelihood of being a full supply of preachers; but when Mr. R. came back from the conference he called a meeting, and required the preachers to declare against camp meetings: so this supply was swept away. I cannot say that this was much of a trial; for by their talk in the field, it appeared to me that they were not in the converting way; so, on the whole, it was well that they were kept away. Cowper, the poet, says—

"Judge not the Lord by feeble sense,
But trust him for his grace;
Behind a frowning Providence,
He hides a smiling face."

My sufferings were heavy, and my sorrows were great; but by labours and diligence, I got all things ready by Saturday evening, August 22nd, 1807; and we had a course of praying, and the Lord was with us, and I so far copied after the Americans, as to sleep all night in one of the tents.

Sunday, August 23rd, 1807, dawned upon us, and we had many in the field before six o'clock in the morning. But I was called into the lane by a young man, Mr. Edward N. Mc.Evoy, a schoolmaster, who was one of the lively Tunstall methodists. He said, the Tunstall methodists had prevailed with the female preacher to stop at Tunstall, and not come to the Norton camp meeting at all; and, he added, the Tunstall methodists do not approve of camp meetings. I asked Mr. Mc.Evoy whether he would not come into the field and help us. He answered, "No; the Tunstall men do not approve of camp meetings, and I will be as they are:" so we parted. At this instant James Bourne was calling me, it being six o'clock in the morning; he said it was time to begin. The morning was fine, and we opened the camp meeting in the name of the Lord. We had a preacher from Macclesfield, and another from Knutsford; so with my brother and I, we were four preachers; and having a pretty good number of pious, praying labourers, the meeting proceeded hopefully. Still my heart was sorrowful. The zealous opposition was known to me before Mr. Mc.Evoy came, but still his account of it made so deep and painful an impression on my mind, that I began to look for a break up; his talk so lowered my exercise of faith, as to induce me to meditate on a failure; and in case it should be so, it was manifest that I and my brother would be clear of the blood of all men; for, being aware that the camp meeting cause was a great movement for promoting the glory of God and the good of mankind, we had spared no expense nor labour in bringing it up ; and should the Lord permit it to be done away, he might at some future time, cause it to be begun again by others.

While I was in this drooping situation, the arrival of a stranger was announced in the field; and this was no less a person than Paul Johnson, M.D., from the city of Dublin, in Ireland. This extraordinary man, moved by the Lord, had come direct from Dublin to Norton, to assist at that camp meeting; and his coming was like light out of darkness. The causes of his coming were these:—our Knutsford preacher, being a native of Ireland, and being acquainted with the doctor, had written him a historical account of the English camp meetings; and the doctor, in waiting before the Lord, believed that the Lord required it at his hands to assist at that Norton camp meeting. It crossed his business, and was unfavourable to his temporal concerns, but he made all give way, and went on board a vessel; and the Lord having the command of the wind and waves, wafted him over to Liverpool: from thence he came to Burslem, and then to Norton.

We had a good supply of pious, praying labourers from the Harrisehead society, in addition to those at Norton. The weather occasionally was rainy; but, by the blessing of God, the air was in a fine, soft state, so that the singing was heard at a great distance ; and the preaching sounded to a considerable extent.

Dr. Johnson being much in the Quaker way, we could not tell when he would preach, but all fell in well. When he stood up, his voice filled the field, and his preaching took surprisingly with the hosts of potters. He appeared to suit the meeting and the people more than any other preacher. I myself had experienced great reluctance to preaching ; but the discourse of a pious sister at Delamere forest had very much removed it, and now the remarks of Dr. Johnson, who had received good under my preaching, cleared away the remainder of my reluctance, so in this respect I have cause to thank God, and to remember the Lord's hand at the great Norton camp meeting.

Thomas Cotton being planned that Sunday at ten and two at Kidsgrove, and Mr. R. not allowing him to get a substitute, he did not arrive till late in the afternoon, and when he was present, we had four of the camp meeting fathers, H. & J. Bourne, M. Bayley and T. Cotton ;—with the exception of Daniel Shubotham, by the mercy of God, we were all there. We closed the labours of the day about eight o'clock in the evening, and by God's Almighty providence, we had a full supply of preachers, and pious, praying labourers. On the Monday, August 24, we commenced about eight o'clock in the morning, and closed at eight o'clock at night. The proceedings of the day were much the same as on the Sabbath. At the close, we had to part with our friend Doctor Paul Johnson ;—his business not allowing him to continue longer. On the Tuesday in the forenoon, we had scarcely any people ; so we had but little service, but we opened at noon, and went on till about six o'clock in the evening, when this extraordinary camp meeting closed. To God be the glory and dominion for ever and ever. Amen."

VARIOUS NOTICES.

1. The coming of Doctor Johnson was looked upon by the camp meeting fathers as a striking manifestation of the providence and will of God. For if he had not come to the Norton camp meeting, we think there would have been a great difficulty in carrying it on to a triumphant close, but as it was, all the movements

made it plain and open that it was the Lord's will that the English camp meetings should be continued; and we may add, thousands have had cause to praise God that such meetings have been continued to this day.

2. The end and design Hugh Bourne intended, or had in view, when he made the appointment, was fully accomplished. The Lord so favoured them, that the whole of the society was preserved; not one member being drawn away by the vanities of the wake. And from that important moment, the English camp meetings were established on an immovable foundation, and could never afterwards be shaken.

3. We shall close this chapter with a few passing remarks on some of the most striking incidents that sprang out of the opposition to the Norton camp meeting. It will be remembered by the reader, that Mr. Mc.Evoy, a Tunstall methodist, called Hugh Bourne out of the camp meeting field, and stated that the female preacher from Macclesfield was prevailed on to stop and preach at Tunstall, instead of coming to the camp meeting, as she intended to do. And be it known, the minister permitted her to occupy the Tunstall pulpit in his own appointment, in the face of the conferential prohibition of female preachers; and on the morrow, when Hugh Bourne learned the circumstances of the female's detention at Tunstall, he made the following observation, on the camp ground :—" It will not surprise me if the Lord does not permit her way to be hedged up at Tunstall." And on some one telling her of it, at Macclesfield, she said, " Mr. R. gave up his appointments to me in Tunstall chapel." Now, reader, mark the sequel. Hear what Hugh Bourne says on the subject :—
" Towards the close of this year 1807, being at the house of Mr. John Smith, at Tunstall, I found him and Mr. James Steele in trial of mind. The female preacher being again at Tunstall, was shut out of the chapel, under a plea of conference.* They

* The preacher, in his zeal to cut off the supply of preachers for the Norton camp meeting, was prepared to bend the conference mandate against female preachers; but when no opposition to field-preaching is called for, he calls to his aid conferential authority, and shuts out of the Tunstall Wesleyan chapel this heretofore-admired preacheress. Oh ! prejudice ; how zig-zag are thy movements !

(Messrs. Smith and Steele) said it was enough to make a secession, and they had determined to fit up Mr. Smith's kitchen for
a place of worship. Their talk gave me alarm! I dreaded a
secession. I spoke strongly to Mr. James Steele; they having
requested me to fall in with them. So they concluded that the
kitchen should be for preaching only, and no society should ever
be formed in it. I then fell in with them, and I obtained a
license from the bishop's court, and it was settled for the preachings to be on Friday evenings; and they were carried on upon
the improved system of extended praying services accompanying
each sermon." And before the close of the year 1807, there was
regular preaching there every Friday night; and this continued
for four or five years, without a single failure. But Mr. Smith
did not appear to open it with the least design of raising up a
separate society; neither was there any class ever raised up in it.

This preaching establishment sprang out of the opposition to
Norton camp meeting. Had not the superintendent given the
Tunstall pulpit up to Mrs. Dunnel, on the camp meeting Sunday,
there would have been no call for Mr. Smith to take umbrage at
his closing the pulpit against her when she paid them a second
visit; for it was well understood that the Wesleyan conference
did not sanction women preachers; but now Mr. Smith will not
brook what he considers an insult to the people, and to the friends
of this female evangelist; so he is determined to have a preaching
establishment, where the female shall have full liberty to exercise
her talents in persuading sinners to fly to Christ; and, although,
as H. Bourne states, there never was formed any class or society
in Mr. Smith's kitchen, yet it formed an asylum for the camp
meeting fathers, and the revivalists, where they could worship God
in their own way.

CHAPTER XVIII.

GOOD RESULTS OF THE CAMP MEETINGS—THE WREKIN—W. CLOWES—J. BOURNE'S LABOURS —KINGSLEY — FARLEY — RAMSOR — TEAN — WOOTON—CAMP MEETING AT BUGLAWTON—MOW THIRD CAMP MEETING—RULES FOR HOLY LIVING—ATTENDS A CONFERENCE OF THE INDEPENDENT METHODISTS, AT MACCLESFIELD — A REMARKABLE DREAM — J. CRAWFOOT—WARRINGTON—P. PHILLIPS—A TRACT ON THE PREACHING OF WOMEN—AN IMPRESSION — HIS EXPULSION FROM THE METHODIST SOCIETY—REMARKS.

The Mow, Brown-edge, and Norton camp meetings were productive of much good ; for in addition to the salvation of many who sought the Lord and found him at these meetings, an effectual door was opened for the spread of gospel truths. The timidity and unwillingness of Hugh Bourne to be a preacher were partially swept away ; first, by a few remarks made by Mrs. Foden, at the forest of Delamere ; and secondly, by Dr. Johnson, at the Norton camp meeting ; and "by the good providence of God," he says, " I was like a new man, and was ready to preach the gospel whenever the Lord in his divine providence opened the way. Laskedge, bordering on Leek circuit, is but a few miles from Bemersley ; and at the Norton camp meeting, a man from that place asked me to come and preach at his house. I took it up, and a society was raised, and we got Leek Wesleyan circuit to take it in ; but as they could only supply it one Sunday a fortnight, I had to provide for the opposite Sundays, and in this I had to look for assistance from my brother, from Thomas Cotton, and from William Maxfield of Mow Cop."

Market Drayton, and other places in Shropshire, were another mission field in which Hugh Bourne was called to labour. In returning from one of the Shropshire excursions, he says :—

"*Wednesday, April 6th*, 1808.—I set out for Staffordshire. To oblige John W. I called at Knutton-heath, but it was too late to call a meeting; therefore, we prayed and appointed a meeting to be held in a fortnight. I had an odd feeling while going by the race-course; surely if any ground be accursed, this is. I called at Tunstall on William Clowes. He spoke of an assurance that he should obey God to all eternity, and of being every moment devoted or given up to God, and clean through the word spoken. William Clowes told me that they have sent from Leek for their rules and method of conducting the law-work for stopping Sabbath-breaking. I find great thankfulness to God for calling me in some degree to stand up in defence of this association. During this journey into Shropshire, I have grown much in grace, and have seen the openings of providence before me, and my labours have not been in vain. O Lord, make me always faithful ! "

Near Wellington, in Shropshire, there is a very high mountain, called the *Wrekin;* and understanding that for time out of mind it had been customary to hold a yearly revel on the top of the Wrekin, on the first Sunday in May, he says, " I and my brother went thither; and getting help, we held a camp meeting on the top of the Wrekin; and the Lord so bridled the revellers, that we had not much trouble from them. This was on Sunday, May 1st, 1808, and the effects of that camp meeting were great and lasting, and this opened our camp meeting course for the year 1808 : and on the Monday, I and my brother walked to Bemersley, a distance of more than thirty miles." In one of their religious excursions, Kingsley,* near Cheadle, in Staffordshire, about fifteen miles from Bemersley, was opened by Hugh Bourne's brother James, and a society raised, and this was joined to the Leek Wesleyan circuit. This place, Lask-edge, and Tean, were all opened early in 1808, by James Bourne. The brothers had to supply them once a fortnight; hence arose the necessity of preachers plans. These were written and supplied by Hugh Bourne to the camp meeting fathers, and others, who now regularly entered gratuitously the home mission field.

---

* There was much persecution at Kingsley; but this was stopped by the law. The persecutors were forgiven on paying expenses, and acknowledging their fault in the public papers.

Farley, a village near Alton Towers, was visited in the order of
providence. Hugh Bourne writes, "At the instance of Miss
Hannah Heaton of Farley, an appointment was made for
J. Bourne to preach at that village, on Sunday, March 20th, 1808,
but his constable duties interfering, I took it up. Through this
appointment I was called to preach at the village of Ramsor, on
Saturday evening, May 7th, 1808, and on the following Sunday;
and when at this place, I took down the names of six destitute
villages, and appointed to preach on Sunday, May 22nd, at
Wooton, a village about a mile and a half from Ramsor, and which
is usually called Wooton-under-Weaver. On Sunday, May 15th,
1808, we held a useful camp meeting at Buglawton, near
Congleton, in Cheshire; and here I first introduced reading as
an additional variety in the services. On Sunday, May 22nd,
1808, I and my brother held our first Wooton meeting. It was
in the open air, and was like a small camp meeting. On Sunday,
May 29th, 1808, I and my brother, Thomas Cotton, and a preacher
from Macclesfield, held the third Mow Cop camp meeting, and
all went on well; but none of my Wesleyan friends from either
Burslem or Tunstall came to assist: and this was the seventh
and last of the camp meetings while I was with the Wesleyans;
and I never knew of any member leaving the Wesleyans on
account of those seven camp meetings : so our hands were clean."

We find the following entry in his journal :—" Sunday, May
29th, 1808. Mow third camp meeting commenced at about nine
o'clock in the morning, and broke up between six and seven at
night. I erected a flag * a little before nine, and the people began
to assemble. We began with a prayer meeting, and then
E. Horthen spoke ; then prayer, and I spoke by impression from
2 Kings ii. 1, ' And it came to pass when the Lord would take
up Elijah into heaven by a whirlwind,' &c. Then we prayed, and
Cotton spoke ; then a prayer meeting, at the conclusion of which
we gave handbill rules for holy living, and then stopped for
dinner.† We had some opposition, and were forsaken by

* This was the anniversary of the first camp meeting ever held in
England; and Hugh Bourne and his coadjutors felt it their duty to cele-
brate it on Mow Cop.

† "A few weeks before this," says H. B. "I drew up rules for holy
living, and got them printed on a large and handsome handbill ; and at

Daniel Shubotham and others, but we had no want of labourers. Glory to God for ever! The Lord in tender mercy tempered the weather, so that it was neither too hot nor too cold; and the place under the mountain was exceedingly pleasant. Towards night a few drops of rain fell; but upon the whole it was the finest day for the purpose I ever saw. Thanks be to God for his mercy, through Jesus Christ. Amen. Before dinner was over, I began to read, and read a long time. I at first thought that I should immediately be exhausted; but I thought the Lord can give strength, and so it was, for as my strength failed, I was supplied with new strength. Glory be to God for ever. The power of God came down upon the congregation in the morning, and never left it all the day; so that the company was solemn. There was a very great company in the afternoon, and about three o'clock a very sharp fire; one was set at liberty, and others were in distress. And the power of God continued strong till the meeting broke up at night."

noon we gave away rather a large quantity, and apparently they were gladly received." We subjoin a copy of the rules, as they seem adapted for usefulness as well now as then. They are as follow:—" Rule 1st.— Endeavour to rise early in a morning, for this is more healthful. Spend some time in private prayer;—give yourself, with all your concerns, up to God; and, if it be possible, get the family together before going to work— pray with them and for them, and recommend them to God. 2.—While at work, lift up your heart to God; and, if possible, get a little time once or twice in a day to kneel in private before God. 3.—At night be sure to get the family together upon their knees:—pray with them and for them; and before going to bed, spend some time on your knees, and pour out your soul before God, and remember God is present. Psalm cxxxix. 4.—If you are able, read a chapter, or a part of a chapter, every day. Regard not the vain words of those who say, ' We have not time to serve the Lord.' You have time—you have all the time that comes; for when you live with a single eye to God, you serve him in all things, even in your bodily labour; for the Lord says, ' Six days shalt thou labour.' Therefore, ' Whether ye eat or drink, or whatsoever ye do, ye have a right to do all to the glory of God.' 1 Cor. x. 31. And you have a right to offer all upon your knees, a sacrifice to God, and he will accept you through Jesus Christ. 1 Peter ii. 5. 5.—If you are not born again, pray to God to show you the need of it, and he will show you your sins, and your lost state. This will bring godly sorrow and repentance. 2 Cor. vii. 10. Follow it. And when you feel your sins to be a burden, (Psalm xxxviii. 4,) and feel that you are condemned already, (John iii. 18,) and satan puts evil thoughts into your mind, pray for mercy and pardon in good matter, (John xiv. 21,) and Jesus Christ will manifest himself unto you, and pardon you. Isa. lv. 7.

The above is the simple entry in Hugh Bourne's journal, respecting the last of what he calls his Wesleyan camp meetings.
On Sunday, June 12th, 1808, by appointment he was at Macclesfield; it being the time of holding the Independent methodist
conference. He says, "they ordained Parker; and I found this
to be a very solemn ordinance. The controversy about women
ministering was brought forward, and I agreed to write an answer
to the propositions. I had a good time with them. O Lord
Jesus support me fully! Monday;—I spent some time with Dr.
Johnson; he earnestly tried to convert me to Quakerism, but
could not succeed. Saturday, June 18th, 1808; last night I
dreamed a remarkable dream. I thought there came a carriage
like a gig, with two horses, to fetch me to Warrington; and the
persons that were with it said, I must get up and start off to
Warrington immediately. I thought that I reasoned thus:—

You will then be born again, and have the witness of God. Rom. viii. 16.
And you will be happy,—'The love of God will be shed abroad in your
heart,' (Rom. v. 5,) and 'Christ will dwell in you.' Ephes. iii. 17. This is
glorious work, and thus your prayers will be gloriously answered; for if
they are not answered, you will lose all your labour. Like a beggar at a
door, praying for alms, if he gets nothing, his labour is lost: but God has
promised to answer, therefore, do not rest without it. 6.—Then, 'As ye
have received Christ Jesus the Lord, so walk ye in him,' (Col. ii. 6,) and
abound more and more. 7.—On the Sabbath, and attend
public worship as often as possible; and rest upon these words of God,
'Remember the Sabbath day to keep it holy.' Exod. xx. 8. This command was given in flaming fire, and a man was stoned for gathering sticks
on the Sabbath day, (Num. xv. 31—36,) and the Mighty God can no more
look upon iniquity now, (Hab. i. 12,) than he could at that time; therefore,
beware of buying or selling, (Neh. xiii. 15—22,) or of talking about
worldly buisness, (Isa. lviii. 13,) or of doing any work that may be
avoided, lest the Lord be angry, 'And ye be consumed from the way, when
his wrath is kindled but a little;' and to say you did it to oblige a master
or a parent, will make the flames of hell no colder, when you come there.
Be sure to shave, and clean the shoes before Sunday; and be at all times
as fearful of sin as you would of burning your finger off, for that will not be
so painful as hell. 8.—If the Lord call you to any public exercise, or to
assist in a Sunday school, he will give you wisdom and patience. 9.—Now
play the man, be strong, never mind being reproached for Christ. 1 Peter
iv. 14. 'If we suffer, we also shall reign with him: if we deny him, he
also will deny us.' 2 Tim. ii. 12. 'And that servant which knew his
Lord's will, and prepared not himself, neither did according to his will,
shall be beaten with many stripes.' Luke xii. 47."

They need not to have been at all this trouble and expense to bring a carriage ; for I was almost minded to go to the forest, and then I should have been sure to go to Warrington :—but I do not remember getting into the carriage."

" I arose early this morning, and despatched some work, and found myself very unwilling to go to the forest, or to Warrington, as I am very busy ; but as I had thought that my worldly business should not hinder me in religious exercises, when I could avoid it, and the dream rather moving me, I set off. I lost my way, and went four miles round, but came to James Crawfoot's in good time. The little peculiarities of James Crawfoot, with regard to certain passages of scripture, had on a former visit prejudiced my mind against him ; and had it not been for visiting my Warrington and Runcorn friends, I might have totally neglected him ; but on his allowing me to correct his improprieties, we hit together, and I certainly received some valuable information from him."

" For years I had been at times much exercised with conflicts of mind, conflicts which in many instances I could not account for ; but I was not aware of its being the case with others ; but on stating the matter to Mr. Miller, he said the case was the same with all he had talked with ; conflicts not brought on by unwatchfulness, nor from any failing they knew of. But the reason of this he could not tell. And others being exercised the same as myself, greatly encouraged me ; but still I wondered why we should be so exercised. To explain and illustrate this matter was a main point with J. Crawfoot. And when he had imparted information, he would say, " you must not take this because I have said it, but read the scriptures for yourself, and pray to God to open your understanding." I took the advice, read commentaries less, and the scriptures more, with prayer to God to open my mind, and give me understanding. His discourse was, that in the exercise of faith we made war against the enemy of souls, and must expect him to make war in return. If we wrestle (Ephes. vi. 12) we must expect the enemy to wrestle in return ; and if that could not be felt, it would be no wrestling. I had thought these conflicts were occasioned by a sinking in grace ; but he shewed that at times it was through a more powerful exertion of faith than usual, and that the consequent exercise of mind was the trial of faith (1 Peter i. 7), the travail in birth (Gal. iv. 19), the conflict (Col. ii. 1). That it was in general a proof that much had been done, an advance made on satan's kingdom. That without going, more or less, through such conflicts, we could not bring forward the work of God,—could not bring souls into liberty,—could not set on foot revivals; and that in such cases we must hold fast the beginning of our confidence, and, like Abraham, against hope, believe in hope, and press on to victory; press on till the cloud disperses, grace or power descends, and faith rests. I believe this view of the work is consistent with scripture and experience, and his imparting this information, caused me to think highly of the old man."

"*Monday, June 20th,* 1808.—I set off to Warrington,—a stranger among strangers. On the road, the Lord fulfilled his promise; he came to me as he once did aforetime, and I gave soul and body into his hands, and I entered into freedom with the Lord. When I came near to Warrington, I met a man who knew me; this I thought providential. He was one of the society, where I was going. He took me to John Mee's, and John Mee took me to Peter Phillips's. I consented to help to hold a meeting, though not to do it all. I spoke after him, with life and power, and it was a tender time. *Tuesday, 21st.*—I almost by impression, went on with remarks on the ministry of women. When I had gone through with it, I shewed it to Peter Phillips, and he requested that I would let him print it. I replied, it wanted correcting; so I corrected and enlarged it. *Wednesday, 22nd.*—I finished the tract about the ministry of women."

Subjoined, is a copy of the tract, which we cannot withhold from our readers :—

Remarks on the Ministry of Women.—In a conversation at a friend's house, this subject was agitated, and the written propositions of an absent friend were produced; and a person in company promised to write some remarks upon them, which gave rise to the following. [Published in 1808.]

REMARKS.

Dear Father Berrisford,—Agreeably to my promise, I shall endeavour to give you a few remarks on the subject of women's ministry: though I have not been accustomed to study this controversy for the following reasons, which have been established among a few of us.

1. If persons who exercise in the ministry are of good report, and the Lord owns their labours by turning sinners to righteousness, we do not think it our duty to endeavour to hinder them ; but we wish them success in the name of the Lord, without respect to persons.

2. We do not think it right to be the cause of any one's going to hell through a proud and fond desire of establishing our own (perhaps vain) opinions.

3. Instead of stopping to reason about various things, we find it best to be pressing on.

4. In general, instead of engaging in useless controversy, we find it more profitable to continue giving ourselves to God, and spending the time in prayer.

But my friends from time to time have spoken to me on this subject; and from their observations, and from other remarks, I shall endeavour to answer your friend's propositions and objections.

We find in Joel ii. 28: "And your sons and your daughters shall prophesy."

In order to enter more easily into the subject, we must first find out the precise meaning of the word prophesy : and on this head you will find full satisfaction in a sermon on the Christian Prophet and his work, by Adam Clarke, which may be had of the methodist preachers, price sixpence. It was first published in the magazine, for 1800. To this I will add the explanation given by Parkhurst, whose authority ranks very high, and it is as follows :—" NABA—to prophesy. It signifies not only to foretell future events, but also to speak, or utter something in an eminent and extraordinary manner. Thus the noun Nabi is first applied to Abraham, (Gen. xx. 7,) as being ' an interpreter of God's will, to whom he freely and familiarly revealed himself.' See Clarke's note ; and comp. Psalm cv. 15. And Aaron is ordained Moses' Nabi, prophet or spokesman, to Pharaoh. Exod. vii. 1, comp. ch. iv. 6. Nabi is also applied to the musicians or singers appointed by King David. 1 Chron. xxv. 1, 2, 3. So in the New Testament, the words propheteuo to prophesy, prophete-s a prophet, and propheteia prophesy, are applied to those, who, without foretelling things to come, preached the word of God. See 1 Cor. xiv. 3, 4, 5, 6, 24, 29, 32, 37. 1 Thess. v. 20. Yea, St. Paul calls a heathen poet prophete-s a prophet, Titus i. 12." See Parkhurst's Hebrew and English Lexicon.

We here see that a prophet was simply one who was employed in the service of God, and that whether as one that sung the praises of God, or one that preached, exhorted, or instructed the people ; and these last were said to preach the gospel. See Heb. iv. 2. 1 Peter iv. 6. Thus Abel, (Luke xi. 50, 51,) Abraham, Aaron, and others are called prophets, though it does not appear that they foretold future events : but as the knowledge of future events was given to those who were eminent in the service of God, the term prophet was, in a secondary sense, applied to them also. And in these later ages of the world, this secondary sense has been used as the primary one ; but on this head you will find satisfaction in A. Clarke's sermon.

I shall now endeavour to follow your friend's propositions. The first of which may be comprised in the following words :—" Is the preaching of women authorized by Jesus Christ ? "

Answer. I think it is. I think he authorized Miriam, (Micah vi. 4,) Deborah, Huldah, and perhaps many others not recorded ; and the gospel was preached in those days, (Heb. iv. 2,) and he is the same God now, and acts in the same way.

But, perhaps, you wish for an example when our Lord was upon earth. Well, besides the Virgin Mary and Elizabeth, you have Anna, the prophetess, who testified of Jesus in the temple ; and this I take to be strong preaching. Well, but you say, whom did he authorize personally? Ans. The woman of Samaria. I believe she was commissioned by the Holy Ghost to preach Jesus, and she did preach him with extraordinary success ; and he authorized her ministry, for he joined in with it, and acted accordingly.

But, perhaps, you want a personal commission,—very well, then you have Mary Magdalene. She was commissioned by an angel to preach, and then by Jesus Christ himself. It is said of Paul, in one place, that he preached Jesus and the resurrection,—so did Mary to the apostles themselves. Thus our Lord ordained her an apostle to the apostles, a preacher to the preachers, and an evangelist to the evangelists.

The second proposition may be stated thus:—"Was women's ministry countenanced by any of the apostles?"

Answer. Philip, the evangelist, had four daughters, virgins, that prophesied—preached. Acts xxi. 9. Secondly, Aquila and Priscilla took Apollos, and expounded to him the way of God. Acts xviii. 26. St. Paul says, "Help those women which laboured with me in the gospel." Phil. iv. 3. He there joins them with Clement and his other fellow-labourers. He also says, 1 Cor. xi. 5, "Every woman that prayeth or prophesieth with her head uncovered," &c. This is rather decisive. He here lays down rules and regulations for this very thing; and even if any woman who prayed or prophesied would not submit to rule, he did not say let her be stopped, but let her be shorn.

The third proposition is about historical documents, which I think is pretty well answered above. And in Acts, Phœbe is called a deaconess. Now a part of the office of deacons was preaching, as appears by the customs of the churches, and by the example of St. Stephen.

The fourth proposition wants scripture prophesy.

Answer. Joel ii. 28, 29. Acts ii. 17, 18.

The fifth proposition may be stated thus:—"Is not women's preaching interdicted by apostolic authority?" 1 Cor. xiv. 34. 1 Tim. ii. 11.

Answer. It is rather harsh to suppose that an apostle interdicted what had been the practice of the church of God in all ages, what had been personally sanctioned by our Lord himself, and what even the same apostle had just been establishing, by giving rules for it. 1 Cor. xi. 5, 6, 7. The question, then, is, "What are we to understand by these scriptures?" I shall not endeavour to give you on this any opinion as my own; for having never studied them very closely, I could not in conscience do it.

*But I am told that these speak of church discipline, and of establishing church authority; and truly, if women must ordain or set apart the men for the ministry, it would be usurping authority, for the greater would be blessed of the less.

I have heard it stated further, that he there says, "If they will learn any thing, let them ask their husbands at home." This they say settles the meaning, for he must be speaking of something that the husbands can inform them of. This well applies to discipline, but if it extends to preaching also, then all who have ungodly husbands are inevitably bound over to eternal damnation, because they are restricted from learning any thing from any but their husbands.

If also this must be stretched out so as to exclude women from teaching men religion, it would reach too far,—it would break the order of God,—it would interdict mothers from teaching their sons; and I believe that I owe my salvation, under God, in a great degree, to a pious mother.

Objection. 1.—I wish to consider prophesying as different to preaching.

Answer. 1.—Preaching Jesus and the resurrection is, in a degree, prophetic. 2.—Prophesying not only includes preaching, but also rises higher, and is greater; for it not only teaches the present generation, but all future generations.

Objection. 2.—But I wish to confine prophesying simply to foretelling future events, and not to be of use to the generation to whom it was delivered.

Answer. 1.—This is contrary to the meaning of the word both in Greek and Hebrew. 2.—It is contrary to plain matter of fact, even confining

* Since this was written, some friends have given me nearly the following information, viz.:—That they understood that it was the manner of the church at Corinth, and some other places, for one of the congregation to ask or require from the preacher an interpretation, or a further explanation upon what had been spoken, or to controvert what he thought wrong;—and that in the course of time, women also took this authority and freedom, and for this they were reproved by the apostle, and directed, if they did not fully understand what was delivered, to ask their husbands at home, for in this way he permitted not a woman to speak in the church. And the husband had more authority to ask questions, and to require interpretations.

ourselves to the ministry of women. See Judges iv. 5. 2 Kings xxii. 14. 2 Chron. xxxiv. 22. 1 Sam. ii. Luke ii. 38. John iv. 29. And Matt. xxviii. 1—9. 3.—This objection would carry things too far. It would be charging the Holy Ghost with neglect; for if he gave the prophecies only for the use of future generations, they must have been recorded, or else they were given in vain; and neither the prophecies of King Saul, nor of Philip's daughters are recorded.

Objection. 3.—St. Paul says to Timothy, " The same commit to faithful men."

Answer. If the word there used had been Anear, this objection might have had a shadow of an argument, for that word generally signifies a man as distinguished from a woman; but Pistois Anthropois might be literally translated faithful persons, for Anthropos is understood to be a name of the species without regard to sex. See Parkhurst on the word. Our Lord lays down another rule, " By their fruits ye shall know them." Now my own eyes have seen the labours of a woman owned in this way, and you have seen many instances wherein the Lord has set his seal to a woman's ministry, by converting sinners to himself. Now, would it not have been hard to have hindered these persons' salvation?

I had been many years in the methodist society, during which I frequently heard of Mrs. Fletcher's exercising the ministry, before I was favoured with an opportunity of sitting under it, and she had Mr. Wesley's approbation, as appears by his letter to her, and I never heard any person express his disapprobation of it. Now supposing her ministry had been stopped by arbitrary measures, what a loss that part of the country would have sustained.

I think all the objections that can be brought may be confined to this, that the woman is the weaker vessel. But this is so far from making against, that it is strongly in favour of it. See 1 Cor. i. 27. And as God chose the ministry of women under darker dispensations, it would be strange if they are incapable of ministering, on account of being weaker vessels, now the gospel shines with a brighter light.

Your servant and son in Christ,

H. B.

A Divine Impression.—We again cite the diary :—" On Thursday, June 23rd, 1808, I set off for home ; and on my way between Holmes Chapel and Congleton, it suddenly came to my mind that I should soon be put out of the old methodist society, and should be more useful out than in ; but having never heard a hint of the kind, being also a chapel trustee, and having expended scores and scores of pounds in promoting the interests of the society, and hundreds of members having been raised up out of the world, by means which the Lord had enabled me to set on foot; and feeling as if wedded to the society, I concluded it could not be, and put the thought from me, hoping it might not arise from a divine impression; but it returned until I found it difficult to walk the road; so, after a struggle, I gave up, and was instantly filled with joy unspeakable, and full of glory; and this enabled me to rest with the Lord, and made me thankful indeed. Perhaps the Lord gave me this notice to prevent the separation from being a trial too heavy for me. On arriving at home, I met the rumour of being likely to be soon put out. This caused me to be thankful to the Lord for having prepared my mind, and my course will be seen in the following extracts from my journal :—

" *Saturday, June 25th.*—I set off for Kingsley. Sunday, June 26th, I led the class. At noon we set off to Tean, and held a meeting out of doors; had a large congregation, and good, I believe, was done. We gave them ' Rules for Holy Living,' and appointed a meeting to be in a fortnight, in the forenoon. This was to give liberty to mission elsewhere. At night I stood up at Kingsley, and the Lord touched many hearts. Monday, 27th, I came home."

Expulsion from the Old Methodist Society.—" On Monday, June 27th, 1808, the circuit quarter-day meeting, held at Burslem, put me out of the old methodist society, without my being summoned to a hearing, or being officially informed of the charge, or charges, alleged against me. This was not upright. I was not a member of the quarter-day meeting; and as a private member of society, I might, if due cause had appeared, have been put out without quarter-day: but in addition to being a private member, I was a chapel trustee, which by rule entitled me to a hearing before expulsion; and in not being allowed this, I was wronged.

I was informed that Mr. Walker, the circuit steward, spoke for justice, saying, that the man ought not to be put out without having an opportunity to speak for himself; but to his words the meeting did not pay attention. Indeed, I had broken no rule or law of Wesleyan methodism, and to have had me face to face, might have brought the meeting into a dilemma."

Had the people assembled at that quarter-day meeting looked at both sides of the question, they might have seen that the Burslem circuit had had grievous sinkings, and did not rise out of the sinkings till the Lord caused Hugh Bourne to begin the mighty work at Harrisehead, and to lead it up to such a height that it raised the circuit up in power, and in particular raised Tunstall out of what one of their own historians calls "a creeping state." That he had spared no expense, but had built the prosperous Harrisehead chapel in a great measure at his own expense, and had spared no expense in other cases The Norton class-leader might have shewed that the Lord enabled Hugh Bourne to begin and raise up the work there, and that H. Bourne had put him in as leader. William Clowes might have said, that mighty work had raised up Kidsgrove, where he was the leader of the second class raised at that place, and which entitled him to a seat in that meeting.

"After all, I believe Mr. Riles was a good man; and as he has since gone the way of all flesh, I trust he died well, and now rests from his labours. What the effect would have been if the Lord had not prepared my mind I cannot say. But on June 28th, 1808, when the rumour reached me, I said, 'The Lord's will be done.' And I felt thankful that the Lord had prepared my mind for what otherwise might have given me a serious shock. I went over to Norton, and the leader informed me that I was put out, but observed that he wished things might have been as they were before. To this I made no reply; but having been out from home for several weeks, I paid up the arrears of class-money, that all might be clear. I originally met in class on Sunday mornings, at Ridgway, about half a mile from our house; but when a class was formed at Norton, about two miles from Bemersley, it met on Sunday mornings; and to strengthen it, I left the Ridgway class and joined the Norton one. I also bestowed

much expense and labour upon Norton; and after the chapel was
built, a second class was formed, to meet on Monday nights; and
Mr. Miller put in a leader who lived at a distance. This was
rather troublesome, as when he could not attend, I had to supply
his lack of service. But the Sunday morning leader took huge
offence at not being put to lead both the classes. The trouble
he made was great; and at length Mr. Riles put him to lead
both classes. But in his hands the second class soon failed, and
this caused me much grief; but I still continued to meet in the
Sunday morning class, although it was seriously inconvenient:
and more so, through the Lord having providentially led me out
in excursions,—to Lask-edge, about four miles; to Macclesfield,
in Cheshire, fourteen miles; Drayton, and Old Park, in Shropshire,
more than twenty miles; Runcorn, in Cheshire, more than thirty
miles; and Delamere forest, twenty-seven miles; Kingsley, twelve,
and Tean, several miles further; and Wooton, Ramsor, and
Lexhead, upwards of sixteen miles; Warrington, Rizley, and
other places in Lancashire, hard upon forty miles from Bemersley.
My time was so filled up in these excursions, besides camp
meetings, that on Sunday mornings I was seldom within reach of
Norton class; but when I was within reach, I attended the Sunday
morning class at Norton, except in one single instance, when I
attended the old class at Ridgway."

" Being in Mr. Piles's company, in regard to trustee business,
I remarked on his having put me out. He intimated something
about my having a tendency to setting up other places of worship.
Of course I was not conscious of such a tendency. He might, it
is true, have Mr. Smith's kitchen in his view; but he said, I
might come into the society again. The matter, however, went
no further, as he did not seem to like to talk of it, and I had
rested the matter with the Lord. After some time, Mr. Walker,
the circuit steward, came over to our house to ask me to join the
society again. I asked him whether he knew for what cause I
was put out. He paused a little, and then said, he understood
that it was for going to a camp meeting upon Mow. This was all
he said on the subject. And not being summoned to a hearing,
nor having received any official statement, it has so happened,
that to this day, May 24th, 1845, I have remained in the dark
respecting the real or pretended charge or charges on which they
secretly put me out of membership."

We cannot close this chapter without a retrospective glance at the objects that have recently crossed our path : but far be it from us (it is not our province) to censure the strange proceedings of the Burslem Wesleyan circuit's quarterly meeting, in excommunicating, in his absence, the father of the English camp meetings. " A constant watchfulness against all those prejudices that might warp the judgment aside from *truth*," would have prevented the intimate friends and companions of Hugh Bourne from taking part in his unrighteous expulsion from the Wesleyan society : but the enemy of truth caught them napping at the post of duty, and the influence of the preachers swayed the mind, and perverted the judgment of every man present, Mr. Walker, the circuit steward, excepted ; but to his honour be it spoken, that good man could not endure the thought, or participate with his brethren, in the act of condemning a man unheard. Our views on this subject may be at variance with those of others; but be this as it may, we fully believe that a divine and over-ruling providence had a hand in Hugh Bourne's expulsion, otherwise, the minds of so many good, pious, and useful men could not have been so prejudiced against him, as they were that day,—they could not have been so blind as to pervert judgment as they did. He had done them no wrong, broken no rule, violated no friendship, nor treacherously betrayed any christian brother. No ! reader, the fact cannot be controverted. Several preachers and leaders that were members of the quarterly meeting, and voted for his expulsion, were his confidents, and had sought the inmost circle of intimacy with him, when encamped beneath the banner of primitive and apostolic practice, in the open air, on the heights of Mow Cop : and he might truly have adopted the language of David, and have said to his Wesleyan brethren, " If ye be come peaceably unto me to help me, mine heart shall be knit unto you ; but if ye be come to betray me to mine enemies, seeing there is no wrong in my hands, the God of our fathers look thereon, and rebuke it." But how few were found in the quarterly meeting of a like spirit to Amasai, who was chief of the captains, and who, in answer to David's interrogations, said, " Thine are we, David, and on thy side, thou son of Jesse : peace, peace be unto thee, and peace be unto thine helpers ; for thy God helpeth thee."— 1 Chron. xii. 17, 18. And the brethren present at that meeting could not be ignorant of the help which the Lord had afforded Hugh

Bourne and his colleagues at the preceding camp meetings.   The
thing was not done in a corner, but before the face of heaven, and
in sight of the multitude under the broad canopy of a summer's
sky, and on the mountain top, for there the Lord displayed his
holy power in the salvation of many souls; yet for all this, they
voted the man of God out of their society, and inflicted the greatest
penalty it was in their power to pass upon him.   Let us, however,
leave the matter until that day when the secrets of all hearts shall
be laid open before the judgment-seat of Christ.

CHAPTER XIX.

TRIALS AND SUPPORT—COLLEAGUES IN THE WORK OF SOUL SAVING—THOMAS COTTON EXPELLED BY THE WESLEYANS — VARIOUS EXCURSIONS AND MISSIONARY LABOURS—A HARD DAY'S WORK—POINTS OF RESEMBLANCE TO THE PROCEEDINGS OF THE BROTHERS WESLEY—A JOURNEY TO LEEDS—HEARS W. DAWSON PREACH—WARRINGTON AND STOCKTON-HEATH —THE QUAKER METHODISTS—SOME CONVERTED UNDER HIS LABOURS— PREACHES ALONG THE HIGHWAY TO THE PASSENGERS—A WALKING SERMON —EARLY CLASSES AT RIZLEY AND RUNCORN—CAMP MEETING AT RAMSOR —MR. JOSEPH SALT BROUGHT IN—TEAN AND WOOTON—LASK-EDGE AND KINGSLEY — PROVIDENCE — BEGINS FAMILY WORSHIP IN HIS FATHER'S HOUSE — VISIT TO J. CRAWFOOT — A VIST TO THE SAME BY THE BIO-GRAPHER — SPIRITUAL SYMPATHY — A STRUGGLE AT THE HOUSE OF W. CLOWES.

"Hitherto," says Hugh Bourne, "I had reposed under the Wesleyan authorities, but that repose being removed, I was necessitated to have no other head upon earth but Christ, and I felt like a solitary being. I did not, however, lose respect to my old friends, although they laboured to set people against me: but I considered that if the Lord had anything for a person to do, he would open the way for him to do it; and the ten thousands of the gold of Ophir would not have induced me to attempt to make a split, and set up a party. My wish was to labour for the conversion of souls, and to have as little to do with management as I could. I allow, in raising the mighty work, the Lord, contrary to my inclination, had kept me in the front, and by his terrors, he had compelled me to take the lead or headship in the camp meeting course : but he had given me J. Bourne, M. Bayley, and T. Cotton, for colleagues. He had formed us in a company for the purposes of his divine wisdom: and shortly after my expulsion, T. Cotton was put out of the methodist society, as it was said, for not giving up preaching at camp meetings. But the company kept united; the Lord opened the way before them, and all attempts to stop them, by expulsions or otherwise, were like attempting to stop a river in its course. The decree of the Lord was gone forth to bring forward open-air worship and the converting work afresh; and every attempt to hedge up their way, or obstruct the course, appeared to have a contrary effect. In their labours, however, there was no seeking for ease, or conferring with flesh and blood. My journal says, 'Saturday, July 9th, 1808, I set off for Kingsley, and had a happy time just before I arrived.' And as I and my brother designed to visit a new place, I waited on the Lord for direction, while the divine impression was upon me, and believed it to be his will that we should visit Wooton."

" *Sunday, July 10th*, 1808.—My brother was to come to Tean with a horse. I was rather foot-sore, but I set off early for Wooton, seven miles, to appoint a meeting for half-past two; and to my surprise, I was told of its being nine or ten miles to Tean, and I was quite a stranger to the road, and very foot-sore; but, the Lord giving me strength, I forced my way, and reached before my brother had read his text. We then rode and ran by turns, and arrived at Wooton in due time; and this second Wooton meeting was extraordinary. The cause took root, and has been kept on to this day; and we took up Ramsor, and Lexhead with it, connecting the whole with Tean; and the Lord opened the hearts of Mr. J. Horrobin of Lexhead, and his wife, to take our preachers in, and the main home of the cause was at Lexhead for several years. After closing this important Wooton meeting, we set off home. The horse had travelled from our house to Tean, seventeen miles,—thence to Wooton, ten,—then back home, about eighteen more. This was one of the hardest days of labour I ever underwent; and if we had not had a horse, I could not have got home, but should have fainted on the road through excessive fatigue; but the Lord greatly owned that day's labour, as well as saving both man and beast."

" The second Mow Cop camp meeting was held to counteract the bad effects of the wake, or parish feast, and the wake was again approaching; and previous to that meeting, the Lord in his providence had caused a company to be formed: but when my expulsion from the methodist society had taken place, with other changes, we were obliged to be a distinct community,—and now our strength had to be tried. The question was, will the second Mow Cop camp meeting have an anniversary, or will it not? The company went on as before, and Sunday, July 17th, 1808,—the wake Sunday,—saw a camp meeting upon Mow Cop. No Burslem nor Tunstall man approached this camp meeting; but the Lord was present, and the meeting went off well. The camp meeting champions now appeared as a distinct company. The Lord opened the way before them; and the expulsions and other matters, had but little effect. The river kept flowing on. The camp meeting company acted somewhat as Messrs. John and Charles Wesley did before they began to form classes; and like those two eminent men, they did not at once take upon them the whole care of societies, and the fruits of their labours fell into other communities, chiefly into the Wesleyan Connexion. And as the Lord was evidently with them, others fell in; as, William Maxfield of Mow Cop, Thomas Knight of Harrisehead, and Thomas White of Runcorn,—all these were preachers,—and others gave assistance. And after a time, I had an admonition from heaven to bring my manual labours to a close, to give myself wholly up to the work of the ministry, and trust to the Lord for food and raiment. This was a trial to nature—a most severe trial. I used every means I could for weeks to avoid it, till at last I was made sensible if I persisted my natural life would be taken; and when I yielded up I received a peculiar blessing from God, a blessing I cannot forget. We had plenty of employment as preachers, and the world was open before us,—we could have had more if we could have done it. And our bond of union was the grace of God,—and our main zeal as a community was for the conversion of precious souls, and the increase and enlargement of the kingdom of Jesus Christ upon earth, and our hands were so pure from proselyting, that we were free to labour in other communities."

" *July 23rd*, 1808.—I was received with a hearty welcome at Warrington. O, my God, bless them a hundredfold, through Jesus Christ. Amen."

" *Thursday, July 28th*.—I set out for Leeds. I took this long journey rather at the instance of Warrington friends, in order

that the extracts to be added in the life of Abbott might be
perfected. I went through Knutsford, Altringham, Manchester,
Middleton, Rochdale, Halifax, and Bradford. There are many
villages, and many methodist chapels. When I first stepped into
Yorkshire, I kneeled down and prayed, and I found that the
Lord would be with me in Yorkshire. Glory be to thy name,
O Lord."

"*Friday, July 29th.*—A little before noon I arrived at Leeds;
my feet were very sore."

"*Sunday, July 31st.*—I heard Dawson, a farmer, preach; but
such a preacher I scarcely ever heard. A man of great abilities,
and great simplicity, and full of life and power. I thought myself fully paid for my journey to Leeds, had it been only to hear
this man."

"*Tuesday, August 2nd.*—I set off from Leeds by the coach to
Manchester, which cost me seven shillings; for my feet being
sore, and all things considered, I thought it to be the cheapest
way. I started with a methodist coachman. From Manchester
I walked eighteen miles to Warrington the same day, and then
went to Stockton-heath, Dr. Johnson being there to hold a
meeting."

Hugh Bourne always spoke as having, for this peculiar people
at Warrington, and Stockton-heath, the greatest respect, and
highest esteem. Forty years after this visit, he writes:—" I
think it was on my second visit to Warrington that the Lord
granted me peculiar success in the Quaker methodist chapel, in
that town. The afterwards eminent Mrs. Richardson was induced
to set out for heaven under my ministry. She was well to do in
the world, and became a mother in Israel among the people.
She soon became a preacheress, and laboured in the ministry many
years. She was a hospitable, eminent member among the Quaker
methodists, and the Lord took her to himself in the year 1848.
Another Quaker methodist's house was blessed to me in an
abundant manner. This was the house of Mr. Thomas Eaton
of Stockton-quay, customarily called London-bridge. I may bless
God that he ever caused me to set my foot in that house. Mr.

and Mrs. Eaton have both finished their course; and in the printed memoir of Mrs. Eaton, it is stated, that her soul was set at liberty in a conversation between herself and me; and that conversion I well remember."

"London-bridge, so called, is two miles from Warrington; and without attending to the order of time, I shall take liberty here to state a circumstance which took place when the Government was first raising the supplementary militia. A large number of them were learning their exercise near Warrington; and on the Sunday afternoon, the lane between London-bridge and Warrington was, comparatively speaking, filled with them. I had that afternoon preached at the Quaker methodist chapel, near London-bridge, and was going down with Mr. and Mrs. Eaton, and others, having to preach at night in their chapel at Warrington: so the road, having in it such an abundance of people, I began to preach as we walked, and preached all the way down, till we reached Latchford, near Warrington. I perhaps preached for a mile and a half; and this was the third course of processioning with which I was acquainted. The first was a walking prayer meeting, among the Stockport revivalists, about the year 1804. The second was the Harrisehead methodists singing on their way to a Burslem lovefeast. The third was this preaching procession of mine in 1808." Here, then, is the true origin of praying, singing, and preaching processions in the Primitive Methodist Connexion, which have been carried out frequently on a large scale, and with powerful effects and success.

Runcorn, in Cheshire, and Rizley, in Lancashire, were at no great distance from Warrington, and claimed a share of Hugh Bourne's labours in 1808. He says, "Thomas White of Runcorn, in Cheshire, was an Independent preacher, and had a small society; and he united with us, and camp meetings were held on Runcorn hill. The society at Rizley, in Lancashire, were an independent people, mainly raised up by Lorenzo Dow; and John Webb was the class-leader, and these determinately united with us: so we had classes in the year 1808, but not of our own raising. After this, Thomas Knight, who might have been termed a converting preacher, pressed in among us. He dwelt in Cheshire, in the year 1808, but he removed into Staffordshire: so we were

a company of six preachers, and had many pious, praying
labourers. For a time we benefited other communities, yet our
own settled places increased. In the Bemersley and Mow Cop
direction, we laboured at Gratton, Gillow-heath, Congleton-edge,
and Brown-edge. In another direction were Tean, Wooton,
Ramsor, and Cauldon-lowe; and other places kept opening."

Mr. Wesley began with labourings without any pre-conceived
plan, and he went on a length of time without forming classes, or
raising up class-leaders; and the Lord led Hugh Bourne and his
colleagues in a similar way. He says, "The Lord in a miraculous
way sent us to Wooton. At Lexhead, near Ramsor, about a mile
and a half from Wooton, the Wesleyans had a small society; and
if we had hastily formed a class at Wooton, it might have caused
a trouble; but Lexhead being inconvenient to the Wesleyans, they
left, and by the blessing of God, Wooton, Ramsor, and Lexhead,
all united in harmony. On my way to Ramsor, on Saturday,
August 20th, 1808, I planned out a camp meeting to be held on
Ramsor common; and at Ramsor, without my speaking of it,
Francis Horrobin proposed the same. I thought this providential,
and gave out the meeting to be on Sunday, September 4th, 1808.
And on my return, I summoned my three camp meeting colleagues,—James Bourne, Matthias Bayley, and Thomas Cotton, and
we were all there that day, besides some pious, praying labourers,
who wished to attend. J. H., a collier, from the neighbourhood
of Mow Cop, and my friend William Clowes of Tunstall, accompanied me to this camp meeting. We were amidst a rainy season,
but the Lord in his loving-kindness gave us fine weather. Thomas
Cotton in particular, had an extraordinary time in preaching; but
the great force of this camp meeting was in the praying services.
The Lord crowned these with his glorious presence."

"*Sunday, September 18th*, 1808.—I preached at Lask-edge,
Gratton, and Gillow-heath. I got a new commission at Gillow-
heath. My brother James provided two saddle-horses for himself
and Cotton, and they were at Tean and Wooton. Cotton brought
word that nearly forty started for heaven at the camp meeting,
and there is a great desire for another. Mr. Joseph Salt, a
respectable farmer, of Wooton, was fully brought to God under
Thomas Cotton's ministry. Before this, Mr. Salt had been

awakened by means of a pious young female. Our Wooton
people met in the Lexhead and Ramsor class; but when it was
judged proper to have a class at Wooton, Mr. J. Salt was made
leader, and Mrs. Salt was a mother in Israel."

"*Wednesday, September* 21*st*.—One of the Harrisehead colliers,
who was at the Ramsor first camp meeting, when he heard of the
good done at that meeting, pressed me to have another, which
induced me to write to Ramsor, and appoint a second meeting, to
be held October 9th, 1808. My brother James provided horses
at his own expense for both the Ramsor camp meetings. It must,
however, be noticed, that this meeting was held in a field belonging to Mr. James Horrobin of Lexhead, near Ramsor. The
Lord favoured us with fine weather at this meeting also; and I
was induced to believe that the Lord was about to give a powerful
call to the people all about this country; and subsequent events
have proved that my faith that day was of the operation of the
Spirit of God. I had had but little faith about this camp meeting, but when I received a letter, informing me that a meeting was
appointed for Saturday night, I felt that the Lord had something
for me to do there. At the camp meeting, there was good
attention all day, and good decorum; but in the afternoon, some
on the other side of a hedge were rather troublesome The
meeting broke up about five o'clock, and we went home riding by
turns. I believe much seed sown at this meeting will take root.
O my God, water it!"

The camp meeting services commenced for that year on the
Wrekin, in Shropshire, on Sunday, May 1st, 1808, and were
concluded October 9th, 1808. At Lexhead, near Ramsor, in
North Staffordshire, Hugh Bourne devoted the following week
chiefly to studying Greek. He says:—"I have been now for
some time very much engaged in the Greek. This week I read
much in the Greek Testament. I have been much assisted in
the languages through prayer. I believe the Lord requires at my
hands to learn the Greek and Hebrew."

"*Saturday, October* 15*th*, 1808.—I set off to Kingsley in order
to go to Tean and Wooton. Sunday, 16th, I took my stand at
Tean, in the usual place, and soon had a congregation. I spoke

in faith, and had a good time.   I then inquired among the people,
and found that a few were desirous to save their souls.   I took
down six names, and got a house to preach in when the weather
is bad, and also to meet the class in.   O my Lord, unite them
together, and strengthen them, through Jesus Christ.   Amen.
I feel myself to be growing in grace,—the Lord's power is con
tinually with me since I have been put out of society.   At Wooton
we got into Phœbe Finney's waggon-house,—there were many
people, and it hailed and rained.   F. Draycott was there; we
both spoke, and it was a good time.   I believe there will yet be a
people raised up at Wooton."

At Lask-edge and Kingsley societies had already been formed,
and now we find Hugh Bourne raising a class at Tean; and
although he and his colleagues, as far as open-air worship, and
turning sinners from darkness to light were concerned, were men
of themselves, acknowledging no head upon earth but Christ, they
as yet do not appear to have had any notion or design of raising
classes for their own immediate benefit, or any wish to take on
their own shoulders the care and management of a separate connexion, otherwise they would have gathered the forty souls turned
from sin to holiness at the first Ramsor camp meeting, and
formed them at once into a distinct church, apart from all other
communities; and it is further evident to us, if such had been
the design of Hugh Bourne, he never would have given the newly-
raised society at Tean to his old friends the Wesleyans, as he
did on this occasion.   At the time of raising the Tean and
other classes, he had received no intimation of divine assistance
in the superintendence and management of societies, apart
from Wesleyan rule and discipline, without which no earthly
power or persuasion could have induced him to take one step
towards the formation of a separate community: for he was a
firm believer in that Providence which has respect to the being
and welfare of every man, woman, and child, but is more
especially manifest in its divine care over christian churches or
societies.

Had Hugh Bourne acted precipitately in forming separate
classes, or endeavoured to make a secession when the Wesleyans
expelled him, we are satisfied the Primitive Methodist Connexion

would not have been permanently founded, or have attained to its present numerical position. His various movements through life, and especially the solicitous parental interest he took in the infant community, then rising into notice, prove that he acted with great cautiousness and circumspection, with prudent care following the openings of divine providence; for he was persuaded in his own mind, that,

> " Eternal Providence exceeding thought,—
> Where none appears, can make herself a way."

" *Wednesday, 19th*," he says, " I was at Harrisehead prayer meeting, and had an extraordinary time. Before this meeting I saw Thomas Knight, and he engaged me to go with him and T. Cotton to Congleton Moss, on Sunday next. I told several of the revival that is now springing up at Ramsor and the neighbourhood thereabout, and asked what other way that revival could have been set on foot; and in general they concluded that it could not well at this time have been set on foot any other way but by the camp meetings.   Friday, 21st, I was at a meeting at J. Smith's, Tunstall,—some are going on well, others are not."

On the following Sunday, he furnished the Bradley-green class with a library, and met his friend Cotton at Congleton, and they then joined Thomas Knight at Cloud, where they held a powerful meeting, and he engaged to write instructions for Hannah Goodwin;—a young girl of whom he said, "she is minded to follow Ann Cutler's steps, and I think she will succeed."

Monday, October 24th, 1808, he tells us, they began family prayer for the first time in his father's kitchen; and then adds, " My father is so violent a man that we have neglected it before." Prior to this they had to hide in secret places from the rage and violence of the father's wrath, when the mother and sons wished to unite in prayer at the domestic altar. He goes on to say :— " Friday, 28, I set out for the Cloud, to Matthew Goodwin's, and read over the directions to Hannah Goodwin. They were new and strange to her. O my God teach her wisdom in the inward parts. Saturday, 29, I thought that Hannah seemed a little sore with being reproved ; she is a precious soul, but she must endure.

O my God make her firm.   I then set out for Warrington, and
had a pretty good journey.—I met with a soldier going to Scotland, to Ayrshire, and by him I sent some of Ann Cutler's life to
Scotland.   O God follow them with thy blessing."

At this period of his eventful life, Hugh Bourne must have
expended a considerable sum of money in printing.   His Scripture Catechism, Rules for Holy Living, Ministry of Women,
Advice to Young Women, and other tracts, he had printed by
thousands, for the express purpose of giving away at camp meetings; and he himself, when travelling from place to place on
errands of mercy, distributed these silent harbingers; and we
make no doubt they were blessed to many a soul inquiring after
the truth as it is in Jesus.   On this journey to Warrington he
laboured with success from the Sunday until the Wednesday following; and then set out to the forest of Delamere, where he the
same evening led the class, and was particularly drawn out to
pray for the Holy Ghost to come upon that church; and then
tarried for the night at James Crawfoot's.   We are induced to give
a short extract from his journal, which to us is very remarkable.
He says:—

"*Thursday, November 3rd,* 1808.—I sat with Crawfoot and
others; they were talking, and I breathed my soul to God for the
Holy Ghost to come upon that church.   I turned my head and
J. Crawfoot was looking at me,—his face shone, I could not bear
it, but was near fainting away.   I felt as if my inside were rising
out of me and going to God.   My soul breathed 'Lord Jesus receive my spirit;' but I did not go down; nevertheless the Lord
made great discoveries to me; and I felt resolute to feel after
this thing; O Lord grant it to me for thy name's sake!"

The following Sabbath, November 6th, he laboured among the
Independent methodists at Macclesfield; and on the Monday he
returned home, visiting and praying with several friends by the
way.   Tuesday, 8th, he went by appointment to Bosley; and remarks, "I was in the keen cutting power, and the Lord went
with me; I had a great service at Bosley.   I had much talk
about the ministry with William Krinks, who is coming out to
preach.   Monday, 9th, as I came away, a great travail came upon

me for brother Krinks. I thought I should have fainted; I lay down by the road; I believe the Lord will deliver him. I called and we had a prayer meeting at M. Goodwin's. Thursday, 10th, I was at Tunstall; Mr. Button preached. We then had a prayer meeting at Wm. Clowes's—a good time; I had much talk with Clowes, and we purposed to go to the forest of Delamere—I on Saturday, and he on Monday next. Saturday, 12, morning; I rose early, prayed, and read Revelations, and Hebrews. I then set off to the forest; I called on Cotton about going to Tean and Wooton. I believe the Lord will be mightily with him. I also sent off to brother Krinks a whole sheet, written on all sides, which I wrote chiefly yesterday; I was happy while writing. I then came to the forest; James Crawfoot had gone to Macclesfield, and had not come home again. The Lord's will be done. J. C. came in a little time, and we fell into conversation. The Lord opened my heart, and his speech dropped upon me."

The Sabbath he spent in worship, chiefly at the chapel, with his forest friends; and, he observes, "I found myself more in the light than ever." He further writes :—" Monday, 14, Wm. Clowes came about noon, and we fell into talk; my heart was opened, and the word seemed to soak into me like rain. I attended to J. Crawfoot's discourse till Thursday morning : when he spoke, that line in ' Parnel's Hermit ' was constantly in my mind—

'Surprise in secret chains his words suspends.'

Just so was my attention chained. He has seen many miracles. He also instructed me in the ministry, and in the labouring spirit. O God make me faithful. Thursday, we left the forest; I stayed at Kidsgrove all night, being taken ill, and was at the meeting, where I found that I had a message."

Perhaps some of our readers may think it strange that Hugh Bourne and William Clowes should so frequently seek advice and counsel from the old man of the forest; to such we would say—

" In such green palaces the first kings reigned,
Slept in their shades, and angels entertained ;
With such old *counsellors* they did advise,
And in their sacred groves grew wise."

Besides, how comely is the wisdom of old men, and the understanding and counsel of men of honour, holiness, and good sense.
The holy counsel and wise instructions given by James Crawfoot
to Hugh Bourne and his friend Clowes, were essential and beneficial to them, both as it respects the mystery of faith, the doctrine of a present salvation, and the deep things of God. We
once enjoyed the favour of an interview with old James Crawfoot,
many years after the time above referred to;—we found him in
all his native simplicity,—unpolished by learning and refinement.
In our first conversation we thought him strangely odd and un-
couth in argument on the subject we were discussing; yet his
words were clothed with such an air of dignity and patriarchal
authority, that our minds were affected with awe and reverence
for the venerable and holy man, especially as we reflected that he
had done our fathers so much good in the early days of primitive
methodism. And we do not wonder at Hugh Bourne's saying,
" his word soaked into me like rain." There was a peculiar unction
accompanying his conversation-preaching ; and he was well instructed in the mystic and obscure parts of the holy scriptures ;
and from this *treasury* he brought things new and old, and set
them before us in a light we had never before seen them in. We were
anxious to learn from him his views on the most effectual method of
winning souls to Christ ; and, in our over hasty zeal to come at
them, we more than once were made to feel the lash of reproof,
and at the same time we received " *a horn full of good news ;* "—
the best instruction on the work of the ministry. We spent a
night and a day with him, and then returned to our labour, much
benefited and pleased with our visit.

We shall conclude this chapter and the year 1808, with a few
extracts from the diary of Hugh Bourne, which are as follow:—

" *Wednesday, December 7th*, 1808.—I begin to write again ; and
as some important things have passed, I shall write rather in the
historical way."

" *Saturday, November 26th.*—I started to go to Ramsor, and
made an appointment at Brown-edge as I went. I called at
Cheddleton, but after awhile, going by the navigation side, it came
into my mind to go to Kingsley. The church at Kingsley is in a

flourishing state. Mrs. Sargent is more convinced of sin. I believe she will now get on better in religion; self seems to be giving way. O Lord, quite strip her! The work has increased in the parish, though not in the village, and they have begun at Cheadle."

"*Sunday, November* 27*th.*—There had been much rain, and the waters were out. I went to Tean; the people are low, but I have good hope of them. I then started to Wooton, and at Alton cotton mill I was obliged to go round because of the flood. While going round, power came on me from H. G., though above twenty miles off. I then knew not how it was, but thought she was praying for me; but the truth was, she then received my letter, and rejected the testimony, and rejected the Lord's messenger, and hereby rejected the Lord himself; and all her power came upon me, and she was stripped as bare as a blasted oak in a forest, and quite fell away."

"*Sunday, December* 4*th.*—I had a great manifestation. I saw friends and all in God. I went to Bradley-green, and purposed, if J. H. required me, to lead the class. I must bear a testimony. He gave me the book,—the Lord was with me, and I bore the testimony. J. H. was displeased, as he was turned against me. In prayer after, I had a manifestation of the Trinity. I had now a greater blessing than I ever before had. After meeting, J. H. took me to task; but the Lord rebuked him, and stood by me. I spent much time in prayer as I went to Harrisehead. A. Lees preached. The Lord shewed me the judgment, and that I should have a reward for standing in the testimony. My heart shouted within me. I had a greater blessing now than ever. At night I was at T. Cotton's house. He preached,—a flat time. I then came back to Daniel Shubotham's, as he had requested me. They had incensed him against me. I stated every point to him, and the Lord enabled him to strengthen my hands. He told me that old James Selby informed him that he was in the habit of praying for a woman, and he saw something in her conduct that was wrong, and told her. She rejected him, and at the next meeting all her power came upon him. She was stripped, and fell away; but after a time was restored again. This shewed me what last Sunday's work was. Monday I spent in prayer and sorrow. I had a most uncommon time at Harrisehead class."

"*Tuesday, December 6th.*—I was with W. Clowes at Kidsgrove class. I led it; we had a good time, and I got through in faith for H. G., T. K. and his wife. I had spent nearly the whole day in sorrow for them, and had been much on my knees."

"*Wednesday, November 30th.*—I filled up the appointment at Brown-edge, with great liberty and enlargement of heart, but was hard tempted to pride."

"*Thursday, December 22.*—I was at Tunstall. Mr. Edmondson preached. I then went to a meeting at William Clowes's. A young man got his heart washed. I remained conversing with W. Clowes. He asked me about J.'s wife at R., who, I believe, is bodily possessed. We prayed, and he was drawn to pray for her, and her state was laid upon him. He had a dreadful struggle. My recollection was taken away. When I recovered, I was some time before I could tell what he was praying for. His wife also was struck with a temptation that he was going mad: he was tempted nearly the same. A backslider's state, that of a person residing in the house with them, was laid upon him; however, he conquered. I was glad he had had this pinch, for he before scarcely knew how to sympathise with a person of a sorrowful spirit."

"*Tuesday, December 27th.*—It is now very edifying to me to read letters on full sanctification. I grow more and more spiritual every day. O Lord, fill me with thy love and thy glory, and guide my steps in all things, through Jesus Christ. Amen."

"*Thursday, December 29th.*—I had a good time at Tunstall chapel. At the prayer meeting I had an uncommon time. It seemed as if Jesus Christ embraced me in his arms. After this he seemed to move to the church at Cloud, and he there sat as he is represented in Isaiah's vision; and he seemed to put his arms round me, and say that I should reign with him. O Lord, let thy will be done! But I felt unutterable things. O Lord, fill my soul and bless me! I have lately laboured much in the closet, and it is most joyful to me, it is always a feast."

"*Saturday, December 31st.*—I set off with W. Clowes to Delamere forest. We went to the watch-night, and prayed the old year out."

CHAPTER XX.

LABOURS OF H. BOURNE AND W. CLOWES IN THE EARLY PART OF 1809—
SYMPATHY OF SOUL IN PRAYER—A TRAVAIL—EXPERIENCING DEEP BAP-
TISMS — UNION WITH W. CLOWES — DEVELOPING OF THE GERM OF
PRIMITIVE METHODISM—SERVICE OF SONG—EARLY HYMNS—W. ALCOCK
— EXCURSIONS — T. KNIGHT—A SPIRITUAL LETTER — SET UPON IN
KINGSLEY—HARSHNESS—VISIT TO THE PRINCIPALITY—VISITS TO BUD-
WORTH AND STABLEFORD MILL—B. HOWEL—REMARKS OF H. PHILLIPS
ABOUT L. DOW — VARIOUS JOURNAL EXTRACTS — REMARKS ON H. B.'S
HABITS—A LETTER FROM MR. STEELE OF CONGLETON.

Hugh Bourne and his friend Clowes commenced the labours of
the new year with their forest friends. We find the following
entry in Hugh Bourne's journal :—

"*Sunday, January 1st*, 1809. — By the tender mercy of
Almighty God we are preserved, and brought to the beginning of
another year. Clowes and I went with James Crawfoot to Norley
chapel. At night we had a stirring time at Crawfoot's house,—
Hannah Dickinson got into liberty ; and Nancy Hassel once more
got into full liberty at the forest chapel."

Monday and Tuesday H. Bourne and W. Clowes were both
lame at J. Crawfoot's, through their long walk to the forest
on the Saturday. On the Wednesday they turned out,
visited and laboured with success at different places in the
neighbourhood until the following Monday, when they returned
into Staffordshire. The following is an extract from H. B.'s
journal :—

"*Monday, 9th.* — Being at prayer, the power settled on
two women, but we were in haste to be gone. When we were

coming past Winsford, I heard something roll before the throne
like thunder. I was solemn, and wondered, till Clowes said,
' Nancy is praying for us.' I was near falling down. After we
got past Sandbach, Clowes said, ' Nancy is praying for us again.'
I was brought into a great agony; the travail was long and
grievous, and affected my eyes, and brought a pain into my face.
But I wrestled on till we were washed and clothed. Glory be to
Jehovah! This cleared up more and more till I parted with
Clowes; and while coming to and by Lane-ends (on the Staffordshire side of Mow Cop), I plainly saw the clothes, &c., and the
scripture was on my mind, ' These have come out of great tribulation, and have washed their robes and made them white in the
blood of the Lamb,' &c. I did not before know that this belonged
to the church upon earth. I had now power over the unclean
spirits, and was sensible that my face did shine."

"*Wednesday, 11th.*—I was drawn to go to Tunstall, and was at
James Steele's class: they are very low indeed,—I was surprised.
I stayed all night with W. Clowes, and in the morning got up
under an impression that N. A. was praying for me. I kneeled
several hours, and was led into the visions of God; so the dream
came through, though not as I expected : I was much humbled.
O Lord, fulfil the whole, that I may be useful in thy church,
through Jesus Christ. Amen."

" *Friday, January 13th.*—Clowes and old Bettesworth were at
our house to go to Ramsor. I was much drawn out in family
prayer."

" *Saturday, 14th.*—We set off to Ramsor, and held a meeting."

" *Sunday, 15th.*—I and Clowes went to pray with Jackson's
wife, but did not fully succeed in bringing the woman into
liberty. Old Bettesworth preached at Wooton and Ramsor, and
I and Clowes were hearers, and assisted in the praying services."

" *Monday, 16th.*—Clowes and I visited from house to house
at Wooton, and talked and prayed with the families. I was
stripped with hard labouring, but was clothed at night while at
closet-prayer."

" *Tuesday*, 17*th*.—We returned, visiting and praying with several families, as we travelled homeward."

" *Saturday*, 21*st*.—I set off with Clowes to Macclesfield, where we were well received, and remained till Monday."

" *Sunday*, 22*nd*.—We were praying at Mr. Berrisford's, and Clowes touched me with his hand, and power came from him, and it was a great blessing. I rejoice that he has the gift of laying on of hands. Peter Phillips and Mary Dunnel preached. Robert Heathcote is a man of deep experience. I had great union with him. O Lord, strengthen him and me! "

" *Tuesday*, 31*st*.—I was at Tunstall; there is a prospect of a revival; and Clowes is appointed to lead a class there. I was with him there,—it was a lively time."

We have now given a brief outline of the labours of H. Bourne and his friend W. Clowes, during the first month of the year 1809. We think the reader cannot but draw with ourselves this conclusion, viz.:—that there existed at this time between these two noble-minded men, a union and holy fellowship rarely to be met with among professing christians. It is true there had been a difference of opinion on camp meetings and open-air worship, but this in no wise affected the high tone of feeling which they bore to each other; for we find them frequently side by side in their excursions to the forest and elsewhere; and we believe H. Bourne thought there was scarcely such a man on the face of the earth as W. Clowes, at that time, for faith, holy zeal, and success with the Lord at the throne of grace.

" *Sunday, February 5th*, 1809," he says, " I went with Clowes and Nixon to Lawton-wich. We visited from house to house, and were at the preaching at the Wich in the afternoon. At night we called at Kidsgrove, and were at Tunstall at the preaching. It was an extraordinary meeting at Clowes's house after service in the chapel. Wednesday, 8th, I kept the national fast. Sunday, 12th, I spent at Tunstall,—I had a great deal of exercise. The revival seems to be coming forward,—the new converts are very steadfast. Monday, 13th, having stayed all night with Clowes, we had a grand time in reading the scriptures and at prayer this morning. Tuesday, 14th, I was at Clowes's class. Two were set at liberty, and there were many seekers. It was a time of wrestling and labouring. Wednesday, 15th, was a rainy day, and we went to fall trees. I had an opportunity of praying, and had a good time. I saw that faith was mighty."

Notwithstanding Hugh Bourne's expulsion, there was no open hostility between the camp meeting community and several of the Wesleyans, his old friends,—they laboured and communed together as brethren should do. On camp meetings and open-air worship they could agree to differ; for on the fundamental doctrine of a free, full, and present salvation, there was a mutuality of sentiment. They thought that their meeting together, and accompanying one another to the house of God, should make the bond of their love indissoluble, and tie them in a league of inviolable amity and lasting friendship. At this time "the little cloud" which first arose upon Mow hill was widely spreading over the moral hemisphere, and there was a "sound of abundance of rain." The great revival of Primitive Methodism, in the camp meeting community, was diffusing new life and animation, and was coming into more general and public notice. The little company, or camp meeting community, was now evidently *founded;* and the object of its first formation was daily more and more developing before the public mind.

THE SERVICE OF SONG.

In the midst of labour and toil in the field of gospel enterprise, Hugh Bourne registered in his memory the general necessities of the infant community : and among other things he turned his attention to the service of song. In this important part of religious worship, he saw and felt among his own people a general want. The sublime and lofty strains of Watts and Wesley were considered to be generally above the capacity of the poor outcasts, whose spiritual interests he and his brethren laboured to promote; and their books were too often above the reach of the poor people's pockets. To meet the case, he made a selection of hymns and spiritual songs, and published and sold them to the people at a low price; and we have great pleasure in presenting to the reader here, a copy of the title-page of the first Hymn Book printed for the use of the Primitive Methodist Connexion. The size was 24's.

"A general collection of Hymns and Spritual Songs, for Camp Meetings and Revivals, selected by Hugh Bourne. Newcastle: printed at the office of C. Chester. 1809."

This collection of hymns went through many editions, and became the book of the masses, giving a melody to open-air worship which raised up the hearts of thousands, and sweetened the affections of the common people toward their God and Saviour Jesus Christ. Here we find specimens of genuine poetic simplicity, which, in our judgment, are not surpassed in the English language; as, "The sinner's alarm," "The invitation," "The good old way," "The dying pilgrim," "The scriptures are fulfilling," "Blow ye the trumpet," and others; and these were soon the admiration of numbers of the commonalty. The rich and simple melody of these hymns acted on the public mind as if by magnetism! Hence, to the hymns and singing has been attributed by some the great accession of hearers and members to the camp meeting community: and we ourselves are persuaded that the service of song played no mean part among the means made use of by the Lord, to induce men to hear the word, and cleave in with the overtures of mercy then offered; and as long as the spirit and power of Primitive Methodism shall exist, the original revival hymn-book will be recollected with admiration and gratitude. But we now proceed with H. Bourne's journal :—

"*Saturday, February 18th,*" he says, "I set out for Kingsley: much persecution, but eight new converts have joined the class. I stayed all night at Ramsor; and had with me some camp meeting and revival hymn-books, which I have got printed in a cheap form."

"*Sunday, 19th.*—I stood up at Tean; they seem to be doing well. I also spoke out of doors at Wooton, there being a large congregation: there are about six at Wooton who wish to join in a class. At Ramsor I spoke of the priestly office, and the labourers Since we began in this country, last May, there have been about thirty brought forward."

" *Monday, 20th.*—I called on William Alcock, at Latheridge, who greatly wanted to see me. I went with him to Leek. The revival is not deep at present, but it spreads. I stayed all night at Latheridge."

H. Bourne now commenced a friendship with this young man, which was continued, with mutual sincerity, until the death of the former.

Saturday, 25th, he set off for the forest, and with James Crawfoot, laboured in that neighbourhood till the Saturday following, when he returned home. He says :—

" *Sunday, March 4th.*—Morning at Ridgway class; afternoon at Lask-edge. I had a heavy travail for that church. At night I was at Great Chell; Clowes preached; I prayed the power upon him with all my might. I went with him to Tunstall, and stayed all night, and all the next day."

" *Monday, 5th.*—We spent the day in reading and prayer ; such a day for growing in grace I never before experienced. At night I went with him and others to Kidsgrove class ;—a girl was saved. He then spoke to the women, and afterward I spoke to the men : it was a good time."

" *Tuesday, 6th.*—I felt a great flow of light and love going through me all the day. At night I was called to Birchenough's, a young woman being in distress ; toward midnight she was brought through."

" *Saturday, 11th.*—This week I have been working with T. Knight—the man who broke my friendship, and used me very ill ; and of whom I prayed, saying, ' Lord take not this friend from me.' And now the Lord has restored him. We are come into confidence, and he into usefulness ; and I explained to him the priestly office, and the deep things of God. Now my prayer is answered, but in no way that I could have thought of. ' Praise the Lord, O my soul, and forget not all his benefits: who healeth thy diseases, and forgiveth all thine iniquities : who covereth thee with lovingkindness and tender mercies.' "

"*Sunday, March 12th.*—For some time it had been impressed on my mind to go to Norton class and lead it, and instruct them in the nature of the priestly office. I went this morning, and John Brindley asked me to lead the class, so I saw the hand of God. I then went and dismissed the Sunday school, and it was a solemn time. Afternoon, at Brown-edge; at night, at Norton; John Brindley desired me to join again; but I did not see my way clear. The class meets on a Sunday, and I am very often engaged. He then desired me to come among them as often as I could:—thus are things come about. O Lord keep me humble and useful."

"*Tuesday, 14th.*—While praying in private, the spirit shewed me how persons are eminently useful in private. I felt a desire, for a few moments, to live like a hermit; but I soon recollected that this was not right. In the afternoon, I had some conversation with Mr. Button, travelling preacher, an eminently useful, pious man. I went at night to Tunstall, and was at Clowes's class. O Lord Jesus keep me humble and useful. I then felt an impression that my work was done at Tunstall, and this was so strong that I could scarcely stay in the meeting. Mr. Edmondson, head preacher, had talked to Clowes about me; whether he had forbidden my coming or not, I know not.* O Lord thou knowest what is best for me; into thy hands I commit soul, body, and spirit; do with me as seemeth good to thee! O blessed Jesus guide me by thy counsel."

About this time he writes to one of his spiritual daughters, as follows:—" I feel thankful to God for the great work he has wrought in you, and I am fully satisfied that the Lord Jesus Christ intends you to be extensively useful. I believe he has called you to enjoy one of the brighter crowns; therefore, you will do well to endure the cross, despise the shame, &c. Heb. xii. 2. It will be a benefit to you to endeavour to reprove sin, and to recommend religion, at every opportunity; to beseech all that you possibly can, to be reconciled to God. 2 Cor. v. 20. Your ignorance of the scriptures, and of divine things, you will find to

* He afterwards learned that Mr. Edmondson had not forbidden his coming to Clowes's class.

be no insurmountable obstacle to filling up your duty in this respect, for God will give you suitable words. The spirit of your
Father that is in you will speak, and will open the scriptures as
need shall be : and hereby also you will greatly increase in knowledge ; and if the people do not immediately hearken, yet you will
receive a blessing in your own soul. I have constantly noticed
that those who have perseveringly gone on in this way have
always increased in knowledge above all others. It is the same
with me ; I seldom endeavour to speak to any one but the Lord
opens the scriptures anew to me. It was the same at your house ;
I never before knew the scriptural meaning of ' a door-keeper ; '
but when you mentioned it, the spirit immediately opened the
matter, so that our conversation was made a great blessing to me.
And this also was a further testimony to me that the Lord had
called you to bring many to Christ, otherwise the spirit would
not have opened the word at that time : therefore I wish you
good speed in the name of the Lord. Hugh Bourne."

" *On Monday, March 20th*, returning from Tean, Wooton, and
Ramsor appointments," he says, " I had the witness of the
spirit that the Lord was blessing me, and had blessed me through
the prayers of others. Coming through Kingsley, I was set upon
by a few abandoned people. I spoke a little to them. I saw the
need of the gift of discerning spirits, that these might have been
cut, and some of them saved. I then saw that I was not before
fit for it. As I looked to the Lord the voice said, ' I will answer
thee in the secret place of thunder.' I listened further, and it
said, ' Whom thou didst prove at the waters of Meribah,' &c. I
saw that Moses was in an improper harshness with the people,
and that I had been in the habit of so being,* which had kept
me out of the higher gifts. I looked unto the Lord till such a
spirit of love came upon me, that it appeared impossible for me
to feel resentment to any one, except I first cast away the faith.

* A harsh and hasty spirit in a preacher dries up the springs of usefulness, and diminishes the dignity and influence of the christian ministry.
In our opinion there is an absolute necessity on the part of open-air
preachers especially, for being vigilantly attentive to the spirit in which
they reprove sinners, and exhort them to fly to Christ for mercy and
salvation, lest an improper harshness with the people should keep off the
" higher gifts," and materially hinder their usefulness.

If a man were to rob or murder me, I believe I should only feel
tenderness, pity, and love. Thanks be to God for his unspeakable
gift. Wednesday, March 22nd, I solemnly engaged with Thomas
Knight,—James's wife, (my sister-in-law Sarah,)—and Hannah
Mountford, our servant, to fast and pray on Wednesdays and
Fridays, for a month, for the Lord to revive his work. O Lord,
assist us through Jesus Christ. Amen."

On Tuesday, 23rd, he set out for Delamere forest, and in this
journey extended his excursions to the principality, and was
made particularly useful in different families. " On the 29th,"
he says, " we came at night into Flintshire, a part barren of
religion;—exhorted and prayed with the family. I had good
liberty, and one of the servant women was cut to the heart.
Before this I was quite bowed down to see their carelessness
about religion. 30th ;—Betty Howel, daughter of the man of the
house, was cut to the heart. We joined in prayer, and she was
born again, and her mother was nearly brought through. 31st, I
came home."

On the next day, Saturday, April 1st, 1809, he set out for
Waterfall and Cauldon, two new places in the neighbourhood of
Ramsor, and he preached on the Saturday night and Sunday with
much power and liberty. " Monday, 3rd," he writes, " I visited
a few families, and was greatly blessed. I find a surprising
increase of love. A woman at Ramsor said she thought they
could not attain as great blessings as I had attained, their strength
not being equal to mine in this respect. I replied that I wished
always to come to Christ in the manner that Mary Magdalene
did, and wished those who prayed for me to consider me in that
light, and as one that in himself was no better than satan, only
that I was touched by the blood of Christ, and that the blood of
Christ kept me out of hell; and I said that people who were
prejudiced against me might perhaps pray for me with more effect
than those who esteemed me too highly, and that in this view she
stood upon as good ground as I. To day is my birth-day. I am
now thirty-seven years of age. Wednesday, 5th, when I came
home I was informed that W. Clowes had wanted me to go with
him into Cheshire, and that he had started without me. Thursday, 6th, I went to Budworth, and there met with Clowes.

Friday, 7th, we got the two women-servants converted. Sunday, 9th, no preacher came ;—Clowes and I took the pulpit with good liberty. Monday, 10th, Clowes started home, and I to Budworth. We had no meeting, the house having been threatened; so I engaged to get a license at Chester. Tuesday, 11th, I set off to Stableford-mill, where I saw my spiritual daughter, Betty Howel. I had had the most vehement desires to see or hear from her. She had had the same to see me, and had prayed to the Lord to send me, and glory be to his name he did, though by a way that I never expected;—surely all things work together for good. Glory be to Jehovah. Amen. I was much comforted in Betty, and she in me. They have had meetings, and some cut to the heart. I believe Betty will be a mother in Israel; I believe she has been the beginning of a revival. O Lord, prosper her! Wednesday, 12th, we had an extraordinary time in prayer this morning. Betty got into the spirit of a labourer. O Lord, establish her! I then set off to Chester, and by the Lord's assistance got a license. At night I stood up and preached at Tarvin. It was a glorious time. I believe Betty Howel will be eminent in the church of God. When the confusion was on about Hannah Goodwin, I prayed to the Lord to give me a spiritual daughter that would be useful in his cause. This prayer he has now answered in Betty Howel. O Lord, may my soul be wholly devoted to thee! O Lord, I beseech thee to raise up more!"

Thursday, 13*th,* he returned to James Crawfoot's, and laboured in the neighbourhood of the forest till the 19th, when he proceeded to Warrington, "where," he says, "they were glad to see me. Hannah Phillips informed me Lorenzo Dow was a man much given up to private prayer, and solemn in all things. Thursday, 20th, I had much enlargement in private. I wrote a letter to Betty Howel. O may the Lord make her a saint indeed. O Lord Jesus, grant me my desire concerning this woman. O let her be filled with thy glory, grant her the faith of Abraham, the chastity of Joseph, the constancy of Samuel, the zeal of Elijah, the purity of Isaiah, the firmness of Shadrach, Meshach, and Abednego, the patience of Job, the meekness of Moses, the self-denial of John the Baptist, the activity of Paul, the love of John, and the lowliness of the Virgin Mary. To-day I also became acquainted with Betty Prescot, a lovely young woman (of Warring-

ton society), full of grace. O Lord, bless her soul, and write her
on my heart to pray for her. Friday, 21st, I kept this the last
fast day of the month, proposed by Thomas Knight; and every
day of them has been marked with a particular blessing except
two. Saturday, 22nd, I had great enlargement in private this
morning, especially in the Lord's prayer. In the afternoon went
with John Webb to Rizley: the people here have been much
persecuted by professors and profane. They had a meeting at
night, and it was a very powerful time;—I was near falling to the
floor."

"*Sunday Morning, April 23rd.*—We had a meeting at
Rizley,—an exceedingly powerful time. I received new light on
the ministry. O Lord Jesus, keep me faithful, and enable me to
go through the awful work. Here each one does that which is
right in his own eyes. They stand, sit, kneel, pray, exhort, &c.,
as they are moved. I was very fond of this way. On my way to
Warrington, another fold of power spread over my soul. Afternoon and evening I was at Warrington. Monday, 23rd, came to
Budworth, and then to the meeting at Charles Spinner's. It was
a glorious time, and I had a good service there. I think the
power will go beyond J. S.'s. I stopped all night at James
Crawfoot's. Tuesday, 24th, set out for Tarvin, where I called on
Mrs. Powel: in prayer it was revealed that the Lord had called
her to the ministry. I spoke to her on the subject, and she was
brought into tears. Perhaps for this the Lord sent me to Tarvin.
Last Tuesday morning, while praying for Betty Howel, I had a
sense that she was not going on well, and it gave me much sorrow. I now found this to be so, but I trust she will still go on.
In the afternoon I felt a great burden for Betty, and the family;
and at night the Lord opened my mouth, in sorrow, to speak;
after which we had an uncommon time in prayer, so that I trust
the Lord will still visit this house. Wednesday, 26th, this
morning I felt a great burden for the family, and was led to
fasting; but I rather got through the cloud, and I trust the Lord
will visit this house. At night I spoke from John vii. 37. I was
exceedingly happy. Thursday, 27th, Mrs. Powel offered me
money to carry me home, but I did not take it, for I had no need.
O my God remember her! In coming home I was led to pray as
I walked,—this was good exercise. I got Abbott's life at Congleton,—there were two hundred for me."

Hugh Bourne's Cheshire round, as he calls it, was now become
an extensive home mission field, extending from the forest of
Delamere to Warrington and Rizley, in Lancashire, and Stockton-
heath and Runcorn, in Cheshire, on the one side; and on the
other, to Tarvin and Stableford, near Chester, and the neighbourhood of Altrey, in Flintshire.   In these localities we find his
calls and duties increase, so that he is now necessitated to devote
a greater portion of time and labour to them than he did formerly
to his visits to the old man of the forest.   Indeed, so numerous
were become his ministerial engagements, that when he arrived
at home, he only tarried one day, in which he visited Hanley and
Newcastle, returning through Tunstall to visit his friend Clowes,
and attend the meeting in Mr. Smith's kitchen.   On Saturday,
29th, he left home on a tour to another favourite field of gospel
enterprise, viz., Ramsor and its neighbourhood.   Here the Lord had
signally owned his and his colleagues' former visits. " This journey,"
he says, " it was shewn me by the way, that F. Horrobin was
called to sound the trumpet; so I told him that he was called to
preach the gospel.   He said it had been in his mind about a
week, that I should come at this time, and that I had something
to tell him, and should find fault with him.   He wished to de-
cline the work, and asked me why I fixed on him instead of others.
I said that our Lord told the Jews if they would answer him
one question, he would satisfy them ; and if he would tell me why
it was in his mind that I had something to say to him, I would
answer him.   At night we had a meeting at Ramsor,—a precious
time, and the power flowed.   Sunday, 30th, I set off to Tean,—
a small company, but a good time, and a great view of the work.
Thence to Wooton,—a large company, and a large prospect, both
above and below.   At night, at Ramsor, we held a meeting three
hours ; it was a great time,—the power flowed abundantly."

Monday, May 1st, 1809, he returned home, visiting the sick
by the way, and counselling others on the great work then springing up on every side.   It was a maxim, or general principle, with
Hugh Bourne, in those days, while seeking the good of others, as
far as it was possible to follow the example of the great apostle
of the Gentiles : " and when I was present with you and wanted, I
was chargeable to no man : * and in all things I have kept myself

* When labouring in the neighbourhood of Delamere forest he took
up his abode with J. Crawfoot, the old man of the forest, always remune-
rating him for his bed and board.

from being burdensome unto you, and so will I keep myself."
2 Cor. xi. 9. To the fact that he pursued this conscientious
line of procedure we have the testimony of the venerable William
Clowes, who says, "I thought brother H. Bourne was a very
singular man, for on his visits to my house I never could
prevail on him to accept of any refreshment."

Hugh Bourne had received what he considered a *divine* intimation to lay aside his manual labours, and give himself wholly to
the work of the ministry; yet to avoid being burdensome to the
people, he, at times, was free to engage in secular employment.
But this was only to supply the needful, or to minister to his
necessities, while carrying out the God-like design of bettering
the spiritual condition of the people among whom he went preaching the everlasting gospel.

He had now been from home several weeks, labouring for the
good of others; and as he was dependant on his own resources, it
is not at all unlikely that at this time his funds were getting low;
hence his journal says—

"*Tuesday, May 2nd*, I went to work at Milton. Monday, 8th,
I worked hard at Milton, and at night was at the fellowship meeting at Norton." This week he had earned a sufficiency to meet
his present wants; hence he again cheerfully and zealously enters
the mission field, directed by the hand of a superintending Providence. By some it might be thought, that the product of a week's
labour, either as a carpenter or a millwright, would be a very in-
sufficient fund with which to meet the temporal wants of an
itinerant minister, engaged as Hugh Bourne was at that time,
journeying from county to county, carrying to the people the glad
tidings of salvation. And we can assure the reader, that such a
fund, in our opinion, was anything but adequate. But Hugh
Bourne's wants were widely different from those of most other
men.

The great Locke tells us, "The masters of the world were
bred up with spare diet; and the young gentlemen of Rome felt
no want of strength because they ate but once a day." Here we
have a sort of archetype of the manner in which Hugh Bourne

was bred up, and thus inured to toil and hardship. We are told, "The first christians were by great hardships trained up for glory." The glory of God and the salvation of men were the main objects of Hugh Bourne's life; but the great hardships he endured to accomplish this good, in the infancy of the Primitive Methodist Connexion, we are well persuaded are known to but few. Happily there are some surviving witnesses of his early toils, whose communications throw a considerable degree of light on this part of his history : and it affords us great pleasure to lay before our readers a few extracts from a letter to us from Thomas Steele, Esq., whose revered father was a particular friend of Mr. Bourne's, and was well acquainted with the economical plans carried out by him on his missionary excursions. Mr. S. writes :—

" Congleton, December 22nd, 1853.

DEAR SIR,—The intimacy that existed between the late Mr. Hugh Bourne and my father, frequently caused him to visit our house in Tunstall, when I was a boy ; and his zeal and activity in the cause of God made him an object of respect and reverence to myself, although only a child ; and from this cause no person's habits and manners are so fresh to my mind as his.   On the subject of his preaching I would observe that he was clear, concise, and short, very seldom exceeding half an hour ; and when on scripture history, he was truly enchanting, being excelled by few. As to his labours in the church, 'they were more abundant; ' and truly it may be said of him that he was always about his Master's business. I know he used frequently to walk forty or fifty miles a day, and that under circumstances of self-denial, little practised, or even known by most.   He used to put into his pocket two or three hard-boiled eggs, and a little dry bread, in the morning ; and during his journey, he would sit down by a well of water, and take his humble fare, and then travel on in pursuit of the great object of winning souls. He was a strict disciplinarian ; and I shall never forget his laborious zeal at quarter-days, district-meetings, &c.   In short, his whole soul was in the work, and he seemed to be altogether indifferent to every thing else but either fishing or mending nets.   The foregoing observations refer to the rise and early times of Primitive Methodism. For some years past I saw and heard but little of this honoured servant of

God; but I understand he continued to 'walk by the same rule,
and mind the same things,' as long as his health permitted; and
on making some inquiries respecting him in his last affliction, I
was told that he was anxiously awaiting his Lord and Master's
summons. Believe me to remain, dear sir,

Yours very truly, in Christ Jesus,

T. STEELE."

From Mr. Steele's letter we learn the secret of Hugh Bourne's
making a little of this world's goods serve his purpose in prose-
cuting the great and noble objects of the ministry. Only picture
to yourselves this pilgrim father seated on a stone, partaking of
so humble a repast as dry bread and hard-boiled eggs, and sipping
at the spring by the wayside; and then say if there be any wonder at the product of a week's toil in the carpenter or millwright's shop being a sufficient supply for his wants during a
missionary excursion into several counties. The astonishment
with us is, how he went through such an amount of labour with
so little sustenance.

CHAPTER XXI.

CAMP MEETING ON RUNCORN HILL—A DREAM—A SCEPTIC—CAMP MEETING
AT RAMSOR — BOURNE AND CLOWES AT MACCLESFIELD — A DISPUTE—
ANNIVERSARY OF MOW COP CAMP MEETING—INSTANCES OF SOUL-SAVING
—BETSEY AND SAMUEL EVANS, OF DERBY—VARIOUS LABOURS—A SECOND
CAMP MEETING ON RUNCORN HILL — ONE NEAR BIDDULPH-MOOR — RE-
MARKS — ANOTHER ON MOW COP — SUCCESS — SOLEMN REFLECTIONS —
SCRIPTURE TEXTS—THREE POINTS—W. ALCOCK—FIRST CAMP MEETING
H. B. MISSED—FASTING AND PRAYER—CLASS AT LASK-EDGE—W. ALCOCK'S
MAIDEN EFFORT AT PREACHING — A VALUABLE HELPER — GROWTH IN
GRACE — WARRINGTON, MANCHESTER, MACCLESFIELD — A JAUNT INTO
SHROPSHIRE—VARIOUS REMARKS.

We have now arrived at the period of the year for renewed
operations in holding camp meetings ; consequently, we find
Hugh Bourne actively engaged in making the necessary preparations, and among other things soliciting the aid of field preachers
for the summer campaign.   He designed to commence the meetings of this year (1809) with one on Runcorn Hill.

" *Wednesday, May* 10*th*, 1809," he says, " I fasted, read, and
worked at home ; and at night I prepared for my journey to
Runcorn."

A REMARKABLE DREAM.

" *Thursday,* 11*th.*—Last night I dreamed that I went into a sown
field, and it was almost covered with rooks, which were picking
up the seed.   I had a gun, but the stock was cracked (as our
gun's is), and I thought it might burst, but I was determined
to shoot.   It drove away some, but many were too bold to be so
driven.   I caught some of these, and twisted their necks, and
was determined to clear the field of them."

CAMP MEETINGS.

"*Sunday, 14th.*—I went to Runcorn Hill. I was glad to see the Rizley people. We had a powerful time. James Bentley told me this camp meeting was exactly the sown field I had dreamed of." On this journey Mr. Bourne had a contest with an infidel, and in the debate the sceptic proposed universalism : to this Mr. B. replied,—" It will not do to go to hell to try if we could get out again." The sceptic argued in various ways, " but being in good liberty," says Mr. B., " I turned all his arguments ; and when he got home he told his wife that he had been with Lorenzo's brother."

Mr. B. returned home on the Tuesday, and was fully employed the remaining part of the week in procuring preachers and making preparations for the forthcoming camp meeting at Ramsor. We find him at Tunstall, on the Thursday, inviting his highly-esteemed friend Clowes, and making arrangements with him for the journey ; and on the Saturday they set off together, and they visited several families on their way, and held a special service on their arrival at Ramsor.

THE CAMP MEETING.

Sunday, May 21st, 1809, the weather was unfavourable, being very showery, so that the meeting was conducted alternately in the open air and in the house ; nevertheless, the services were very powerful, and some of the hearers fell down under the power-ful preaching of William Clowes. Hugh Bourne says, " this re-moved prejudice, as they had said none ever fell at Ramsor. My brother James had a bad eye, very bad indeed, and the anguish was so great that it affected the other eye, so that he could not read, and could scarcely look at anything ; but, how-ever, he thought to come and be present, if he could not exercise. When he had been at the place a few minutes, both his eyes were instantaneously healed ; and they continued sound and well." The meeting closed about six o'clock, p.m. ; and afterwards, Hugh Bourne and W. Clowes visited several families at Wooton, resting for the night at J. Horrobin's, of Lexhead. He says—

"*Monday, 22nd.*—Joseph Elks came to thank us for what we did for him the day before. We then came to Kingsley, and I wrote a paper to go to Lichfield for a license for the place at Ipstones;—they have trials at Kingsley. Coming to Norton, Clowes invited me to his class, and then went home; and I called at Norton chapel, where I had a most glorious time; and I then went home in company with T. Knight. Tuesday, 23rd, I was at work at Milton; at night went to Tunstall, when Mr. Sedgwick, missionary from Stafford, preached, and the classes were put by. Clowes said he had been sent for to go to Macclesfield, and he had prayed for the Lord to send me also, if it was his will for him to go thither. I agreed to go, though in opposition to worldly work."

Wednesday, 24th, Hugh Bourne and Wm. Clowes set out together on a visit to the Independent methodists of Macclesfield; they found this church very low, and under great trials. But through a number of special services held by these two Primitive fathers during a week's labour, a revival commenced, the members were quickened, and many sinners were converted. While on this excursion, Hugh Bourne was violently assaulted by the enemy of souls, about spending his time in the manner he did; but the Lord delivered him when he was praying in private.

While at Macclesfield, a subject was discussed on which these two devoted men were of opposite opinions;—an extract from Hugh Bourne's journal will show what was the matter in dispute : " calling at Mr. Higginbottom's, a fund for leaders and preachers was mentioned; I spoke against funds, saying, I never knew them do any good to the cause of Christ, but that they had done much hurt. This was not agreeable to Clowes, so he teazed me so much that I was obliged to stop or hold my ears. But I mean to examine this point." This difference of opinion on the fund-matter in nowise interfered with the unity of their efforts to better the moral and spiritual condition of the labouring masses, or lessened for one moment their feeling of esteem for each other. On subjects such as this, they were free to differ in their opinions, while still their cordiality and good brotherhood remained the same.

The anniversary of Mow Cop first camp meeting was the last Sunday in May; but this year, the authorities (differing as we suppose from Hugh Bourne on the matter) arranged for the ser-

mons to be preached for the benefit of Harrisehead Sunday school
on that day; consequently, the camp meeting was deferred till
June 18th; under which date we find in his journal the
following entry:—"My brother James and I fixed the standard
pretty early, and waited; a few came and we began, and there
was a mighty flame. It was windy, and we removed to the side
of the grove of firs, and there it was very pleasant. We prayed,
and got into the full power. In a short time there was a good
congregation, and I stood up and spoke from 'Joseph is a fruitful
bough,' &c. Then James Bourne and Thomas Knight preached,
and after a course of prayer we retired for dinner. We began
again in less than an hour, and continued till between five and six
o'clock, when we broke up. There was a great company in the
afternoon, and much power all the day, and the wicked gave us
little disturbance; all the people appeared much satisfied with
the meeting, and very desirous for the camp meetings to be kept
up. Thus hath God wrought. We had some difficulty to thrust
this meeting in, and had not the Lord stirred up old James Clark
of Congleton, there perhaps would not have been any more meetings on Mow. Now the people are vehement for camp meetings,
and complain that this was not published more. Isaac Dale of
Ollery-lane, a young man that was started by a handbill, (rules
for holy living,) at one of the last year's camp meetings, goes on
well. He is one of the most earnest and exemplary characters in
all the country. Martha Hamblet, a child that was converted at
the first camp meeting, was taken to heaven about a week ago.
I was informed that a man from Sitheton came, (I believe to the
second camp meeting,) to see what was to be done; and he there
got changed, and was a means of awakening the family at home,
and many in the neighbourhood, and is now gone to heaven.
Glory to Jehovah!"

We think it impossible to calculate the good done at the Mow
Cop camp meetings, or to enumerate the many instances in which
the seed sown afterwards sprang up, producing fruit unto eternal life,—of which there was no sign at the time.

"*Saturday, June 24th,*" H. B. writes, "I set off for Ramsor;
on the way I read Mr. Wesley's sermon on self-denial, and was
determined to endeavour to follow it. O Lord help me! I went

through Cheddleton. I stood up at Cauldon-low,—we were out-of-doors, and we had a good time. They have begun to hold meetings on Friday nights, and I believe there will be a work. O my God bless them ! "

"*Sunday, June* 25th.—I led the class in the morning at Wooton. There were but few present, but they are very promising. We were informed that Betsey Evans, Samuel Evans's wife, from Derby, would speak at Wooton. Her husband also is a local preacher. She began about two o'clock,—her voice was low and hoarse at first, from having preached so much the week past; but she got well into the power. She appears to be very clear in scriptural doctrines, and very ready in scripture, and speaks full in the spirit, and from the little I saw of her she appears to be as fully devoted to God as any woman I ever met with. O Lord help her and establish her! Her husband also spoke. He appears to be an excellent man. O my Father bless and keep him! My brother James spoke next, and then I went up ; so that we occupied most of the afternoon ; and we had, after that, a plead with sinners near the ale-house. We had but little persecution, although it was wake time. I spoke at night, at Ramsor, and we had a powerful time."

"*Monday*, 26th.—I went with Joseph Buxton to Stanton, and stood up in the street ;—the people were very hard. I spoke to a great many, till I was almost exhausted ; and when I had concluded, some fell to arguing ; but the Lord enabled us to answer all their arguments. Glory be to his name. J. Buxton's sister-in-law came at night, from Wirley, near Cannock ; she said the colliers there go on well, but are very noisy. O Lord bless them. Amen. I then came to Ramsor, and there stayed all night."

Tuesday, 27th, he returned home. Wednesday, Thursday, and Friday, he worked at Shieldscroft, attending every night a place of worship.

" *Friday*, 30th.—He says, " I heard a man curse in a field at a distance, but did not reprove him, so I suffered loss."

" *Saturday, July* 1st.—I set out for Cheshire. I felt the effects of neglecting to give reproof, but the Lord healed me, and I was minded not to neglect again. At night I came to Frodsham, much fatigued."

A SECOND CAMP MEETING UPON RUNCORN HILL.

"*Sunday, July 2nd*, 1809.—When I arrived at the hill, there had nobody come. I kneeled down and prayed; and after awhile a few came, and it rained, but we began, and prayed through the heaviest shower. We then sheltered a little and began again, and the Lord sent a fine day. There were scarcely any labourers that exercised in public except Thomas White and myself; so it lay very hard upon me. Nevertheless, the Lord supported us, and there was much power in the meeting: we broke up between five and six o'clock, and then came to a preaching out-of-doors, at Warrington." Mr. B. laboured in the neighbourhood of Warrington till the Friday following, when he returned, taking Budworth, Congleton, and Mow Cop, on his way home.

A CAMP MEETING ON A MOUNTAIN NEAR BIDDULPH-MOOR.

"*Sunday, July 9th*," says H. B., "we began a camp meeting, on a mountain called the Troughstones, about six o'clock. The weather was rather cold and windy. After I and James had preached, and many had prayed, we removed our station to the end of the mountain, where the ground was convenient, being like a gallery. Here we were sheltered from the wind, and full in the sun. People crowded in, and there was much power in the congregation. One or two were set at liberty, and it was a powerful time. We could not stop for dinner, the people so crowded in, and they had a grand and awful appearance. We had plenty of preachers. We concluded before six o'clock."

REMARKS ON THE CAMP MEETING, BY H. BOURNE.

"There was great power in the morning. I and James spoke in great power, and the people prayed in great power. At the end of the mountain we spoke in great power; and so did Thos. Knight, and he said the Lord had told ———— that he should be set at liberty. ———— was in distress, and was strangely brought in. I exhorted, and there was great power; many were

caught. Then James preached; and then ————; he spun
out, and the spirit and the power left the meeting. William
Maxfield and Thomas Cotton also spoke. The power came down,
but the people wanted to go, and we had to break up."

"*Monday, 10th.*—I was at work at Shieldscroft; at night Mr.
Butters preached at Norton, on ʻthese are they which came out
of great tribulation,' &c. This was suitable to me, as I had been
tempted that great tribulation was before me, if I continued in a
public station."

ANNIVERSARY OF MOW COP SECOND CAMP MEETING.

"*Sunday, July 16th,*" he writes, "the camp meeting came on at
Mow; there was plenty of preachers, and a vast company in the
afternoon, but rather turbulent; however, we managed pretty well.
At night I was at Lane-ends, and got higher in faith. I clearly
believed that God would check the wake, and I believed for the
work at Mow, and that sinners would not be able to shake the
power off."

To counteract the evils of the wake Mow Cop camp meeting
was first appointed, and now, in 1809, Hugh Bourne's soul is fired
with the same zeal as at first; and we are happy to say that the
design was in a great measure accomplished: for the standard of
truth planted on the mountain finally prevailed, and the brutal
sports practised at the annual feast were for ever banished from
the Staffordshire side of Mow Cop. And the colliers were led to
regard the work of the Lord, and to consider with veneration the
operation of his hands.

"*Friday, July 21st,*" he writes, "I left off fasting some time
ago, on account of my health, but have since been regularly in
bad health. I believe it is my duty to fast on Wednesdays and
Fridays, and to leave the event to God. Since I left off fasting,
I have been less spiritual, and likewise have suffered more in
body; so I have been a loser every way. O Lord make me faithful to death, through Jesus Christ. Since I have come to the
conclusion again to fast, I have grown in grace rapidly; O Lord
Jesus, make and keep me faithful. Amen."

"*Monday, 24th,*"—returning from Macclesfield, where he had
been highly delighted with two preachers from Manchester, he

writes :—" I have grown much in grace this journey, especially
by the sermon on Monday night.* I was found fault with for
staying too long ; I must not attempt to please man, but endeavour to follow the spirit. Saturday, 29th, working at Shieldscroft; at noon I started to Tean in mistake. I went through
Bucknall. In the church chapel-yard, at that place, lie interred
many of my former schoolfellows ; I felt very solemn while ex-
amining their tombs. I almost felt as if I should not long be an
inhabitant of this world. I then went to Fordhays, where I
was born, and where I lived sixteen years. I went over the field
in which I was convinced of sin."

There is no doubt while thus employed our friend would recall
the ideas planted in his mind in childhood, when the Lord
in this very field revealed to him for the first time that he was a
sinner, and unfit for the kingdom of heaven. Recollection would
wake up in his soul the liveliest emotions of gratitude to the
Father of mercies, who had delivered him from the condemnation
of a broken law, and from the guilt and consequences of sin; and
although death had levelled with the tomb (in thirty years) many
of his former associates, and the thought pressed heavily upon
his mind that ere long he himself should quit the stage of mortality, yet the hope of future happiness would buoy up his spirit,
and fill his soul with heavenly anticipation. He goes on to say—
"Tuesday, August 1st, T. Knight preached at Birchenough's.
I had a glorious time. Two scriptures were applied to me—
' Count it all joy when ye fall into divers temptations,' and, ' Ye
took joyfully the spoiling of your goods.' I saw that ' count it all
joy ' was a commandment, and that if we obey it, the spirit will
set his seal to it, and make it ' all joy.' This strengthened me in
a weak part, for when losses and other disappointments have
come, I have been rather accustomed to count it trouble : but
this failing was now removed by an instantaneous act. O Lord
Jesus, establish me firmly in this to the end. Amen. There
were three points as to which I was troubled:—the first was
unbelief; the second was a lack of that ministerial power in which
Ann Cutler and old Benjamin Abbott lived ; and the third was a
want of the reproving power which old James Crawfoot was in.

* After the Monday night's service, he tells us, he came home,
(15 miles,) by impression.

The first was now removed by an instantaneous work, and I
expect to be brought into the other two instantaneously. O Lord,
grant me the desire of my heart, for the sake of Jesus Christ.
Amen. Yesterday I was informed that Mr. Furness, the head
preacher at Leek, found fault with the letter upon faith, which
I wrote to William Stonier. He objected to an instantaneous
work, which may almost be called the soul of methodism. I
am again linked in contrary to my expectation. There is a revival at Biddulph-moor, and they are much opposed, and they have
linked me with those that are spoken against. Billy Alcock is, I
believe, called to preach the gospel. I some time ago felt an
impression of that sort, and told him of it. He was backward,
but made it a matter of prayer; and he dreamed that a sound
went through him which alarmed the country round, and it was
said that if the country was not alarmed he could not enjoy the
witness of the spirit. He said he would put his trust in God,
and betook himself to prayer; and in the agony of prayer he
awoke. He then prayed to the Lord, that if he had called him to
preach he would give him a sign. He then fell asleep again,
and dreamed that a man in white came to him, and called—
'preach, preach, preach!' &c., and with the calling he awoke, and
the words 'Prepare to meet thy God' ran through his mind.
As to the first dream, I told him that if he was called to preach,
and refused, he could not enjoy the witness of the spirit; for he
would not be obedient, and except he stood in perfect obedience
he could not put his trust in God, for disobedience would throw
him out of God."

" *Wednesday, 2nd.*—I worked at Shieldscroft, and fasted. At
night I went to see William Clowes, having heard that he was
ill. He had been ill, and near death, but was getting better
again, but could not exercise in public. While praying for him I
was brought up into his state, and was stronger than I ever was
before. When I came home I felt resigned to God in all things,
and willing to go or stay as the Lord willed. I never before felt
such an absolute dependence upon God. I was saved even from
all timidity. O Lord I thank thee. O Lord guide my soul.
Friday, 4th, I fasted and worked at Shieldscroft. At night I
again went to Tunstall to see Clowes,—still mending. I had not
such a time as on Wednesday night, nevertheless I was

strengthened. O Lord Jesus, establish me. To-day I felt full power to love my enemies, and to desire and expect that we should dwell in heaven together—this was sweet. O Lord, I thank thee."

Saturday, 5th.—Up to this date Hugh Bourne had been present at every camp meeting held in England. "But to-day," he says, "I received a letter informing me that the camp meeting at Whitley-rede was to-morrow, so I could not go. I started to Ramsor, and it rained all the way. While going through Endon I seemed to have a call to Standley, Bagnall-grange, and Bagnall. The Lord's will be done. Tuesday, 8th, I worked at Milton, and at night I was at Birchenough's. Here it was opened to me what it was to be, 'a pillar in the temple, to go out no more.' When a man is in the spirit, and lives in the spirit, he is a pillar; but if he is drawn into wrong tempers by temptation, he then goes out: but he that always abides in the spirit, and lives in the will of God, is a pillar, and goes out no more. I received the evidence that I should be a pillar in the temple to go out no more. I was gloriously happy. I was also sensible of being in Mount Zion, and the building was of fair colours, and these words ran through me, 'The Lord, the king of Israel is in the midst of thee,' and, 'the enemies thou hast seen to-day thou shalt see no more for ever.' I had also a great opening into the ministry. O Lord, make thou me a faithful minister of the New Testament, through Jesus Christ. Amen. Wednesday, 9th, I fasted and worked at Milton. I was stronger than ever. At night I went with T. Knight,—he preached at Etruria at six o'clock. I then went through Tunstall, and called on Clowes,—still bad in body. J. Sproston, who was reckoned an 'oaf,' and who was converted some time ago, goes on well, and is got into such a degree of light and power as few attain to. Glory to Jehovah. Amen."

"*Thursday, 10th.*—To-day I was led to meditate on the law of faith, and the law of works, and they were much opened to me."

"*Sunday, July 20th,*" he says, "I set out to Bagnall-grange. Wm. Turner seemed much affected, and desirous to start afresh. Going back through Standley, some boys were pitching; I spoke

to them, and some women engaged me, and we had a strong
campaign : I spoke a good while, but the people were very hard;
there were many hearers. I then came to Lask-edge, and had
some liberty. I was informed that the class was all dashed
to pieces;—some reasoning having been propagated about allowing something for the preachers' refreshment, and for benches.
On this I stayed till night, to lead the class, instead of going to
Biddulph-moor. We visited some, and I had a glorious time. I
had 'that sacred awe that dares not move, and all the silent
heaven of love.' At night I led the class,—we had a good time,
and I endeavoured to put the reasoning away.   O Lord Jesus,
bless, protect, and unite them.   Amen."

This class was raised by the camp meeting community, and
generously given to the Wesleyans, as had been others ; still the
Bournes and colleagues supplied the place, each alternate Sunday,
with preachers ; and Hugh Bourne, as was his wont, took the
liveliest interest in the prosperity of this church ; and to allay
the tumult or reasoning, he at once paid for the benches out of
his own pocket, besides using every effort of parental care to
raise the infant society.

"*Monday*, 21*st*," he says, "I worked at Milton. Thomas
Knight spoke of a present and instantaneous salvation through
faith, and that it ought constantly to be preached. I saw that I
had fallen short in this, which I believe is one cause why I have
not had more success. I felt repentance on this account, and a
determination to follow the Lord more fully. O Lord, make me
faithful ! "

MR. W. ALCOCK ATTEMPTS TO PREACH.

"*Tuesday*, 22*nd*.—I worked at Milton, and in the work gave
way to some impatience, which hurt me. At night W. Alcock
was by appointment to preach. This was the first time he ever
attempted to preach. There were four preachers present, viz. :—
H. Bourne, J. Bourne, T. Knight, and W. Maxfield. I prayed
much for him. He gave out a hymn and prayed in power. He
then sang again, and read out a text, ' When they had
nothing to pay,' &c. He spoke about two sentences, and then was
fast, and stopped. He stood awhile, and then asked one of us to

pray. He then stood up again, but still could not speak. He then kneeled down and prayed, and arose, and stood up again; and W. Maxfield asked him to tell his experience, which he did, and then spoke a little from the text, and delivered a strong, weighty exhortation. His word was much blessed to me. We concluded with a prayer meeting. Upon the whole it was a very powerful time. At night I discoursed much with him in order to strengthen his hands, and direct him. O Lord, bless him! I believe he will be a useful man."

Perhaps few, if any, ever took a more active part or a livelier interest in calling talent into exercise than did Hugh Bourne; indeed, this was one of the characteristics by which Hugh Bourne and the camp meeting community were distinguished from others. Praying companies he ever considered the main stay of camp meetings, believing that on them, next to the influence of the Holy Spirit, depended the success of those meetings. From this source also sprung the staff of open-air preachers; and where there was a lack of ministers, these praying exhorters were sent, two by two, to hold religious services, and fill up the appointments; and to this class of labourers we attribute a large share of the success that crowned the efforts of the Primitive Methodists in the infancy of the connexion.

In Mr. William Alcock Hugh Bourne found a valuable accession to the staff of open-air preachers. This young man first entered the mission-field, and laboured for some time at his own expense; afterwards he travelled with success in the Primitive Methodist Connexion; and after some years' servitude as an itinerant, he located, and is now, in 1854, we believe, a respectable farmer in Derbyshire, and a local preacher with the Wesleyan methodists.

Hugh Bourne says, " *Friday, 25th.*—To-day I ventured to tell Thomas Knight of an impression that had followed me ever since I was last in Bucknall chapel-yard, where lie some of my schoolfellows. The impression was that I should not live long. But whether this is to impress me with the shortness and uncertainty of life in general, or whether it is that I shall soon go away out of this life I cannot tell. But God knoweth, and that is enough. But if it were God's will I should like to live till Francis Horrobin and Billy Alcock are gated* in preaching.

"*Monday, 28th.*—I went to see Clowes; better in body, and driving on as usual." He said at class—'I have always Christ, and he always satisfies me. I am always satisfied.'"

"*Tuesday, August 29th.* — I had an opening into *faith*— 'all things are yours'—I saw that all things were mine, fully bought and paid for, by Jesus Christ; and through him I had a claim upon all. I wondered that I had never thought of this before. I was even almost ready to knock my head against the wall, that I had never thought of this before. I felt godly sorrow and unfeigned repentance for all my past labours. I almost even wished that I had never preached, I had done it so much out of faith. But after preaching at Brown-edge, I found faith was imputed to me for righteousness, just as if I had done all right. This hath Jesus wrought. This day faith made me new; I was as if I had jumped into a new world, and I felt a desire to spend my life in preaching faith. O Lord, pour thy blessings upon me, through Jesus Christ. At night I endeavoured to explain faith to Billy Alcock and Hannah Mountford. To-day has been a wonder of wonders, a day of days. I saw that in the law of faith any one might in an hour grow up into a higher state of grace than I, if he could believe; and through this I could esteem others better than myself. This faith brought a fulness of universal love. Some-time ago I could not have borne this doctrine. To say that I had fasted, prayed, laboured, &c., and yet another might almost instantaneously grow up into the same, or greater grace and usefulness than I, this I could not have borne, but now I rejoice in it."

"*Wednesday, 30th.*—I increased much in faith. All things are mine; all spiritual gifts; and they will come forth to be used as my heavenly father pleases."

* *Gated*—a provincial word of the same meaning as the word begun, or started. Hence he wished to live till his two friends had begun to preach.

For EU product safety concerns, contact us at Calle de José Abascal, 56–1°,
28003 Madrid, Spain or eugpsr@cambridge.org.